Said Aljoumani, Zahir Bhalloo, Konrad Hirschler

Catalogue of the New Corpus of Documents from the Ḥaram al-sharīf in Jerusalem

Said Aljoumani, Zahir Bhalloo, Konrad Hirschler

Catalogue of the New Corpus of Documents from the Ḥaram al-sharīf in Jerusalem

DE GRUYTER

ISBN 978-3-11-125314-5
e-ISBN (PDF) 978-3-11-133024-2
e-ISBN (EPUB) 978-3-11-133083-9
DOI https://doi.org/10.1515/9783111330242

Library of Congress Control Number: 2023940057

Bibliographic information published by the Deutsche Nationalbibliothek
The Deutsche Nationalbibliothek lists this publication in the Deutsche Nationalbibliografie; detailed bibliographic data are available on the internet at http://dnb.dnb.de.

Cover image: Amal Abul-Hajj, Linda Northrup and Donald P. Little (from left to right), Islamic Museum/ al-Ḥaram al-Sharif, spring 1978 (taken by Martin Lyons), © Linda Northrup
Typesetting: Integra Software Services Pvt. Ltd.
Printing and binding: CPI books GmbH, Leck

www.degruyter.com

Acknowledgements

This book was made possible with the help, support and advice of many colleagues. Chief among them are our Jerusalemite colleagues Bashir Barakat, Arafat Amro (Islamic Museum, Jerusalem) and Yusuf al-Uzbaki (al-Aqṣā Library). Christian Müller (Paris) helped by offering his intimate knowledge of the documents and Linda Northrup (Toronto) generously shared her knowledge of the documents' discovery in the 1970s. Mohammad Ghosheh (Jerusalem/Amman) has supported this project (and many other related ones) in numerous ways. Suzanne Ruggi converted our various English vernaculars into a more legible shape.

Jost Gippert and his team on the European Research Council project *The Development of Literacy in the Caucasian Territories* project at CSMC (Universität Hamburg), and David Maisuradze (Tbilisi University) provided invaluable help in reading the Armenian and Georgian texts in the documents. Nimet İpek (Sabancı University) generously agreed to take on the documents in Ottoman Turkish. Ken'ichi Isogai (Kyoto University), Ryoko Watabe (Tokyo University) and Takao Ito (Kobe University), helped to improve considerably the readings of the Persian and Persianate documents, while the intervention of Yoichi Yojima (Nara Women's University) was crucial for deciphering their Mongolian and Turkic witness clauses.

The research for this book was funded by the Deutsche Forschungsgemeinschaft (DFG, German Research Foundation) under Germany's Excellence Strategy – EXC 2176 'Understanding Written Artefacts: Material, Interaction and Transmission in Manuscript Cultures', project no. 390893796. The Persian and Persianate documents were examined as part of DFG project no. 449163880, 'The Persian Documents from al-Ḥaram al-Sharīf in Jerusalem, 1300–1353'. The research was conducted within the scope of the Centre for the Study of Manuscript Cultures (CSMC) at Universität Hamburg.

https://doi.org/10.1515/9783111330242-202

Contents

Acknowledgements —— V

Figures —— IX

Symbols used —— XI

Preface: Bringing the Ḥaram documents to light – A memoir —— 1

I Introduction: The making of a documentary corpus —— 20

II Arabic documents concerning Jerusalem, Bilād al-shām and Cairo —— 35

II.1 Decrees, petitions and *muṭālaʿas* —— **35**
II.2 Sale and rent —— **45**
II.3 Accounts, debts and receipts —— **54**
II.4 Estates and inheritance —— **69**
II.5 Endowments —— **78**
II.6 Letters —— **85**
II.7 Poetry —— **89**
II.8 Prayers —— **92**
II.9 Other documents —— **96**

III Ottoman-language documents concerning Jerusalem and surroundings —— 100

IV Persian and Persianate documents concerning Transcaucasia, Anatolia and Northwestern Iran (including Georgian, Armenian and Arabic documents) —— 106

IV.1 Documents belonging to the dossier of Amīr Ādūjī's family —— **106**
IV.2 Documents from Anatolia (Kayseri and Sīwās) —— **119**
IV.3 Further documents —— **127**
IV.3.1 Decrees and receipts —— **127**
IV.3.2 Sale and lease —— **133**
IV.3.3 Inventories —— **143**
IV.3.4 Other legal documents —— **145**
IV.3.5 Prayer —— **151**

Appendix 1a: Edition of five Persian documents (Zahir Bhalloo) —— 153

Appendix 1b: Edition of five Arabic documents (Said Aljoumani) —— 171

Appendix 2: List of edited Ḥaram al-sharīf documents —— 185

Appendix 3a: List of the documents in order of catalogue entry number —— 193

Appendix 3b: List of the documents in order of Islamic Museum classmark —— 197

Bibliography —— 201

Index of persons (Arabic script) —— 205

Index of persons (Latin script) —— 211

Index of places (Arabic script) —— 215

Index of places (Latin script) —— 217

Figures

Figure 1 Linda Northrup, Amal Abul-Hajj and Martin Lyons (from left to right), Islamic Museum/al-Ḥaram al-Sharif, spring 1978 (most likely taken by Donald P. Little), © Linda Northrup —— **4**

Figure 2 Amal Abul-Hajj, Islamic Museum/al-Ḥaram al-Sharif, spring 1978 (taken by Martin Lyons), © Linda Northrup —— **6**

Figure 3 Linda Northrup (left) and Amal Abul-Hajj reading Document #333, Islamic Museum/al-Ḥaram al-Sharif, spring 1978 (taken by Martin Lyons), © Linda Northrup —— **8**

Figure 4 Linda Northrup spraying document with water to flatten, Islamic Museum/al-Ḥaram al-Sharif, spring 1978 (taken by Martin Lyons), © Linda Northrup —— **9**

Figure 5 Amal Abul-Hajj, Linda Northrup and Donald P. Little (from left to right), Islamic Museum/al-Ḥaram al-Sharif, spring 1978 (taken by Martin Lyons), © Linda Northrup —— **17**

Figure 6 Ia (67)/#911v Transfer of *iqṭāʿ*, 711/1312, © Mohammad H. Ghosheh —— **155**

Figure 7 Ib (67)/#911r Witness clauses, © Mohammad H. Ghosheh —— **156**

Figure 8 IIa (70)/#942 Marriage contract for a deferred dowry, 769/1367 (top), © Mohammad H. Ghosheh —— **159**

Figure 9 IIb (70)/#898 Marriage contract for a deferred dowry, 769/1367 (bottom), © Mohammad H. Ghosheh —— **160**

Figure 10 IIIa (71)/#913 Draft of Ilkhanid decree, undated (top), © Mohammad H. Ghosheh —— **162**

Figure 11 IIIb (71)/#892 Draft of Ilkhanid decree, undated (bottom), © Mohammad H. Ghosheh —— **163**

Figure 12 IV (76)/#906 Decree on collection of revenues, 740/1339, © Mohammad H. Ghosheh —— **165**

Figure 13 Va (82)/#975 Sale contract of two *dāng* of the village of Azād, 723/1323 (top), © Mohammad H. Ghosheh —— **168**

Figure 14 Vb (82)/#893 Sale contract of two *dāng* of the village of Azād, 723/1323 (bottom), © Mohammad H. Ghosheh —— **169**

Figure 15 VI (3)/#966 Report on a Sultanic decree and a judge's order, 797/1395, © Mohammad H. Ghosheh —— **172**

Figure 16 VII (8)/#946 *Muṭālaʿa*, most likely late 700s/1300s, © Mohammad H. Ghosheh —— **174**

Figure 17 VIIIa (10)/#922r Sale contracts (cotton), 776/1374, © Mohammad H. Ghosheh —— **177**

Figure 18 VIIIb (10)/#922v Sale contract and accounts (cotton), 776/1374, © Mohammad H. Ghosheh —— **178**

Figure 19 IX (12)/#923 Rent contract for baths, 737/1336, © Mohammad H. Ghosheh —— **181**

Figure 20 X (30)/#945 Estate inventory *(wuqūf)*, 795/1393, © Mohammad H. Ghosheh —— **183**

Figure 21 XI/#867 Autograph witness clause of Zakariyā, son of Shams al-Dīn Juwaynī, © Mohammad H. Ghosheh —— **184**

https://doi.org/10.1515/9783111330242-204

Symbols used

| | interlinear text
[ ] editor's insertion of letters or words
[ˀ] tentative reading
[/] alternative reading
[. . .] non-legible or missing word(s)
* = vertical strikethrough of name

https://doi.org/10.1515/9783111330242-205

Preface: Bringing the Ḥaram documents to light – A memoir

In early February 1976, I was on my way home from a year of doctoral research in Cairo.[1] My husband, Martin Lyons, a professional photographer, and I were on the same flight from Cairo to Amman, Jordan as a close friend, Stephen Emmel. Stephen, a Coptic specialist, was on his way to Jerusalem to study with a renowned authority in that field.[2] Steve tried to convince us to go with him to Jerusalem—just for the weekend. Ordinarily, we wouldn't have hesitated for a second, but at this moment we were not easily persuaded, not only because we had planned other travels as we made our way back to Canada, but also because of the political tensions in Jerusalem and the surrounding region at the time. Steve, however, insisted, and prevailed. Little did we imagine that our "weekend" in Jerusalem would not only be life-changing but also have a significant impact on scholarship in the field of Islamic history and historiography.

Travelling by taxi, we descended from Amman to the Allenby Bridge (now also known as the King Hussein Bridge), crossed the Jordan River and the border into the West Bank and Israel, and then ascended from the river valley up through the hills to Jerusalem where we arrived in a snowstorm! We alighted at the British

1 This is not an article of the usual scholarly kind but rather a memoir, a reminiscence of an extraordinary time nearly 50 years ago in the lives of all involved on both the personal and professional levels. We were about to embark on a scholarly adventure of a most difficult and challenging kind. Recently, I have come to the astounding realization that I am the only one of the original core participants still living or able to tell the tale. This memoir is therefore written first and foremost in gratitude and as a tribute to Amal A. Abul-Hajj (now Hull) who first recognized the potential significance of the documents she had uncovered and ensured that they would be preserved. Amal is unable to co-author this memoir with me for health reasons. I also wish to dedicate this memoir to the memory of Crystal M. Bennett (d. 1987), Martin Lyons (d. 2002), my esteemed professor Dr. Donald P. Little (d. 2017), Dr. Michael H. Burgoyne (d. 2021), and Dr. Christel Kessler (d. 2022 just a few days short of her 100th birthday but who remained forever young in spirit), all of whom played key roles in bringing the Haram documents to light. I wish also to thank Dr. Nicholas Stanley-Price and the late Lynda Burgoyne, both of whom facilitated our research stay at the British School of Archaeology in Jerusalem in a variety of ways, and Edmund J. Hull for his continuing assistance and unfailing friendship.

2 Dr. Stephen Emmel studied Coptic language and linguistics with Prof. H.J. Polotsky, Emeritus, Hebrew University, Jerusalem, 1976–1977. From 1996 to 2019, he was Professor für Äygyptologie und Koptologie, Münster, Germany. Coincidentally Stephen and I were both born in Rochester, N.Y., USA and attended Monroe High School though we did not know each other before meeting in Cairo in 1975. We recently met again more than 40 years later at a conference of the Coptic Studies Society of Canada held in Toronto in 2017.

https://doi.org/10.1515/9783111330242-001

School of Archaeology in Jerusalem (BSAJ) in the Shaykh Jarrah neighbourhood where Steve would be in residence and were stunned when Prof. Christel Kessler, whom we had come to know in Cairo, opened the door. Christel, had just retired as professor of Islamic art and architectural history at The American University in Cairo.[3] On her retirement, she had told us that she was returning to Cambridge, UK, but in fact, she had gone to Jerusalem to advise and assist in the preparation of the BSAJ exhibition, an inventory and mapping of the medieval Islamic monuments of Jerusalem for the World of Islam Festival in London that year. In those days, for political and security reasons, she had been unable to reveal that her true destination was Jerusalem. Christel was delighted to see Martin land on her doorstep since, as it happened, she needed a photographer to prepare for the exhibition. And so began the adventure! Working with Prof. Kessler and the director of the project, Dr. Michael H. Burgoyne, a Scottish architectural historian,[4] Martin photographed the western and northern walls of al-Ḥaram al-Sharif for the BSAJ exhibition.

Meanwhile, however, Michael introduced me to Amal Abul-Hajj, the Palestinian Director/Curator of the Islamic Museum at al-Ḥaram al-Sharif, now more officially known as the Islamic Museum of al-Aqsa Mosque,[5] which operated under the auspices of the Jerusalem Council of the Awqaf (religious endowments) which in

3 Prof. Kessler had been an assistant to K.A.C. Creswell during his lifetime and was his literary executor upon his death. She is author of *The Carved Masonry Domes of Cairo*, among other studies. While in Cairo, Martin Lyons photographed a series of the Mamluk domes in the Qarafa or northern Cemetery for Prof. Kessler. Christel visited us in Montreal and I her in Cambridge and we remained in touch until shortly before her death.

4 Michael Burgoyne served as Lead Architect of the survey of Islamic monuments in Jerusalem sponsored by the BSAJ from 1975–1979 while also completing his DPhil at Oxford under the supervision of Dr. Michael Rogers. Michael held several positions before joining Historic Scotland as Senior Architect in 1989, a position he held until his retirement, but he never lost interest in the architecture of the Middle East. See the interesting account of Michael's life and career in the obituary by Denys Pringle, *Michael Hamilton Burgoyne 1944–2021*. Michael's daughter was born unexpectedly early while visiting us in Montreal and now lives in Toronto. We exchanged many visits to Edinburgh and Toronto over the years.

5 Amal Abul-Hajj held the position of Director of the Museum (1973–1979) in all but name, for the title of Director was then held nominally by the highly trusted custodian during those tense times. Amal received her BA from the American University in Beirut in 1971, an MA in Arabic Studies from the American University in Cairo in 1994 where her thesis dealt with thirty *ṭirāz* fragments from The Textile Museum in Washington, DC. She also spent a year at St. Cross College, Oxford University, 1986–1987. She is author or co-author of several articles in addition to the article in which we announced the discovery of the Haram Documents: Northrup/Abul-Hajj, *Collection of Medieval Arabic Documents*. See also Burgoyne/Abul-Hajj, *Twenty-four Mediaeval Arabic Inscriptions*; Walls/Abul-Hajj, *Arabic Inscriptions in Jerusalem*. Amal also collaborated with Esin Atıl on the translation into English of *Kalilah wa Dimnah*.

turn was responsible to the Awqaf officials in Amman,[6] a detail that would eventually be of critical importance to our work as will become apparent below. On her appointment as Director/Curator in the fall of 1973, Amal had insisted on carrying out an inventory of all the Museum's holdings. This included the contents of some locked display cabinet drawers that the Awqaf officials in charge of the Museum were reluctant to open, telling her that they contained only some old papers. Amal insisted and so, in the presence of officials of the Jerusalem Council of Awqaf, the drawers were opened on August 19, 1974. They did, indeed, contain some very old papers, papers dating from the thirteenth to the fifteenth centuries CE. Though not knowing precisely what these papers were, she realized that they likely had historical importance. When she found them, some, if not all of them, had small notes attached to them, indicating that they had previously been perused, but by whom is not known. In fact, it is still not known how or when these papers found their way into the Museum.[7] In any case, Amal sought the advice of a UNESCO expert in the conservation of written artifacts of this sort who recommended as a first step that they be fumigated to exterminate any insects that might be dining on them. That task was completed before my arrival in Jerusalem. The UNESCO expert also provided further instructions for their conservation. However, Amal was already involved in a project to study 25 or so of the more than 600 unpublished, unstudied Qur'an manuscripts in the Museum collection. Moreover, since discovering the documents in 1974, she had not found anyone interested in helping her to examine them, so given the lack of interest, resources, and her other curatorial projects at the time, she had temporarily set the documents aside.

That is. . .until I came along. . .a young historian of the Mamluk period (1250–1517 CE) and PhD candidate at the Institute of Islamic Studies, McGill University in Montreal, but with little experience of medieval Islamic legal or administrative documents. I had, however, developed an interest in and appreciation for original source materials that had evolved while carrying out research, using not microfilms or photocopies, but manuscripts dating to the Mamluk period in the libraries of Cairo. My excitement over the discovery of the Ḥaram documents was further fueled by the fact that I had somehow miraculously come across the shelf number for the *waqfiyya* (endowment deed) for the hospital (*al-bīmāristān al-Manṣūrī*)

6 Little, *Significance*, 194, no. 16.

7 Müller, in his article, *Mamlūk Court Archive*, on the basis of some painstaking analysis of the Ḥaram corpus, proposes that these documents had been gathered selectively in the context of an investigation into the affairs of a corrupt judge in Jerusalem, and suggests that because the case had never been closed, the documents related to the case were kept at the al-Aqsa mosque. Yet the evidence is circumstantial and, as he says, the mystery of the true nature of this collection remains unsolved. On the making of this corpus see also the *Introduction* to this catalogue.

Fig. 1: Linda Northrup, Amal Abul-Hajj and Martin Lyons (from left to right), Islamic Museum/ al-Ḥaram al-Sharif, spring 1978 (most likely taken by Donald P. Little), © Linda Northrup.

founded in Cairo by the Mamluk Sultan, al-Manṣūr Qalāwūn (r. 678/1279–689/1290) in the late thirteenth century kept at the Ministry of Awqaf in Cairo.[8] Without knowing the shelf number, such a document for all practical purposes did not exist, for there was no way to ask to see it. At that time, there were few documents in the Cairo collections accessible to anyone and Prof. Muhammad Muhammad Amin of Cairo University had not yet published his *Catalogue*, which, once available, had the effect of opening the "archives" to interested scholars.[9] Gaining permission to read Qalāwūn's waqfiyya took months of weekly interviews at the Central Agency for Public Mobilization and Statistics (CAPMAS), Egypt's national security agency. Success was achieved just two weeks before my departure from Cairo, so there was little time to acquire the skills or experience to read and analyse it.[10] I did, however, succeed in obtaining a photocopy of the original waqfiyya preserved at Dār al-Ku-

8 The *waqfiyya* is filed as #1010 *qadīm* in the Daftarkhāna of the Ministry of Awqaf in Cairo. On the hospital, see Northrup, *From Slave to Sultan*, 119–25; Northrup, *Mamluk Historiography Revisited*; Northrup, *Qalawun's Patronage of the Medical Sciences*.

9 Amin, *Catalogue des documents d'archives du Caire*. Since then, Prof. Amin has published the text of the document and some plates in the appendix to his edition of Ibn Ḥabīb, *Tadhkirat al-nabīh*, Vol. 1, 296–396.

10 In Little, *Use of Documents*, 3, he complains of not having had training in documentary studies at the graduate level. I had suffered the same fate! Documents were scarce and documentary studies were in their infancy.

tub al-Miṣriyya (Egypian National Library) before leaving Cairo.[11] Although I had been reading original manuscripts of contemporary chronicles, biographical dictionaries, scribal handbooks, and other kinds of narrative texts all year in Cairo, I had never until then encountered an original document. Qalāwūn's waqfiyya was clearly penned in what I now consider to be a relatively legible script, certainly as compared to many of the Ḥaram documents, which though physically well preserved, are frustratingly written in what I call "scribal scrawl". The result of my find in Cairo? – a budding interest in documents and the kinds of historical evidence they could provide!

Michael had introduced me to Amal almost immediately upon our arrival in Jerusalem. She showed me the documents retrieved from the display cabinets which by now were kept unceremoniously in an old wooden crate. So scruffy looking were they that if one didn't know what they were, one might have thought them wastepaper. The first document I fished out of the crate to examine was, as fate would have it, a *marsūm* (decree or administrative order)[12] dated to the last ten days of Jumāda I 664/28 February – 8 March 1266 issued to my amazement by the Mamluk Sultan al-Ẓāhir Baybars (r. 658/1260–676/1277), my Sultan Qalāwūn's predecessor.[13] My excitement grew as we examined a few more documents that morning and Amal proposed that we work together on them.

There was no turning back. Martin and I agreed to a change in plans. I would stay in Jerusalem to work with Amal if he could obtain a visa for Yemen, a country he had been longing to explore since meeting some young Yemenis (where else but) at the top of the Great Pyramid (Khufu) in Giza, from which the Inspector of Antiquities at Giza then, the now famous Dr. Zahi Hawass,[14] had asked Martin to photograph. The Yemenis would soon become our close friends and visited us in Montreal. On completing the photography in Jerusalem for the BSAJ exhibit, we both returned to Amman where Martin succeeded in obtaining a visa for Yemen,

11 Document #15/2 at Dār al-Wathā'iq al-Qawmiyya (Majmūʿāt Maḥkamat al-Aḥwāl al-Shakhsiyya). What I did not know when I was granted permission to see the *waqfiyya* in the Awqaf collection was that it (#1010) was a copy of document #15/2 in Dār al-Wathā'iq. Document #15/2 is, in fact, the original *waqfiyya* and was the basis for Prof. Amin's edition of Qalāwūn's *waqfiyya* published in the appendix to his edition of Ibn Ḥabīb, *Tadhkirat al-nabīh*.

12 On *marsūm* (pl. *marāsim)*, see Little, *Catalogue*, 24/5.

13 Little, *Catalogue*, 27, #34.

14 Dr. Zahi Hawass, an Egyptologist and archaeologist by training and Inspector at Giza in 1976, who later served as Minister of Antiquities of Egypt, and who has now become a media celebrity, sometimes referred to as "the Indiana Jones of Egypt." So steep are the pyramids and so large the stone blocks from which they are constructed that climbing them is extremely dangerous and so not permitted to the public. Exceptionally, we climbed at the request of Dr. Hawass to photograph from the summit.

whereupon I returned on my own to Jerusalem to work with Amal. There was no room available at the British School just then and so at this point I wish to acknowledge the generous and warm hospitality of Amal's family, but especially of her mother, Wasilah Abul-Hajj, who invited me to stay with them. I lived with Amal and her mother in their family home in the Bāb al-Ẓahra neighbourhood in East Jerusalem around the corner from the National Palace Hotel that had been owned by her parents, Ali and Wasilah, and just a stone's throw from Damascus Gate and the Ḥaram. Amal's mother was a wonderful cook and so not only did my knowledge of medieval Arabic documents expand but so too did my experience of and appetite for Palestinian cuisine. I learned how to cure olives, how to stuff carrots, and many other delightful things, but unfortunately, I've never achieved results to equal Wasilah's delectable cuisine. It is thus also in remembrance of Amal's mother, Wasilah, that I dedicate this memoir with love.

Fig. 2: Amal Abul-Hajj, Islamic Museum/al-Ḥaram al-Sharif, spring 1978 (taken by Martin Lyons), © Linda Northrup.

Amal and I immediately began a preliminary survey of the documents in the collection which at that stage numbered approximately 354 complete documents and many other small fragments.[15] Of these we read perhaps 70 or so but focused more closely on about 50 documents, a sample that we believed would suggest the nature of the collection until a catalogue of the documents could be produced. We

15 Northrup/Abul-Hajj, *Collection of Medieval Arabic Documents*, 283.

described them briefly in our article announcing the find.[16] We began by sorting the documents into categories. This we were able to do quite easily in most cases simply by reading the introductory phrases—*ḥaṣala al-wuqūf ʿalā* ("the viewing occurred on. . .", i.e., an estate inventory), *hādhā mā ishtarā* ("this is what [so-and-so] purchased. . .", i.e., a purchase), etc.[17] The Ḥaram documents contained specimens of decrees (*marsūm, marāsim*) and petitions (*qiṣṣa, aqṣāṣ*), court records (*maḥḍar, maḥāḍir*), legal depositions (*iqrārāt, ishhādāt, shahādāt*), property deeds and rental contracts, a few endowments (*waqfiyyāt*), quittances of debt, accounts, and letters.[18] As it turned out the estate inventories constituted the largest group among these various types. We were also able to determine that most of the documents in the Ḥaram collection, as it existed then in the spring of 1976, bore dates, the majority of which were issued in the late fourteenth century.[19] We were also aware of the frequent appearance of the name of the Shāfiʿī judge, the qāḍī Sharaf al-Dīn ʿĪsā b. Ghānim al-Anṣārī, as well as of another Jerusalem resident, Burhān al-Dīn Ibrāhīm al-Nāṣirī, who seemed always to be seeking employment in various religious capacities in and around the Ḥaram, but we had no time to investigate these interesting people at that time.[20] Nevertheless, as we sorted and read the documents, the significance of the Ḥaram collection became increasingly apparent. This was one of the few collections of documents known to exist before the Ottoman period pertaining to or emanating from mainly ordinary people, rather than from a civilian or military elite as is the case with most other surviving collections, the Cairo Geniza excepted, and one of the only sources of this kind for Jerusalem. The Ḥaram documents promised to yield a wealth of economic, social, cultural, and other data not found in narrative texts.[21]

---

16 We described them only briefly because we had limited time and lacked the resources that would allow us to investigate them more thoroughly, as will be explained below.

17 But now see Müller's careful analysis of these opening phrases and some variations, *The Ḥaram Collection*, 437.

18 Northrup/Abul-Hajj, *Collection of Medieval Arabic Documents*, 283. The various types of documents are now described in greater detail in Little's *Catalogue*.

19 Northrup/Abul-Hajj, *Collection of Medieval Arabic Documents, 283*. After further study, we realized that a large number dated to the last decade of the fourteenth century. It would later become apparent that of these a significant number were dated between the years 793–796/1390–1395. See Little, *Significance*, 195.

20 Haarmann, however, published an article on Burhān al-Dīn's library, *The Library*. See also Aljoumani/Hirschler, *Owning Books and Preserving Documents*.

21 The Geniza documents, discovered in the late nineteenth century in the basement of one of the oldest Jewish synagogues in Cairo, is another such collection. Though associated with the Jewish community, the Geniza nevertheless contains many documents in Arabic or Judaeo-Arabic that have received intense scrutiny though they are scattered in libraries all over the world. We were acutely aware that the Haram documents could provide a wealth of information not always found

The documents were not easy to read or should I say decipher. Whereas Amal could read more quickly than I could, she might read what she expected or wanted to read whereas I, struggling to decipher a word or phrase, would sometimes deliberately read a phrase backward to determine where the ligatures between letters were, sometimes even correcting Amal. This strategy worked! Together we were able to resolve many, though not all difficulties, that would have perplexed us had we been working alone.[22] Amal also commented on one occasion that many of the phrases in these "medieval" documents were like those she had encountered while going through her father's "modern" papers after his death. Indeed, we realized that to a large extent the Ḥaram documents not only contain some turns of phrase used in Mamluk times, but also resemble modern legal or other forms with set phrases. Once one becomes familiar with the legal jargon, the documents become, if not easy, at least easier to read. The problems most often arise in deciphering the detailed information that fills in the blanks, so to speak, between the set phrases.

Fig. 3: Linda Northrup (left) and Amal Abul-Hajj reading Document #333, Islamic Museum/al-Ḥaram al-Sharif, spring 1978 (taken by Martin Lyons), © Linda Northrup.

in literary sources and thus would be of incalculable importance. See also Northrup/Abul-Hajj, *Collection of Medieval Arabic Documents*, 284.

22 See Little's comments on our article, *Significance*, 189 and *Catalogue*, 2, no. 1. It should be remembered that we were working without resources of any kind and with limited time to study the collection in any greater detail. The situation required creativity, improvisation, and resourcefulness resulting in our bringing the Haram documents to light, thus making a new source of historical information known to modern scholars.

Amal and I worked together on the documents for the next two months or so without news of and not knowing when Martin would return from Yemen, for in those days we did not have the advantage of cell phones, text messages, or email. In other words, we did not know how much time we had for our project. Early each morning we would leave for Amal's office in the Museum housed in the Zāwiya al-Fakhriyya (dating to before 732/1332),[23] situated at the southwest corner of the Ḥaram to the west of al-Aqsa, adjacent to the Maghribi gate, and overlooking the Wailing Wall, where we would work until mid-afternoon.

Following the instructions of Amal's UNESCO advisor, we applied a fine spray of water to each document to enable us to unfold or unroll it as the case might be and flatten the paper or parchment so that it could be read and eventually photographed. We then placed each document so dampened between sheets of absorbent archival matting paper and improvised a press to weigh them down, using the two huge, heavy volumes of K.A.C. Creswell's *Early Muslim Architecture*, the only objects of sufficient size available to us in the Museum that could serve the purpose. The same technique was employed again in the spring 1978 phase of the project. The UNESCO advisor had assured Amal that centuries-old ink does not run, and though apprehensive, we accepted his advice which proved correct, and so the written texts when dampened were not damaged. As far as I know an analysis of the several types of paper and ink found in the collection has yet to be undertaken but would be an interesting project.

Fig. 4: Linda Northrup spraying document with water to flatten, Islamic Museum/al-Ḥaram al-Sharif, spring 1978 (taken by Martin Lyons), © Linda Northrup.

23 Burgoyne with additional historical research by D.S. Richards, *Mamluk Jerusalem*, 258–69.

We left the documents we had prepared each day in this way overnight so that by the next morning they were dry and flat and could be read and eventually photographed. The original folds and the glued or stitched joinings in some of the documents remain clearly visible in the photographs, a point of some importance as, for example, in the case of the *murabbaʿ* (a so-called square decree as opposed to a scroll), only one specimen of which had been known to exist before those found in the Ḥaram collection, but which display a manner of folding particular to that category.[24] A number of documents were stitched together with string as is evident either in the string holes which remain or in documents in which the string still remains in place. We determined that these documents consisted mainly of accounts, a fact that Little later confirmed.[25] With one exception we left the string in place when found, recognizing that it constituted evidence. We also measured and assigned a number to each document and took notes regarding each. We did this as systematically as possible at this early stage of our survey. Documents assigned to each category together were for the most part clustered and numbered in their group consecutively, though not ordered by other important criteria such as date, etc. Eventually strict order was impossible to maintain for a variety of reasons beyond our control at the time, but also because additional documents were subsequently found and added to the original cache.[26]

Reading the documents was the most difficult task facing us, but we encountered other challenges as well. The Museum was closed to the public at the time and lacked facilities to make our work easier. The Zāwiya remained nearly in its original state. The cut, thick stone ith which it was constructed retained the cold and dampness in February and March 1976 when we began our survey. Our only source of heat was a small electric heater. Our hands froze as we worked during these winter months! The lighting was also poor. Yet, despite the difficulties, it was a thrill to work in this environment soaking up the history in these stones as one does in such a place and as I had also had experienced while working at Dār al-Wathāʾiq al-Qawmiyya (Egyptian National Archives) then housed up at the citadel in Cairo before its move down to the new Dār al-Kutub al-Miṣriyya (Egyptian National Library) on

---

24 Little, *Catalogue*, 24 and 28–35. See also Richards, *'Square' Decree*, 63–7.

25 Little, *Significance*, 207 for a discussion of the documents stitched together with string. See Little, *Catalogue*, 335 for further discussion where he states that most of the documents bound together with string are accounts related to estate inventories. With just one exception, these accounts are referred to as *makhzūma, makhzūmāt*, meaning something that has been pierced, a term, it seems, ultimately derived from camel terminology, i.e., the nose of a camel.

26 Little's *Catalogue* takes this problem of catalogue numbers into account by providing an index of the documents by number which gives the page number in the *Catalogue* for each. He groups each category together although the numbers in each category are not always consecutive.

the banks of the Nile. Nor did we have a library (Creswell's tomes excepted) available on site to consult. Indeed, only a few document collections were then known to exist. Nor were there many models for this kind of scholarship available in those days.[27] We were working in the dark so to speak, the blind leading the blind, yet learning from the experience as our project progressed.

Our work was also frequently interrupted by disturbances in and around the Ḥaram. Unfortunately, given the tensions at the time, it was difficult to consult Israeli colleagues, visit museums,[28] or even to purchase books that might provide guidance. One day as we were walking from the Ḥaram up through the Old City to the bookstore of the Franciscan Custodia Terrae Sanctae to purchase Norberto Risciani's *Documenti e Firmani*,[29] all the shop shutters began to be drawn. Fearing that something sinister might be afoot in the neighbourhood, we rushed back to the Ḥaram to take refuge there before the gates closed.

Political tensions were not the only threat posed to the documents. Windstorms also proved to be a menace. One afternoon we had left some documents on the desk for processing the following day, but overnight a huge windstorm arose. The next morning, we found that the old windows in this early fourteenth-century building that did not close firmly in the best of times had blown open. We were shocked in the morning to find that the documents had flown all over the office. We didn't lose any, but we were more careful after that to secure our precious specimens.

One day, later that spring, Martin suddenly reappeared at the door, thinner than when he had left, but safe and sound. He had walked all over Yemen from its mountain tops to the Tihama Red Sea littoral, north to south, east to west photographing the architectural wonders of that country and especially the people he had met along the way.[30] At that point, our initial survey of the documents had advanced to the extent that we had a good idea of the nature of the collection as it existed then. Martin spent several days informally photographing some of the doc-

27 See Little, *Significance*, 189–92, who summarizes in some detail the scholarship available when we were working with the collection, and as he was preparing the *Catalogue*.

28 I did meet with the late Prof. David Ayalon, the doyen of Mamluk studies, and here acknowledge with gratitude his hospitality and generosity in introducing me to the resources pertinent to my thesis research available in the Hebrew University of Jerusalem library. Amal and I also did manage a visit to the L.A. Mayer Museum for Islamic Art in Jerusalem.

29 Risciani, *Documenti e Firmani*. We returned another day to the bookstore where, I believe, we purchased the last 3 copies available of this rare publication. The book has no title page! It includes photographs, transcribed Arabic texts and translations in Italian of several decrees and other documents, some bearing Mamluk chancery style royal signatures as well as commentary.

30 His Yemen photographs were exhibited at the Notman Photographic Archives at the McCord-Stewart Museum in Montreal and are now held in the permanent collection of the Notman Archives.

uments, though not the entire collection, for it was now time to return to Canada. Our serendipitous weekend trip to Jerusalem had turned into a stay of several months and into an exciting adventure, a project that would have a lasting impact on us and on scholarship concerning the history and historiography of Mamluk Jerusalem and the region.

That summer Amal and I co-authored an article published in December 1978[31] announcing the discovery of the Ḥaram documents. Reflecting our preliminary survey, it included a brief description of each of the 50 sample documents in the collection that we had read a little more closely. Donald Little later described us as having published the article "quietly and modestly",[32] but in fact, we not only lacked time and resources, but we were also hesitant to draw too much immediate attention to the find. There was some apprehension given the Israeli military presence just outside the Ḥaram gates and the Maghribi Gate next to our office and the frequent intrusions of groups such as Gush Eumunim,[33] an ultra-orthodox right-wing Jewish group, that the documents among other artifacts in the museum might be at risk of damage or even confiscation if their value were recognized. Perhaps our fears were unfounded or exaggerated, but tensions were palpable, so we deliberately decided not to make too big a splash, one that might attract unwanted kinds of attention.

On my return to Montreal in the summer of 1976,[34] I showed the photographs of the sample of Ḥaram documents to my PhD supervisor, Prof. Little. He was interested and excited, but realizing the enormity of the task at hand, declared that he already had his life's work before him and so was unable to help. Meanwhile, I was in the midst of writing my PhD thesis and, having just spent a research year in Cairo, could not easily abandon my study of the Sultan al-Manṣūr Qalāwūn to begin a new project on the Ḥaram documents as attractive as that possibility might have been.[35] And so, except for the brief article that Amal and I published announcing the find, the documents languished in Amal's office. Nevertheless, she continued to work on them intermittently as time permitted until a turn of events threatened to close the window of opportunity available to study this cache of documentary evidence that promised to illuminate the history of Mamluk Jerusalem between the thirteenth and fifteenth centuries.

31 Northrup/Abul-Hajj, *Collection of Medieval Arabic Documents*.

32 Little, *Significance*, 189.

33 Gush Eumunim was founded in 1974 and still plays a role in Israeli society and politics today.

34 Not 1975 as Little mistakenly states in *Significance*, 193.

35 It should be said that I have never regretted following through on my study of the Sultan Qalāwūn, an intriguing character who still commands my interest today. The Sultan has become a lifelong companion!

First, there were changes in the organization of the Museum. Amal reported that a new Department of Islamic Monuments had been created.[36] Although she didn't believe this development would have an impact on our project, it nevertheless created some uncertainty regarding the future direction and development of the Museum. In December 1976, Amal also wrote that while continuing as Director/Curator of the Museum, she would be spending a year at St. Cross College, Oxford. In the fall of 1976, still more documents were found resulting in a near doubling of the size of the original find. In February 1977, about one year after our first visit to Jerusalem, Amal wrote that she had found several more documents including three *marsūms* signed by the governor of Jerusalem (*nā'ib al-salṭana bi-al-Quds*), among others.[37]

Of most significance, however, was that by early 1978, Amal had announced her imminent marriage to an American diplomat and member of the US Consular Corps in Jerusalem. We realized that if the documents were to be brought to light, we had to seize this moment or lose the opportunity to study them since not only was the fate of the Museum unclear, but Amal would almost certainly be leaving her position after her marriage. At this point Prof. Little was persuaded to become involved. He succeeded in procuring the funding that would finance the return of our team (my husband Martin Lyons as photographer, Donald Little, and myself) to Jerusalem in the spring of 1978 to work with Amal systematically to conserve, photograph and catalogue the entire and now expanded collection.[38]

On our return to Jerusalem in the spring of 1978, however, we encountered still more challenges. Martin and I flew to Amman where we met Crystal Bennett, Director of the BSAJ, who, as it happened, was returning from Amman to Jerusalem. From Amman we traveled together. When we reached the Bridge and the border, Crystal and I initially had no problem crossing. However, Martin, our photographer, carrying all the film and photographic equipment, was detained. We could see him in a separate room, signalling frantically that he was being refused entry to the West Bank/Israel. To make matters worse, perhaps sensing our plight, the soldier or border guard in charge of Crystal and me, hearing Crystal speak a few words of Arabic to a porter, accused her of speaking Arabic, while not knowing Hebrew (this in fact was not the case), creating some unpleasantness and delay. Eventually,

36 According to Amal, the head of the new Department, whose name I regret not to know, was a graduate of Cairo University who had been transferred from Amman.

37 Personal communication with Amal Abul-Hajj.

38 With continuing gratitude, I acknowledge the financial support for our endeavour provided by the Institute of Islamic Studies and the Faculty of Graduate Studies, McGill University, and by Mr. James George, Director of The Threshold Foundation for funding the processing of the prints, and by Kodak Canada for photographic paper.

with a little negotiation and the payment of a small bakshish, whatever issue it was that had caused Martin's detention was resolved. Much relieved and the three of us reunited, we continued on our way to Jerusalem. Prof. Little had travelled separately flying directly to Tel Aviv. On this trip, we all stayed at the British School of Archaeology in Shaykh Jarrah.

Whereas Amal had won the respect of the Awqaf administration in Jerusalem as Director/Curator of the Museum, the announcement of her impending marriage to an American diplomat was met with rancor from the local Awqaf officials, hostility which also affected us. Having applied for and been assured permission to undertake the necessary conservation, photography, and cataloguing of the entire collection, which after all would benefit the Museum, politics came into play. We had been looking forward to our first meeting with the Director of the Jerusalem Awqaf administration at the time, but our reception turned out to be a chilly one. Clearly, all was not well. We were informed that we would be allowed to study only a small number of the documents, not the entire collection as originally planned. Not only was the scope of the project severely threatened, but we were also working within scheduling restrictions that allowed little time to negotiate and complete our task. It was then that the Director of the British School of Archaeology in Jerusalem and Amman, Crystal Bennett, once again came to the rescue. Crystal was scheduled to return to Amman and offered to meet and plead our case with the Jordanian Awqaf officials who had authority over the Awqaf administration in Jerusalem. Thanks to Crystal Bennett's intervention, the negative decision of the Jerusalem Awqaf office was overturned and permission to proceed with the project was restored. Consequently, we were able to photograph and catalogue the entire collection which by that time had grown in number to approximately 900 documents of which 850 are in Arabic. An intriguing subgroup of about 28 documents in Persian and another 14 documents, related to the Persian documents, in Arabic form part of the now greatly expanded collection.[39]

We worked quickly over approximately three weeks to spray, flatten, measure, assign a number, photograph, and make notes regarding each document, as described above. Some were photographed in Amal's office despite the lack of light, but many more were photographed in full daylight and open air in the small walled yard behind the Zāwiya/Museum office overlooking the Wailing Wall. On at least one occasion, it was decided to take the documents to the Aqsa Mosque whose windows had deep sills in the thick walls, sills that were filled with beautiful, filtered sunlight at certain times of the day, perfect light for photographing. At that time al-Aqsa and

39 See Little, *Catalogue*, 5–8 and 377–87 for the documents in this subgroup catalogued in Section IX of the *Catalogue*. See also Chapter IV *Persian and Persianate documents concerning Transcaucasia, Anatolia and northwestern Iran* in the present catalogue.

areas of the Ḥaram were undergoing renovations to repair damages suffered during the fire in 1969. The chief engineer in charge of the repairs in the Ḥaram at that time, Ibrahim Dakkak, and the supervising architect of the Ḥaram restorations, Issam Awwad, appreciating the historical importance of our project and indeed of all finds made during the repairs, facilitated our work, including occasional photography of the documents in the mosque. Martin would take the black and white 35 mm films made each day back to the BSAJ where he would develop them in the evening. On our departure the documents themselves remained in the Museum, conserved as well as possible given the limited resources available, between sheets of archival matting paper and laid flat in display cabinet drawers. Of the two sets of black and white photographs made, one remained in the Museum and one is kept at McGill University.[40] A microfilm copy was given to the University of Jordan and I obtained another microfilm copy that is now catalogued in the collections of Robarts Library at the University of Toronto.[41] The sample photographs that Martin made in the spring of 1976, printed on scraps of photographic paper left over from the BSAJ inventory project, remain in my possession.

In the fall of 1979, Prof. Little offered a graduate seminar on the documents in which my friend and classmate, Dr. Huda Lutfi, also a PhD candidate at the time, and two other students were enrolled. In our seminar, we not only read a selection of the documents, but also explored different types of early or contemporary source materials including Mujīr al-Dīn's *al-Uns al-jalīl bi-tārīkh al-Quds w'al-Khalīl* (one of the only contemporary "histories" of Jerusalem in the "medieval" period),[42] biographical dictionaries, legal treatises, scribal manuals (e.g., al-Qalqashandī (d. 821/1414),[43] al-ʿUmarī (d. 749/1348–1349),[44] al-Nuwayrī (d. 743/1332),[45] chronicles, and *shurūṭ* manuals used by notaries such as al-Jarawānī's *al-Kawkab al-mushriq fī mā yaḥtāj ilayhi al-muwaththiq*[46] and al-Asyūṭī's *Jawāhir al-ʿuqūd wa muʿīn al-qudāt wa'l-muwaqqiʿīn wa'l-shuhūd*,[47] that might assist us in our efforts to understand the documents we were studying. We also read secondary sources such as Stern's *Fatimid Decrees* and his edited volume, *Documents from Islamic Chanceries*,[48]

40 Little, *Significance*, 194.

41 It may be that other sets of microfilms are now available in other libraries of which I am unaware.

42 Al-ʿUlaymī, *al-Uns al-jalīl*,

43 Al-Qalqashandī, *Ṣubḥ al-aʿshā*.

44 Al-ʿUmarī, *Al-Taʿrīf bi-muṣtalaḥ*.

45 Al-Nuwayrī, *Nihāyat al-arab*.

46 Al-Jarawānī, *al-Kawkab al-mushriq*.

47 Al-Asyūṭī, *Jawāhir al-ʿuqūd*.

48 Stern, *Fatimid Degrees*.

Goitein's studies on the Geniza documents,[49] Aziz Atiya's,[50] Kenneth Clark's,[51] and Hans Ernst's works on the Sinai documents,[52] among others., and familiarized ourselves with technical dictionaries, geographical works, numismatic studies, etc. At least partially based on our work in this seminar, Prof. Little prepared his preliminary article, "The Significance of the Ḥaram Documents for the Study of Medieval Islamic History,"[53] and began work on his *A Catalogue of the Islamic Documents from al-Ḥaram aš-Šarīf in Jerusalem*. Subsequently, he published a series of articles dealing with various aspects of the contents and format of the Ḥaram documents.[54] These articles dealing with topics such as slaves, Jews, rugs, institutions, legal practice, the estate of a merchant and his wife, etc., demonstrate the wide variety of topics and new areas of research that the discovery of the Ḥaram documents has made it possible to address. An interesting discovery regarding scribal practice made on the basis of the Ḥaram documents is that the *siyāqa* script, the earliest known usage of which was previously dated to the Ottoman period, had been used even earlier in the Mamluk period as our documents reveal.[55] Dr. Huda Lutfi's PhD dissertation, "A Study of al-Quds (Jerusalem) during the late Fourteenth Century, Based Primarily on the Ḥaram Estate Inventories and Related Documents," submitted to McGill University, 1983 and published as *al-Quds al-Mamlûkiyya: A History of Mamlûk Jerusalem based on the Ḥaram Documents*,[56] in which she focusses on the estate inventories, especially those concerning women, had its origins in our seminar and were also the subject of her article, "A Study of Six Fourteenth Century Iqrārs from al-Quds Relating to Muslim Women."[57] The documents had by now also become Donald Little's research priority and life work!

The bringing to light of this collection of documents for which Amal Abul-Hajj deserves our utmost appreciation, has had a profound impact on the study of medieval Jerusalem and the surrounding region and on the history and historiography of the medieval Middle East. It has invigorated discussion of legal and judicial practice, the scribal profession, pious institutions, interfaith relations in medieval Jerusalem, provincial administration, and relations with the Mamluk capital Cairo, slavery, the material culture of the region, in fact, Mamluk economic, political, and social history

49 Goitein, *Mediterranean Society*, among others.
50 Atiya, *Arabic Manuscripts of Mount Sinai*.
51 Clark, *Checklist*.
52 Ernst, *Sultansurkunden*.
53 Little, *Significance*, 189–219.
54 See *Publications of Donald P. Little*, 1–14, covering the years 1962–2005 and forthcoming, where most, if not all, of his Ḥaram related articles are listed.
55 Little, *Catalogue*, 334.
56 Lutfi, *al-Quds al-Mamlûkiyya*.
57 Lutfi, *Six Fourteenth Century Iqrārs*.

Fig. 5: Amal Abul-Hajj, Linda Northrup and Donald P. Little (from left to right), Islamic Museum/al-Ḥaram al-Sharif, spring 1978 (taken by Martin Lyons), © Linda Northrup.

and historiography in general. Research on the Ḥaram documents is also contributing to the burgeoning discussion of the existence of archives and archival practices in the Middle East.[58] The problem of the existence (or not) of centralized archives in the medieval Middle East comparable to those that are well known in the West, has constantly perplexed scholars who have studied various collections of pre-modern documents. It also challenged those of us who were seeking to understand the provenance of the Ḥaram documents at this early stage of investigation, and it is receiving renewed attention today. Whereas Little hypothesized that these documents, many of which bore the name of the Shāfiʿī judge, the qāḍī Sharaf al-Dīn ʿĪsā b. Ghānim al-Anṣārī may have constituted the private archives of this judge, Christian

58 See, for example, Bauden, *Mamluk Era Documentary Studies*; Reinfandt, *Mamluk Documentary Studies*; Paul, *Archival Practices*.

Müller has more recently argued that these documents were not part of the qāḍī's archive but more likely had to do with an embezzlement case in which the qāḍī was involved: they had been selected and collected for their relevance to an ongoing investigation.[59] Meanwhile, Konrad Hirschler has been questioning the existence of centralized archives in the Islamic world at least before the Ottoman period.[60]

Since the opening of the display cabinet drawers in the Museum on that day in August 1974, not only have more documents been found in the Museum, but other collections have also come to light. In fact, while in Jerusalem in the spring of 1978, Prof. Little was introduced to Mr. Haydar Khalidi, Chief Custodian of the Khalidi Library who invited him to visit the Library housed in the tomb complex of Barakat Khān (d. 644/1246), a Khwarazmian chieftain in military service with the Mamluk Sultan al-Ẓāhir Baybars, mentioned above, located in Ṭarīq Bāb al-Silsila, a street leading to one of the main gates of the Ḥaram (Bāb al-Silsila, the Chain Gate), a street that also overlooked the Wailing Wall. Mr. Khalidi's home, belonging to the tomb complex, was adjacent to the tomb/library separated by a courtyard, the site of the burials of Barakat Khān and his two sons. When shown the contents of the famous Khalidi Library, whose holdings Little has described in the article cited, Mr. Khalidi produced a portfolio of 46 family documents.[61] Little, by now as preoccupied with documents as Amal and I were, proposed to Mr. Khalidi that they be photographed to ensure their survival in the tense atmosphere that existed at the time, tensions that were directly affecting the Khalidi family whose home had been confiscated by the Israeli military alleging that a bomb had been found or set off in that street thus implicating Mr. Khalidi's properties.[62] The Library was consequently also in jeopardy. Mr. Khalidi agreed and so Donald Little, Martin and I photographed the Khalidi documents in that file. As at the Ḥaram, two sets of photographs were made one of which remains along with the documents with the Khalidi family in the library while a second set is kept at McGill University in Montreal. This bonus project proved to be yet another adventure in scholarship, one that offered further insights into the treacherous political situation affecting life in Jerusalem then (and now).[63]

59 Müller, *The Ḥaram Collection.*

60 Hirschler, *From Archive to Archival Practices.*

61 Little/Turgay, *Documents from the Ottoman Period*, 44. Little's introduction is followed by a brief description of each of the documents from the Ottoman period. Little describes the Arabic documents whereas Prof. Turgay describes the Turkish documents.

62 Little/Turgay, *Documents from the Ottoman Period*, 44–6. Mr. Khalidi, as Little reports, was a member of a prominent Arab family in Jerusalem and a former official in the Palestine Ministry of Education.

63 Little/Turgay, *Documents from the Ottoman Period*, 46/7.

The spring 1978 phase of the project coincided with Easter celebrations in Jerusalem and these events brought this phase of our project to a spectacular close. We attended the Maundy Thursday services in both the Armenian and Syriac churches. Though both churches commemorated the same event in the life of Jesus (the washing of the feet of his disciples), this event was re-enacted in very different but interesting ways. On Holy Saturday evening, we climbed to the roof of St. Stephen's chapel, the Ethiopian or Abyssinian church next to the Holy Sepulchre, to attend the "searching for the bones"[64] ceremony in which the faithful perform a counter clockwise procession circumambulating the chapel dome (resembling the counter clockwise circumambulation [*ṭawāf*] of the Ka'ba in Mecca during the *ḥajj*), though here to the accompaniment of drums, with all in attendance illuminating the procession with handmade beeswax candles, while some carried ceremonial parasols, a symbol of royalty. The climax of this Holy Week came on Easter Sunday for us not with traditional Easter celebrations, but rather, in a most extraordinary and memorable way. Invited by the engineers in charge of restorations in the Ḥaram, we climbed to the gallery above the rock circling at great height the interior of the Dome of the Rock (Qubbat al-Ṣakhrā). The reason for this invitation was that yet again, as at the Pyramids in Giza, Martin had been asked to climb to the top of the dome, which can be opened, to photograph. He climbed to the top with his guide up between the outer dome and the inner "skin" on a rickety metal ladder that curves with the shape of the dome. I found that climbing to the gallery on the inside of the dome was quite scary enough for there was nothing between those who found the courage to ascend and the rock below. Nevertheless, I bravely attempted to follow while refraining from joining Martin and his guide at the very top. We all survived, and I lived to tell this story! As we descended, the Easter bells rang out, celebrating Easter and our mission accomplished.

Since our first encounter with the Ḥaram documents in early 1976, others have taken up the scholarly baton to explore this important, but still challenging new source of information for Mamluk Jerusalem, immersing themselves in this difficult but fascinating material that offers, unlike narrative accounts, relatively unfiltered glimpses into the life of this city in these centuries. What began as a serendipitous weekend escapade resulted in a lifelong passion for the study of documentary sources and this intriguing find, as well as lifelong personal friendships and professional relationships that have enriched our lives. Who says documents are tedious?!

Linda S. Northrup

64 As I understand it, the bones searched are those of St. Stephen, not of Jesus!

I Introduction: The making of a documentary corpus

The Ḥaram al-sharīf corpus from Jerusalem with its 980 documents is a collection of outstanding importance for the history of pre-Ottoman Western Asia. As will be discussed below, numerous editions have been undertaken and these documents have proven to be of pivotal importance, especially for the field of Mamluk Studies. Yet how and when these documents converged into a single corpus is still largely unexplored. Even its (scholarly) discovery, which began in the 1970s, has been a convoluted process. The first batch of documents came to light in August 1974 and some two years later, in October 1976, another, larger batch was discovered.[65] The present work is the catalogue of a third batch of these documents that was discovered in the late 1990s. The first two batches, catalogued by Donald Little in his 1984 *Catalogue of the Islamic Documents from al-Ḥaram aš-Šarīf in Jerusalem*, came to light in rather undramatic circumstances; they were simply lying in the drawers of modern display cases in the Islamic Museum on the Ḥaram al-sharīf. As described in this catalogue's preface, the main protagonists in the bringing of the documents to the attention of the scholarly community in the late 1970s and early 1980s were Amal Abul-Hajj, Linda Northrup and Donald Little.[66] Of particular importance for the subsequent scholarly work were the black and white photographs of the documents taken by Martin Lyons in 1978. These photographs were subsequently microfilmed and made available to the wider community to serve as the basis for almost all publications in the next decades.[67] Yet notes accompanying the documents show that they had in fact already been 'discovered' at least once before the 1970s: A member of the museum staff must have started to work on some documents before the 1970s as is evident from notes on papers that have regrettably since been lost.[68]

Unfortuntely for researchers, who love narratives of discovery, the third batch (or new corpus) described in this catalogue was found (or rather identified) in a similarly unspectacular location: the cupboard of an office in the museum. Even though this new corpus came to light in the late 1990s, its documents have thus far hardly played a role in scholarship and the mere fact of its existence was not known

65 Little, *Catalogue*, 1984, 1.

66 Northrup/Abul-Hajj, *Collection of Medieval Arabic Documents*; Little, *Catalogue*. On Donald Little see the volume dedicated to his memory, Massoud, *Studies in Islamic Historiography*.

67 The 1978-set was deposited at McGill University and most editions until well into the 2010s de facto relied on (microfilm) copies of these images. They were made available online in 2021: https://mcgill.on.worldcat.org/oclc/1102813166.

68 Little, *Catalogue*, 2.

https://doi.org/10.1515/9783111330242-002

outside a handful of experts. The only documents from the third batch discussed in scholarship to date are two accounting books on repair works on the Ḥaram al-sharīf (23)/#926 and (24)/#927)[69] described in an article by Khader Salameh.[70] In this article he did not note that these two accounting books came from a new batch – a batch comprising documents that had neither been included in Donald Little's catalogue nor photographed by Martin Lyons. In consequence, the article published in 2014, did not really introduce the idea that a new batch had been found and scholarship failed to understand how important this publication was. The first (implicit) reference to the existence of a third batch of documents in the Islamic Museum had been made even earlier, in another article by Khader Salameh in 2001 in which he speaks of '950 items' in the museum, that is clearly a higher number of documents than those in the first two batches catalogued by Donald Little. Yet the ramification of this number – that new Ḥaram al-sharīf documents had been discovered – was not explicit.[71]

Our personal 'discovery' of the third batch came in 2019 when two of us, Said Aljoumani and Konrad Hirschler, went through the set of colour photographs taken in 2014.[72] While Donald Little's catalogue stopped at classmark #883, the photos continued right up to classmark #980, adding a further 97 items. The documents in this new corpus turned out to be crucial for our book *Owning Books and Preserving Documents in Medieval Jerusalem. The Library of Burhan al-Din al-Nasiri* (2023). The third batch has also been key for the research project *The Persian Documents from al-Ḥaram al-sharīf in Jerusalem* (2021–24) led by Zahir Bhalloo, who worked closely with the Japanese Society for the Promotion of Science (JSPS) project led by Masatomo Kawamoto.[73] The Transcaucasian documents, in turn, proved to be of significant interest for Jost Gippert and his team on the European Research Council project *The Development of Literacy in the Caucasian Territories*. While working on our various projects at Universität Hamburg's *Centre for the Study of Manuscript Culture* we repeatedly came together to discuss these new documents and it was clear that a catalogue was required to ensure that these documents finally take up the place they deserve in future scholarship.

69 Numbers in brackets refer to the entry number in this catalogue. Numbers preceeded by '#' refer to the classmarks in the Islamic Museum in Jerusalem. Only the classmark numbers should be used for citing documents in future scholarship.

70 Salameh, *Renovations*.

71 Salameh, *Primary Sources*, 3–5.

72 Another set of photographs was produced under the supervision of Christian Müller (Paris) and Khader Salamah (Jerusalem) in December 2010 with some additions in February 2011.

73 A comprehensive edition and study of the Ḥaram al-Sharif Persian documents is being prepared in the framework of this collaboration.

Archival histories

When the documents in what we call today the Ḥaram al-sharīf corpus actually became one single corpus is entirely unclear, as has been argued elsewhere.[74] The Islamic Museum was founded in the early 1920s. Was the corpus (or parts of it) already part of the collection at this point? Where were the documents before they came to the museum, whether in the 1920s or at a later date? What is clear is that the corpus is highly heterogeneous and is neither a single court archive nor a judge's archive, as previous scholarship has sometimes assumed.[75] Rather, it consists of clearly distinct documentary sub corpora that were merged at some point in history. Previous work has shown that within the Ḥaram al-sharīf corpus there are several clusters of documents and that each of these sub corpora had its own archival history and trajectory before becoming part of today's corpus. Among them are at least two estate archives (those of a wealthy trader called Nāṣir al-Dīn al-Ḥamawī (d. 788/1386) and a reciter called Burhān al-Dīn al-Nāṣirī (d. 789/1387), both from the late eighth/fourteenth century),[76] an archive of the (Persianate) Ādūjī family (mostly from the first half of the eighth/fourteenth century), a collection of documents for a legal case against the late eighth/fourteenth century Jerusalem judge Sharaf al-Dīn ʿĪsā b. Ghānim (d. 797/1395),[77] an archive of sultanic Mamluk decrees (mostly from the ninth/fifteenth century) and an administrative endowment archive of the Ḥaram al-sharīf itself (again mostly dating from the eighth/fourteenth century).

The Ḥaram al-sharīf corpus as we know it today is thus not one single medieval 'archive' with a continuous and linear shared history. It is rather an amalgamation of sub corpora that lends itself to inquiry into practices of collecting and preserving documents in West Asia up to the twentieth century. It is entirely unclear at what points in history the various sub corpora of the 'Ḥaram al-sharīf corpus' started to have a shared history. This is quite similar to the case of the 'Cairo Geniza corpus' (or rather corpora) that Rebecca Jefferson has so elegantly analysed. These documents also have a far more complex and rich history than the narrative of the dormant storeroom discovered by European scholars and travellers implies.[78] Neither the Ḥaram al-sharīf corpus nor the Geniza corpus is just a medieval corpus, they are rather corpora that continued to grow right up until the point when schol-

74 Aljoumani/Hirschler, *Owning Books*.

75 Aljoumani/Hirschler, *Owning Books*, 81.

76 Research on al-Ḥamawī's accounts is part of the PhD thesis of Michail Hradek (Munich). On Burhān al-Dīn see Aljoumani/Hirschler, *Owning Books*.

77 Müller, *Mamlūk Court Archive*.

78 Jefferson, *Age of Discovery*.

arship discovered them as sites of inquiry – and to some extent even after their discovery. Nick Posegay has, for instance, shown that we find Yiddish newspapers issued in Leeds in 1897 and in London in 1902 within the Geniza corpus, as well as a book price list printed in Berlin-Steglitz as late as 1929.[79] In the same vein, the Ḥaram al-sharīf corpus' youngest member dates to the beginning of World War I in 1914 ((60)/#887).

The Islamic Museum has been home to the Ḥaram al-sharīf corpus since the founding of the establishment in the early 1920s. Its foundation was part of a wider process in which new cultural institutions were set up across Ottoman and Mandate Palestine from the late nineteenth century onwards. Part of this development saw private initiatives 'from below' such as the foundation of the Khalidi family library as a public library in 1900.[80] These bottom-up projects were part of a wider reconfiguration of the cultural topography, in which the Ottoman state also played a prime role. For instance, in the field of redrawing the map of libraries Ṭāhir al-Jazā'irī (1852–1920) acted as the state's representative and was a driving force in the late Ottoman period throughout Greater Syria.[81] In the Mandate period the Supreme Muslim Council emerged as one of the main actors of Arab civil society founding, for instance, the Islamic Library in Jaffa in 1923.[82] This council also set up the Aqṣā Library in Jerusalem on the Ḥaram al-sharīf as well as the Islamic Museum. The creation of these new institutional frameworks went hand in hand with the reconfiguration of existing collections. For instance, when the al-Jazzār Library in Acre was 'revived' in the early twentieth century, a process in which Ṭāhir al-Jazā'irī was also involved, a large number of new manuscripts were added to its existing collection.[83] In the same vein, the Aqṣā Library absorbed collections that were not previously in the building. The foundation of the Islamic Museum was accompanied by a similar reconfiguration of existing collections of material objects in Jerusalem and wider Palestine. It is thus highly likely that this moment was also a decisive milestone (though certainly not the first milestone) in the gradual merging of documentary (sub)corpora into what we know today as the Ḥaram al-sharīf corpus.

---

79 Posegay, *Searching for the Last Genizah Fragment*.

80 Conrad, *The Khalidi Library*; Khālidī, *al-Maktaba al-Khālidīya*.

81 On him see El Shamsy, *Rediscovering the Islamic Classics*, 158–70.

82 *Bayān al-majlis al-sharʿī al-islāmī al-aʿlā fī Filasṭīn sanat 1341/2 (1923/4)*, Jerusalem: Maṭbaʿat madrasat al-aytām al-islāmīya, 1343/1924, 33.

83 Hirschler, *A (Mostly) Local Story*.

The material and textual logic of the new corpus

This catalogue presents the documents found in the third batch, the new corpus, and sees itself as a supplement to Donald Little's 1984 catalogue. Rather than just noting that there are now more documents in the Ḥaram al-sharīf corpus, we want to take the opportunity of this introduction to reflect upon the cultural process that led to the formation of this third batch. The aim is to highlight the characteristics and profile of this batch so that it might serve as a contribution to the effort to disentangle the archival histories of the modern-day Ḥaram al-sharīf corpus. For that purpose, we want to make two principal arguments: Firstly, this third batch is indeed part of the mishmash that we call today the Ḥaram al-sharīf corpus as we find a very clear overlap with the first and second batch in terms of period (mostly pre-Ottoman period with a large cluster from the 'classical' period of the Ḥaram al-sharīf corpus, the 790s/1390s), in terms of documentary genres (such as the importance of documents linked to estate inventories) and in terms of geography (Jerusalem and a distinct group of documents from Persianate Transcaucasia, Anatolia and northwest Iran). Secondly, we want to propose that the third batch only came into being in the twentieth century as the result of a sorting process of the Ḥaram al-sharīf corpus that took place in the museum. This formation of the third batch was underlain, the argument continues, by a material, visual and textual logic so that those documents considered to be too fragmentary in material terms, too untidy in terms of visual organisation and too strange in textual terms were set apart. This is evident from the fact that most of the documents in the third batch are much more fragmentary and incomplete than those of the first and second batches catalogued by Donald Little. In addition, we find in the third batch relatively more drafts, more non-Arabic documents (in particular Persian and Ottoman), more multi-lingual documents (including texts in Armenian, Georgian, Mongolian and Turkic) and more non-documentary texts (such as prayer texts). The new corpus thus seemingly came into being during a process of putting aside such fragmentary and 'strange' documents, while the more complete, more Arabic and more documentary texts went into the first or second batch. This sorting must have occurred before 1974 as Linda Northrup is certain that the documents of the third batch were not known when she and Amal Abul-Hajj worked on the first two batches in the 1970s.[84] Regrettably we no longer know which of the documents catalogued by Donald Little belonged to the first batch and which belonged to the second batch as this was not recorded. It is thus impossible to know whether the formation of these two batches was also underlain by comparable material or textual logic. In consequence, from now onwards we will refer to these two batches simply as the 'old corpus'.

84 Personal communication to Konrad Hirschler in 2021.

The first argument, that the third batch belongs to the Ḥaram al-sharīf corpus, is clearly evident from those documents that are in our catalogue's second chapter on (mostly) Arabic documents concerning Jerusalem, Bilād al-shām and Cairo. They strongly match the Arabic documents of the old corpus in terms of content and period as the following four examples demonstrate. We have for instance a document linked to the Ṣalāḥīya Khānqāh in Jerusalem ((1)/#884) and we find several documents on this *khānqāh* in the old corpus. The new corpus also has documents linked to trade such as accounts for (sale of soap, (14)/#890 and (15)/#924; wheat and honey, (20)/#971; and food products such as onions and meat, (19)/#979); as well as merchants' letters ((43)/#899) and sale contracts (for cotton, (10)/#922; lambs, (16)/#940; and land, (9)/#974). These are strikingly similar to the numerous trade-related documents in the old corpus. Moreover, the new corpus encompasses documents linked to estates and inheritance ((29)/#901, (30)/#945, (31)/#978), (32)/#939, (33)/#897, (34)/#921, (35)/#968, (36)/#944 and there are hundreds of such documents in the old corpus. Finally we find in the new corpus: endowment-related paperwork ((37)/#931, (38)/#970), (39)/#937, (41)/#947; receipts ((13)/#948 and (28)/#907); a rent contract ((12)/#923); a lease contract ((21)/#941); a Sultanic decree ((2)/#973); judicial certifications ((53)/#933 and (74)/#888) –all of which have counterparts in the old corpus.

Apart from the thematic overlap, the close connection between the old corpus and the new corpus is evident from documents linked to the same persons. The missive *(muṭālaʿa)* (7)/#943, for instance, is linked to the household of the above-mentioned officer al-Yaghmūrī, for whom we have several documents in the old corpus (for example #023, #024, #600, #602 and #841). To cite another overlap in terms of historical personae, the old corpus has more than fifty documents linked to the little-known reciter Burhān al-Dīn.[85] In the new corpus we find an estate inventory (33)/#897 that is linked to Fāṭima, the wife of Burhān al-Dīn, and document (35)/#968: a list of receivables drafted during the process of settling Burhān al-Dīn's estate. The same overlap of individuals applies to the Persian and Persianate documents. The old corpus contains fifteen documents relating to the Ādūjī family and the new corpus adds another eight documents from the Ādūjī family dossier. Finally, we not only find the same actors in the main texts of documents across the two corpora, but also the same witnesses who sign documents. The sale contract (9)/#974 from the new corpus, for instance, was signed in the year 800/1398 by ʿAlī b. Muḥammad al-Ḥijāzī and the same witness signed several documents of the old corpus (#237 and #390 in the year 796/1394 and #290 in the year 797/1394).[86]

85 Aljoumani/Hirschler, *Owning Books*, Appendix 1.

86 Müller, *Der Kadi und seine Zeugen*, 554 (witness ID P313). For further overlaps in the identitiy of witnesses see (29)/#901, (36)/#944 and (31)/#978.

That documents that had once shared archival histories within Burhān al-Dīn's estate archive, the Ādūjī family dossier and other sub-corpora, ended up in two distinct corpora, the new corpus and the old corpus, brings us to our second argument. While there is a strong historical overlap between the documents in the third batch and those in the first and second batches, the material profile of the third batch's documents is in many cases strikingly different. Most of the documents in the new corpus are incomplete or almost illegible: In many cases large parts of the original document have been lost or the documents have numerous holes or have been exposed to humidity so that most of the text is lost. Readers of the catalogue will also see that there are lots of cases of cutting and trimming documents. These documents thus often look like the 'poor cousins' of their more complete peers in the old corpus. For instance, only two lines have survived of what we believe to be the petition for a position in a *madrasa* ((40)/#951 and of document (54)/#976 only the witness signatures are extant so that it is impossible to determine the content of the actual document. In document (53)/#933 humidity has caused the the ink to fade to such an extent that all our attempts to read the text have failed except for a few words. In another case, letter (45)/#935, another document must have been attached to it and the ink traces left by the missing document make (45)/#935 illegible. Most of the Persian and Persianate legal documents and decrees in the new corpus are fragmentary with either the top, bottom or middle parts missing ((71)/#892 and #913, (75)/#904, (76)/#906, (78)/#959, (79)/#980), (85)/#958 and (92)/#912.

The fragmentary nature of the documents was thus clearly an important factor underlying the material logic behind why some documents were put into the third batch. There is another distinct profile to this third batch, namely that many of them them share particular features in terms of their visual organisation so that they often look like the 'wild cousins' compared with their more orderly peers in the old corpus. This appearance goes back to two factors. First, we have many drafts, among them drafts of petitions, decrees and inventories that by definition look rather untidy. Second, the new corpus encompasses a relatively high number of cases of reuse, that is cases where a written artefact was reused to write a further text on it.[87] These reuse cases include the following, which are discussed at greater length below: a petition and the folio of a Sufi text that were both reused for writing estate inventories; legal and accounting documents both reused for writing prayers; and accounts reused for writing poetry.

Apart from the material and visual logic that underlies which documents ended up in the third batch, there are also distinct clusters of documents in the new corpus that do not really match those of the old corpus in terms of content

87 On reuse practices see the overview in Liebrenz, *Archive in a Book* and Hirschler, *Monument*.

or period, those probably considered to be 'weird cousins' in textual terms. These textual outliers include, for instance, a letter of introduction for a *murābiṭ* in Maghribi script ((42)/#889) for which there is no counterpart in the old corpus as it has no such letters of introduction nor any items in Maghribi script. Particularly striking are non-documentary texts for which we have no counterparts in the old corpus such as a sheet from a Koran commentary ((55)/#954), prayers ((49)/#952, (50)/#956 and (97)/#917), poetry ((46)/#930 and (47)/#961) and instructions on how to write amulet prayers ((52)/#965). Among the Arabic-language material the final cluster into which the documents from the third batch fall is defined by period, namely those going back to the Ottoman period ((22)/#932, (23)/#926, (24)/#927, (25)/#936 and arguably (26)/#949) – there are no Arabic-language documents from the Ottoman period in the old corpus. That the person(s) conducting the sorting process considered Ottoman documents to be distinct from the core focus of the collection is also evident in the fact that the new corpus includes six documents in the Ottoman language. Four of these documents either request an official letter of investiture, a *berat,* ((60)/#887) or are actual *berats* ((57)/#929, (58)/#928 and (59)/#934). The other two Ottoman-language items carry a prayer ((62)/#903) and private letters ((61)/#972). It will come as no surprise at this point that the old corpus has no Ottoman-language documents. Perhaps the sifter thought the Ottoman documents would not suit the Ḥaram al-sharīf corpus, a 'medieval' corpus and chose to exclude them, among them the abovementioned youngest document in the new corpus, which dates to the beginning of World War I in 1914 ((60)/#887).

The Persian and Persianate documents in the new corpus

In his work on the old corpus, Donald Little identified that the 'foreign' documents from the fourteenth century produced outside Mamluk Jerusalem written in Persian, Arabic or in other languages under the influence of Persian, what he termed 'Persianate', came from three neighbouring geographic regions: Transcaucasia[88], Anatolia and northwestern Iran.[89] One striking characteristic of the new corpus is the significantly higher ratio of Persian and Persianate documents. In the third batch, these documents constitute about one third of the total, while they represent less than five percent in the old corpus. Despite this significant difference in volume there are firm connections between the Persian and Persianate documents

88 Transcaucasia or the South Caucasus roughly corresponds to modern Armenia, Georgia, and Azerbaijan.

89 Little, *Catalogue*, 5–8.

in the two corpora and in order to understand them one must get to know a particular officer. The most important cluster across the two corpora is related to the activities of officer Amīr Ādūjī b. Amīr Yāzilī b. al-Nāʾib (d. c. 1331) and his family. Donald Little did not further identify this Ādūjī. His role, however, is indicated in a Persian deed of acknowledgement (*iqrār*) in the old corpus dated 711/1311 (#871). Ādūjī is described here as the vice-regent (*nāʾib*) of the supreme military commander of Iran, Chūpān Bēg (d. 1327). Chūpān Bēg's name only appears in the margin based on the Mongol custom of moving the most significant name mentioned in a document to the margins.[90] Chūpān Bēg, better known as Amīr Chūpān, claimed de facto control over former Mongolian core territories of Azerbaijan and Mughan in north-western Iran, as did his descendants, the Chubanids.[91]

Ādūjī was clearly employed in the service of the Chubanids, most probably in Transcaucasia.[92] The documents are not only linked to Ādūjī himself, but also to his descendants so that we can speak of an Ādūjī family dossier.

The Transcaucasian connection in the Ādūjī cluster is also visible in Ādūjī's dealings with a certain Zakariyā b. Ṣāḥib Dīwān. Zakariyā was the son of Shams al-Dīn Muḥammad b. Muḥammad Juwaynī (d.683/1284), the Ilkhanid *wazīr* and *ṣāḥib-dīwān*, minister of finance, executed in 1284 near Ahar in Azerbaijan by the Mongol ruler Arghūn (r. 1284–91) on charges of financial misappropriation.[93] In 1289, Arghūn ordered the execution of all Juwaynī's male offspring. Four of his sons were indeed put to death in Iran, but Zakariyā, who was in Abkhāz (Abkhazia)[94] at the time, survived.[95] Zakariyā's Georgian exile might explain some of his transactions with Ādūjī, including the transfer of a benefice (*iqṭāʿ*) he owned ((67)/#911)[96] and the presence of the Georgian language among the papers of the

90 See the right hand-margin of #871 and the x marked in the blank space in line 5 indicating the removal of the name from the main text to the margins. An even earlier Chubanid link is attested in #857 (1291 or 1292). An individual, probably Armenian, agrees to transfer to Amīr Chūpān the ownership of a village that had been given to Chūpān's grandfather Tūdāʾwn. In this document, Amīr Chūpān is called *amīr-i aʿẓam*, the Greatest Amīr, and his name and his grandfather's name are respectfully written in the right margin. I am indebted to Ryoko Watabe for sharing her reading of this document.

91 Hope, *Political Configuration of Late Ilkhanid Iran*.

92 Ādūjī's grand-son Amīr Khiḍr Shāh is described as *mashhūr-i arrān*, well known in Arrān in #859. Little notes that Arrān corresponds to the district in Transcaucasia between the Kur (Kura) and Aras Rivers, see Little, *Catalogue*, 380, footnote 4.

93 Biran, *Jovaynī, Ṣāḥeb Dīvān*.

94 Abkhazia is today an autonomous republic in northwestern Georgia. Historically, however, the term Abkhazia was used in Georgian and non-Georgian sources to refer to the whole kingdom of Georgia.

95 Rajabzadeh, *Jovayni Family*.

96 For an edition of this document, see the appendix 1a.

new corpus ((96)/#885 and #920). The legal Persian and Persianate documents in the new corpus, which have no comparable counterpart in the old corpus, all belong to the Ādūjī family dossier. They include the sale contract of a mine bought by Ādūjī ((64)/#896), a marriage contract of the grand-daughter of Ādūjī (fragments (70)/#898 and #942)[97] and the sale contract of an underground water canal involving Ādūjī's grand-sons ((65)/#909).

In addition to the Ādūjī family dossier, we can identify two further Persian and Persianate document clusters across the old and new corpora based on their geographic provenance. One cluster is linked to Anatolia. Donald Little has pointed out the significance of Anatolia based on an *iqrār* in the old corpus which mentions the Mongol Tīmūrtāsh (#357), the son of Amīr Chūpān, who served as viceroy of the Seljuq Sultanate of Rūm from 716–23/1316–27. Several documents in the Anatolian cluster of the new corpus refer to Qayṣarīya (Kayseri) in central Anatolia. These include fragments of a draft decree in Persian issued in the name of the Mongol ruler Abū Saʿīd Bahādur Khān ((71)/#892 and #913)[98] and a judicial certification (*ishhād*) in Arabic on the invalidity of a loan security which also contains texts in Persian ((74)/#888). The Anatolian *iqrār*s in both the old and new corpora are written in Arabic ((84)/#886). Two documents in the new corpus were issued in the town of Sīwās (Sivas) in central Anatolia. The first is a tax receipt issued by the royal treasury in 681/1283 ((72)/#918) of which we have a comparable example in the old corpus (#661) and a loan agreement dated 742/1341 ((73)/#919). These Persianate Anatolian documents shed light on the legal and administrative practice of Anatolia in the period after the Seljuq Sultanate of Rūm had become a dependency of the Mongol Ilkhanate. The second cluster is related to places in northwest Iran. As in the old corpus, this accounts for only a small proportion of the Persian and Persianate documents. The new corpus includes two Persian sale deeds, one of which mentions Tabriz ((81)/#900) and the other the village of Azād, which might correspond to the present-day village of Azād in West Azerbaijan province, Iran ((82)/#893 and #975).[99]

In addition to these documents, the new corpus also contains several fragmentary Persian decrees of uncertain geographic provenance ((75)/#904, (76)/#906 and (78)/#959), two mention a certain Sarfarāz ((77)/#969 and (79)/#980) and one contains a black seal (*qārā ṭamghā*) used in Mongol orders issued by officials lower in rank than the ruler ((76)/#906).[100] There is also an undeciphered inventory of expenditure relating to a Mongol (?) woman ((89)/#963), an estate inventory (?) ((90)/#977) and a receipt for grain ((80)/#955).

97 For an edition of this document, see the appendix 1a, for images see fig. 8 and 9.
98 For an edition of this document, see the appendix 1a, for images see fig. 10 and 11.
99 For an edition of this document, see the appendix 1a, for images see fig. 13 and 14.
100 For an edition of this document, see the appendix 1a, for an image see fig. 12.

At the present state of research, there appears to be no clear link between the different clusters of documents of the Persian and Persianate sub-corpus. Donald Little felt that since these documents contained references to places in the same general area and contiguous territory, all of which was contested by Mongol and Turcoman dynasties, they may have formed a single entity.[101] This remains to be proven. Similarly, it is difficult to establish when and why these Persian and Persianate documents were deposited with the other Arabic documents of the Ḥaram al-sharīf corpus produced in Mamluk Jerusalem. According to Donald Little, their arrival in Jerusalem might be linked to the migration of a family from Transcaucasia. He suggests they were subsequently brought to the Shāfiʿī court in Jerusalem in connection with legal claims and thus entered the archive of the judge Sharaf al-Dīn ʿĪsā b. Ghānim (d. 797/1395).[102] This hypothesis, as Donald Little himself notes, is difficult to prove. Moreover, there is little in the documents themselves, which mainly concern transactions in Transcaucasia, Anatolia and northwest Iran more than half a century earlier, to suggest why they might have become relevant in the Jerusalem investigation against Sharaf al-Dīn. It is not impossible that the Persian and Persianate sub-corpus was collected at a much later stage, perhaps even as late as the Ottoman period, from one or several families with origins in Transcaucasia or Anatolia. The documents eventually entered the Islamic Museum, either as a collection or in batches after its founding in the 1920s. As 'antique' looking papers they were piled together with the much larger Mamluk corpus of Arabic documents to form the modern Ḥaram al-sharīf corpus. When this corpus was subsequently sorted, many of these Persian and Persianate documents were put into the third batch.

The historical importance of the documents in the new corpus

The fact that the documents in the new corpus are in many ways the poor, wild and weird cousins of their peers in the old corpus does not mean they are of any less historical significance. This is particularly relevant because although scholarship has produced numerous editions of Ḥaram al-sharīf documents (see Appendix 2) their analytical potential remains underused. The turning point in this regard and thus a milestone for understanding important parts of the Ḥaram al-sharīf corpus, has been the work of Christian Müller, in particular, but not exclusively, with regard to legal practices.[103]

---

101 Little, *Catalogue*, 8.

102 Little, *Catalogue*, 13–4.

103 Especially Müller, *Der Kadi und seine Zeugen*.

The Arabic documents of the new corpus provide, for instance, important new insights into land administration and the property market in Mamluk-period Palestine. Document (1)/#884 is a governor's decree intervening in a land dispute between one of the most important endowments of that period, the Ṣalāḥīya Khānqāh, and peasants in the vicinity of Jerusalem. Documents (9)/#974 and (84)/#886 record the sale of land between individuals, (12)/#923 is concerned with renting baths (the same baths are subject to a rent contract ten years later in document #046 in the old corpus), (13)/#948 is a receipt for the payment of rent and document (21)/#941 records the lease of orchards. The new documents also shed further light on the day-to-day administration of endowments. Documents (37)/#931 and (38)/#970 are fragmentary endowment deeds, (1)/#884 and (12)/#923 refer to endowment deeds, (39)/#937 is a petition to become the supervisor of an endowment, (40)/#951 is most likely a similar petition for a position in a *madrasa* and (41)/#947 is a rare travel permit for endowment business with its accounts.

The Arabic documents in the new corpus also add significant new material for understanding trade in Mamluk Jerusalem. This concerns in particular the previously mentioned accounts on the sale of soap ((14)/#890 and (15)/#924), of wheat and honey ((20)/#971) and of various food products such as onions and meat ((19)/#979) as well as a merchants' letter ((43)/#899) and sale contracts on cotton ((10)/#922) and lambs ((16)/#940). The new documents also provide insights into the sale of estates, such as accounts (34)/#921. The estate inventories, in turn, shed light on money-lending practices, as they list debts and claims of the deceased ((29)/#901 and (31)/#978). Such practices are also evident from documents such as a receipt (28)/#907, a loan agreement (73)/#919, a debt slip (27)/#962 and a desperate letter from a father to his daughter after he has run up too many debts ((44)/#925).

The new documents will also complete stories that had already been apparent from the old corpus. For instance, in our work on the documentary and bookish life of reciter Burhān al-Dīn al-Nāṣirī, the discovery of documents (33)/#897 and (35)/#968 proved invaluable for our understanding of the documents from the old corpus that had up to that point appeared rather enigmatic.[104] Document (7)/#943, in turn, will be crucial for any project on Jerusalem's short-term governor al-Yaghmūrī. This report bears witness to the communication within an officer's household in the middle of the corruption scandal involving the Jerusalemite judge Sharaf al-Dīn ʿĪsā b. Ghānim – a scandal that gave birth to a substantial part of the Ḥaram al-sharīf corpus.[105]

The documents in the new corpus are not only important because of their content, but also crucial because they add to our understanding of the different

104 Aljoumani/Hirschler, *Owning Books.*
105 Müller, *Mamlūk Court Archive.*

stages of documentary practices. Documents (32)/#939 and (33)/#897, for instance, are first drafts of estate inventories that do not carry any witness signatures. Such drafts provided the basis for the subsequent and legally valid estate inventories bearing witness signatures, which have been much more frequently preserved. In the same vein document (41)/#947 is the draft version of accounts of endowment-related products or income from the village of Bayt Dajan; document (6)/#964 is most likely the draft of a petition to the viceroy of Bilād al-shām; documents (71)/#892 and #913 are the draft of an Ilkhanid decree.

Such drafts provide insights into another crucial documentary practice, the reuse of written artefacts mentioned above. Here we see scribes reusing the draft of a petition ((4)/#897) and the folio of a Sufi text ((56)/#939) to write documentary drafts (estate inventories). Yet documents could also be reused to write prayers such as the legal document (94)/#917 and the accounts (22)/#932 as well as to write poetry such as accounts (16)/#940. The new Arabic documents are also important to understand the use of different numerical systems in documents, especially what we have called the Arabic Documentary Numerals ((14)/#890, (15)/#924, (16)/#940, (17)/#953, (19)/#979, (20)/#971, (21)/#941, (28)/#907, (34)/#921, (35)/#968 and (41)/#947).[106] Finally, the new documents are crucial for future research on archival practices. This includes the presence of 'archival holes', that is perforations that were made in order to string documents together ((13)/#948, (14)/#890, (15)/#924, (29)/#901, (33)/#897, (35)/#968 and (84)/#886, arguably (43)/#899, perhaps (28)/#907, (70)/#898, (74)/#888 and (94)/#917). Another important feature of these documents is the presence of archival dorsal notes ((6)/#964, (7)/#943 and (29)/#901). The most significant discovery in the new corpus in terms of archival practice is related to the Persian and Persianate documents. Among the documents relating to the Ādūjī dossier is an archival list ((63)/#891). This list is an inventory of deeds which were preserved in a 'bag' (Per. *kīsa*) and it thus provides us with evidence of the Ilkhanid Mongol material practice of using archival bags to store documents. Such an archival list mentioning an archival bag is in itself a very rare find indeed, but there is more: Several entries on the list record documents that we find today in the Ādūjī dossier in both the new and old corpora so that we get a sense of how scribes drew up such lists. This is particularly fascinating as the wording of the entries in the list is often directly linked to the wording of the archival dorsal notes on the documents.

106 Aljoumani/Hirschler, *Owning Books*, Chapter 6.

The present catalogue

Our catalogue of the documents in the third batch is organised in three broad linguistic groups, Arabic (under the responsibility of Said Aljoumani), Ottoman (under the responsibility of Nimet İpek) and Persian (under the responsibility of Zahir Bhalloo). These three groups also have geographical connotations. The Arabic documents were generally produced in Jerusalem and surrounding regions such as Gaza with a few exceptions from wider Bilād al-shām, Cairo and perhaps modern-day Libya. The vast majority of the Persian documents, in turn, were produced in Transcaucasia, Anatolia and northwestern Iran. It is clear that the multi-lingual world prior to the twentieth century did not work within neat lines and frontiers. There are also, at points, additional languages and scripts, such as Georgian, Armenian, Turkic and Mongolian in Uyghur script. A particular challenge for organising a catalogue by language is posed by the intertwined worlds of Arabic and Persian that can hardly be separated. Catalogue entry (70), for instance, is a fourteenth-century marriage contract in which the writer constantly switches between Arabic and Persian. As it belonged to the Ādūjī dossier it ended up in the catalogue's fourth section on *Persian and Persianate Documents*. Catalogue entry (46) is Persian poetry yet with an Arabic colophon and written in Aleppo, so we slotted it into the catalogue's second section on *Arabic Documents Concerning Jerusalem, Bilād al-shām and Cairo*.

Above we stated that the third batch contains '97 documents', but quantifying such a corpus is an inexact science. What we have are 97 items according to the classmark system of the Islamic Museum. The classmarks from the museum did not, however, directly translate into the entries in our catalogue on account of two decisions we took when cataloguing the documents. Firstly, there are four cases where two fragments of the same document were given distinct classmarks as the cataloguers did not see a link between them: #942 and #898 (both belonging to the same marriage contract from the Ādūjī dossier), #913 and #892 (both belonging to the same Ilkhanid decree), #885 and #920 (both belonging to the same Georgian/Armenian/Persian document) as well as #975 and #893 (both belonging to the same sale contract). In our catalogue the fragments of the same artefact are merged into one single entry: #942/#898 became catalogue entry (70), #913/#892 became catalogue entry (71), #975/#893 became catalogue entry (82) and #885/#920 (became catalogue entry (96). Secondly, we decided to create two distinct entries for those cases where a document carries two distinct texts on the recto and verso as a result of reuse practices. This applied to five documents: #897 (a petition reused for an estate inventory) became catalogue entries (4) and (33); (16)/#940 (accounting reused for poetry) became catalogue entries (16) and (48): #932 (accounting reused for a prayer) became catalogue entries (22) and (51); #939 (a Sufi text reused for an estate inventory) became catalogue entries (32) and (56); and #917 (a legal document reused for a prayer) became catalogue entries (94) and (97).

Our hope is that this catalogue will make the third batch of the Ḥaram al-sharīf corpus more accessible and manageable. With the cataloguing of the documents of the first and second batch and their availability as microfilm copies from the early 1980s onwards, numerous documents have been edited and published in recent decades, particularly in the 1980s. Recent years have seen a pleasing stream of publications in Arabic (see Appendix 2).[107] A major challenge that remains is the dispersed nature of the printed editions, which are often difficult to track down. The Munich *Arabic Papyrology Database* provides the texts of many of these documents in digital format, but not images.[108] A major milestone was the launch of the Paris *Comparing Arabic Legal Documents* database with (often improved) editions of documents previously published in print.[109] It not only provides text and image, but has also started to offer online-only editions of previously unpublished documents. The ultimate aim has to be that the editions and photos are one day available on the website of their home institution, the Islamic Museum on the Ḥaram al-sharīf in Jerusalem.

---

107 Muḥammad, *Idārat amwāl awqāf*; Muḥammad, *Marsūm al-Sulṭān al-Ashraf Īnāl;* ʿAbd al-Raḥmān, *al-Taʿāmulāt al-qaḍāʾīya;* ʿAbd al-Raḥmān/Anas, *ʿAqdā zawāj.*

108 https://www.apd.gwi.uni-muenchen.de/apd/project1c.jsp, accessed 9 November 2022.

109 https://cald.irht.cnrs.fr, accessed 9 November 2022.

II Arabic documents concerning Jerusalem, Bilād al-shām and Cairo

II.1 Decrees, petitions and *muṭālaʿas*

(1) #884 Decree *(marsūm)* by a governor settling a land dispute

Arabic
undated; most likely dated to the 8th/14th century as most of the documents linked to the Ṣalāḥīya Khānqāh in the Ḥaram al-sharīf corpus, such as (12)/#923, date to that century. Line 5 refers furthermore to 'ʿĪsā, the shaykh of the Ṣalāḥīya Khānqāh', most likely Sharaf al-Dīn ʿĪsā b. Ghānim (d. 797/1395) who led this institution for the last five years of his life (see Müller, *Der Kadi und seine Zeugen*, 208). This would place the document in the classical period of the Ḥaram al-sharīf corpus, the 790s/1390s.

76 x 27.4 cm, 42 lines,[110] 3 witness clauses, paper. The document suffered material damage, especially on the left-hand side where there are numerous holes and water damage. The material damage makes it difficult to ascertain whether archival holes existed.

Summary: Decree concerning lands *(arḍ)* disputed between the Sufis of the Ṣalāḥīya Khānqāh in Jerusalem and peasants. The document identifies the boundaries of these plots and stipulates that they be handed over to the Sufis. The exact location of the lands is unclear, but the reference to 'Dayr Abū Thūr' might indicate that they were south of Jerusalem. The decree was most likely issued by the governor of Gaza (see the beginning of the decree) who had access to notary witnesses from Jerusalem, a representative of the *bayt al-māl* and the governor of Jerusalem. The decree refers to a previous document, most likely an endowment deed, issued in Jerusalem and dated to 12 Muḥarram [year cut off].

Beginning of text:

[. . .] المرسوم العالي المسمى [. . .] المعظم بغزة المحروسة والأعمال الساحلية [. . .] الجناب العالي [. . .] بالقدس الشريف [. . .] عيسى شيخ الخانقاه الصلاحية بالقدس الشريف [. . .] يعتمد المرسوم [. . .] القدس الشريف

110 The number of lines refers to the document's main text.

https://doi.org/10.1515/9783111330242-003

End of text:

[. . .] والدرب الآخر وبه وضع خطه بذلك من وقف على ذلك وتسلمت الصوفية الأرض المذكورة المحدودة ووضعوا أيديهم عليها في تاريخه المذكور أعلاه [. . .]

Names mentioned in text:

زين الدين بن الحاجب،[. . .] عيسى شيخ الخانقاه الصلاحية، الجناب العالي العلائي متولي القدس الشريف

Places mentioned in text:

غزة، القدس الشريف، الخانقاه الصلاحية بالقدس الشريف، الأعمال الساحلية، جورة زين الدين الحاجب، دير المجاذمة، مربعة البنات أو مربعة النساء، بئر الصرارة، دير أبو ثور، درب الخليل، القناة السلطانية، جورة القباب السفلى، جورة القباب العليا

Names of witnesses:

عبد الله بن يحيى، أحمد [بن عبد الله؟] بن سعد، أحمد بن عبد الله بن محمد

(2) #973 Sultanic decree

Arabic
undated
60.6/59.4 x 12.5 cm, 6 lines, paper. The document is torn and most of the text is lost. There is substantial damage to the extant text. The decree consisted of at least four sheets glued together. Sheets 1 and 4 are torn. Sheets 2 and 3 are extant in their entirety and are both 24 cm long.

Summary: Most likely a *muṭlaq* decree addressed to minor lords of castles with an *'alāma* at the top of the document.

Beginning of text:
ومجالس الأمراء الأجلاء الأكابر الغزاة المجاهدين المؤيدين الأنصار أمجاد الإسلام بهاءات الأنام

End of text:
[. . .] الأجل الكريم [. . .] البليغي الأمجدي الحاكمي

We have classified this document as a *muṭlaq* decree addressed to minor lords of castles on the basis of a comparison with such decrees in al-Qalqashandī, *Ṣubḥ al-a'shā*, VII, 225.

(3) #966 Report on a Sultanic decree and a judge's order concerning the confiscation of an (officer's?) estate (edited in Appendix 1b, VI, see fig. 15)

Arabic
Beginning Ramaḍān 795/1393
19.4/15.5 x 25.7 cm, 11 lines, paper. The lower end of the document is missing. The extant part is torn horizontally.

Summary: Report on a public reading of a Sultanic 'square' decree *(murabba' sharīf)* and a written executive order *(mithāl karīm)* concerning the confiscation of the estate of the rebellious (officer?) Khiḍr al-Turkmānī. The decree was issued by the Sultan al-Ẓāhir Barqūq (d. 801/1399) and the order was issued by *mudabbir al-mamālik al-islāmīya* Abū al-Faraj.[111] The documents were read out by the officer 'Alā' al-Dīn Alṭunbughā. The decree, issued a month earlier on 11 Rajab 795/1393, stipulates that Sayf al-Dīn Jaqmaq al-Ẓāhirī was to receive the estate of Khiḍr, who was accused of involvement in the Minṭāshī rebellion.

Beginning of text:
بتاريخ العشر الأول من شهر رمضان المعظم قدره سنة خمس وتسعين وسبعماية ورد مربع شريف ملكي ظاهري خلّد الله ملكه وأدام اقتداره ومثال كريم

End of text:
بضبط تركة خضر التركماني وفيه [. . .]، الألفي علاء الدين [ألطنبغا]

Names mentioned in text:
أبو الفرج مدبر الممالك الإسلامية، علاء الدين ألطنبغا البريدي، سيف الدين جقمق الدوادار، خضر التركماني

Places mentioned in text:
القدس الشريف

111 This might be Muwaffaq al-Dīn Abū al-Faraj, listed as wazir in Onimus, *Les Maîtres du Jeu*, 439 (on him see also https://ihodp.ugent.be/mpp/actor-muwaffaq-al-dīn-ʾabū-l-faraj). We thank Jo van Steenbergen for his advice on this issue.

(4) #897 Petition to officer (subsequently reused, see catalogue entry (33))

Text #897/1 (recto)
Arabic
before 789/1387 (proposed on basis of the inventory on the petition's verso, see catalogue entry (33))
26.3 x 13.4 cm, 18 lines, paper. The extant sheet of the document is in good condition. However, the original petition consisted of at least two sheets glued together. What was originally the upper sheet was cut off in its entirety except for a small piece that remains visible on the top left corner of the extant second sheet. In addition, the lower end of this second sheet was trimmed, probably in order to write the text on the verso of the document.

There is an archival hole on the left-hand side between lines 6 and 7 (most likely linked to the subsequent reuse stage of the sheet).

Summary: A '*mamlūk*' writes to an officer after being slandered by his colleagues. The writer insists that he is innocent of the accusations made against him and asks the officer to look into the matter and hold those responsible to account. With the beginning and end of the text missing most historical information (including the name of writer and addressee as well as date) is missing.

Beginning of text:

[الباقي من بداية النص] قطع مصانعة أحدا أو تعرّض إلى مال المخدوم بقشة أو ظلم أحداً ومهما
قالوه مصدّق في المملوك فالمملوك ما يغفل عن غرضه وإن حصل إهمال من المخدوم

End of text:

للمملوك يتقدم له ركوب، مليح يركبه وهبة لا إعادة فيه [فيها] والله تعالى ختم [. . .]

Names mentioned in text:

علاء الدين دوادار، غرس الدين خليل [الحكمي؟]

Places mentioned in text:

القاهرة، القدس

The verso of this extant sheet of the petition was originally blank before it was subsequently reused as paper in the process of settling an estate. The missing first sheet, by contrast, might have carried text, such as the addressee's response, but was discarded when the document moved into the reuse stage.

(5) #908 A plea for funds to an officer

Arabic
undated
63.4 x 13 cm, 51 lines, paper. The beginning of the document is missing.

Summary: An administrator *(mamlūk)* writes to his officer to inform him that financial matters are desperate. He has already had to use his own money to carry out his duties by hiring five camels for fifty dirhams, buying barley and straw, shoeing the horses and, more burdensome still, hosting the officer's retinue. Yet he is not in a position to make any further payments as he has nothing to eat and no further funds. He mentions previous, seemingly futile, attempts to receive monies from the officer, including sending an envoy, and now desperately urges the officer to quickly respond and send funds.

Beginning of text:
[. . .] [المـ]ـملوك المرسوم واستدنا دراهم من جديد واصرفنا على الكرى الجمال عشرة خمس جمال كل جمل بخمسين

End of text:
والجواب سرعة سرعة حتى يطيب خاطر المملوك فيما ذكرته أول وآخر والسلام

Names mentioned in text:
الحاج خليل، صدر الدين علي، محمد، شهاب الدين الحنفي، المملوك زين الدين

Lines 38 to 51 are written in the text's margin. The verso is blank and it seems that the officer replied with a separate letter (assuming that he did indeed reply). This means that the letter most likely came out of the administrative 'archive' of this officer, not the administrator. Such windows into the inner workings and modes of communication within an officer's household are rare.

(6) #964 Most likely a draft of a petition to the viceroy of Bilād al-shām

Arabic
undated
11 x 14.1 cm, 6 lines, paper. The extant text has substantial lacunae because of holes.

Archival note recto on top of document:

شيخ عباس [. . .] المكرم [. . .]

Summary: The extant lines are taken up by honorifics addressing the viceroy of Bilād al-shām. An actual text that would have provided insight into the content of this petition (?) is missing. This text might be lost because a further lower part is missing. Yet it is not certain that such a text ever existed as there is still sufficient space at the lower margin for the writer to have started the next line. Perhaps this text was a draft or a training exercise by a scribe.

Beginning of text:

الجناب الكريم العالي الأميري الكبيري العالمي العادلي المؤيدي

End of text:

ظهير الملوك والسلاطين سيف أمير المؤمنين أعز الله نصره نائب السلطنة الشريفة بالشام المحروس

Places mentioned in text:

الشام المحروس

(7) #943 *Muṭāla'a* concerning the contested judgeship in Jerusalem

Arabic
undated (probably between 796/1394 and 797/1394)
55/30.4 x 14/4.6 cm, 37 lines, paper. The document is torn into three pieces. The lower piece has suffered substantial textual loss on the right-hand side.

Archival note on verso:
الشهابي، مطالعة المملوك عبد الرحمن [الظاهري؟]

Summary: The writer, 'al-mamlūk 'Abd al-Raḥmān', writes a report addressed to Shihāb al-Dīn Aḥmad b. Muḥammad al-Yaghmūrī (d. 811/1408). He praises the benevolence of the current judge of Jerusalem, the *sharīf* Sharaf al-Dīn 'Īsā b. Ghānim, and Ghānim's care for the weak, popularity in the town among all sections of society and devotion to Shihāb al-Dīn. 'Abd al-Raḥmān emphasises in particular that the judge constantly prays for Shihāb al-Dīn and makes sure that many others do so as well. He continues that Sharaf al-Dīn's rival, 'Alā' al-Dīn Ibn Kamāl al-Dīn, had travelled to Damascus to gain the judgeship of Jerusalem. He leaves no doubt that he sees Ibn Kamāl al-Dīn as unfit for holding a judgeship and states that he should not be appointed.

Beginning of text:
بسم الله الرحمن الرحيم الشهابي المملوك عبد الرحمن يقبل الأرض وينهي أن العلوم الكريمة محيطة بصدق محبة المملوك باثٌ لمحاسنه

End of text:
له على المملوك حقوق [...] الغفلة عنه وهو [...] له على ذلك [...] المملوك [...]

Names mentioned in text:
عبد الرحمن، الشهابي، شرف الدين ابن غانم، علاء الدين ابن كمال الدين

Places mentioned in text:
القدس الشريف، دمشق

With this report we are in the midst of the corruption scandal that gave birth to a substantial part of the Ḥaram al-sharīf corpus (Müller, *Mamlūk Court Archive*). The Sharaf al-Dīn mentioned in this report is the judge of Jerusalem who held the town's judgeship twice (see Müller, *Der Kadi und seine Zeugen*, 251–2, 793–7) and died in Shawwāl 797/1395 (see Müller, *Der Kadi und seine Zeugen*, 207–8). During his second tenure he was accused of misappropriating estates and an investigation was launched into his alleged malpractices. The Kamāl al-Dīn mentioned in this report is another judge of Jerusalem who held the judgeship twice (see Müller, *Der Kadi und seine Zeugen*, 247–8, 770–1 and 774). He was probably trying (unsuccessfully) to take advantage of the accusations against Sharaf al-Dīn to try to secure the judgeship for himself once again. The officer, Shihāb al-Dīn Aḥmad b. Muḥammad al-Yaghmūrī, was the supervisor of the administration in Damascus and also governor of Jerusalem for seven months from 796/1394 to 797/1394 as well as supervisor of the endowments of Jerusalem and Hebron.[112] The writer of the report, ʿAbd al-Raḥmān, is a member of Shihāb al-Dīn's household, the officer Zayn al-Dīn ʿAbd al-Raḥmān b. Ṣārim al-Dīn Ibrāhīm al-Khalīlī al-Fakhrī. He is known from two other *muṭālaʿas* (#600 and #841) and from his participation in drawing up three estate inventories from the Ḥaram al-sharīf corpus in 796/1394 in which he explicitly acted on behalf of Shihāb al-Dīn al-Yaghmūrī.[113] All these inventories were drawn up during the tenure of Sharaf al-Dīn and ʿAbd al-Raḥmān might himself have had a strong interest in supporting this judge against accusations of embezzling estates.

112 On him see Al-ʿUlaymī, *al-Uns al-jalīl*, II, 166.
113 #572, #663 and #722.

(8) #946 *Muṭālaʿa* with instructions for judge regarding the visit of an officer (edited in Appendix 1b, VII, see fig. 16)

Arabic
undated (most likely late 700s/1300s)
9.2 x 12.7 cm, 8 lines, paper. Substantial material and textual loss on the document's lower end.

Summary: The writer, 'al-mamlūk Muḥammad al-Damāmīnī', writes to the chief judge of Jerusalem and informs him of the imminent arrival of the officer Burhān al-Dīn Ibrāhīm al-ʿIrāqī, who will come to Jerusalem on a pilgrimage *(ziyāra)*. He asks the judge to treat the officer with the appropriate care, hospitality and generosity.

Beginning of text:
بسم الله الرحمن الرحيم الشرفي المملوك محمد الدماميني يقبل الأرض وينهي بعد شوقه وثنائه وإخلاصه في وده ودعائه أن الماثل بها

End of text:
مضاعفة الوصية به والعناية والملاحظة ويكون نظره عليه ويحسن إليه ويعامله

Names mentioned in text:
محمد الدماميني، برهان الدين إبراهيم العراقي

Places mentioned in text:
القدس الشريف

The second line of the letter reads 'al-Sharafī' so that there is a substantial onomastic overlap with the influential Egyptian judge and administrator Sharaf al-Dīn Muḥammad al-Damāmīnī (d. 803/1400), who held numerous positions including *wakīl bayt māl, nāẓir kiswa, nāẓir dīwān al-mufrad, nāẓir sawāqī, nāẓir al-jaysh and muḥtasib* of Cairo, as well as judge of Alexandria.[114]

114 For him see https://ihodp.ugent.be/mpp/actor-sharaf-al-dīn-b.-al-damāmīnī within Ghent University's *Islamic History Open Data Platform*. The prinicipal source for him is Ibn Taghrī Birdī, *al-Manhal*, 11: 21–2.

II.2 Sale and rent

(9) #974 Sale contract (lands)

Arabic
29 Jumādā I 800/1398
18.5/10.1 x 19.5/15 cm, 15 lines, 2 witness clauses, paper. The top and the right of the document are torn off with substantial textual loss.

Summary: Sale contract for a share of lands in Marj ʿArab outside Jerusalem. The contracting partners are a woman (seller) and a man (buyer), but their names are lost. However, the boundaries of the plot are preserved. One of the two witnesses at the end of the document, Bilāl b. ʿUmar Ibn Abī al-Qāsim is the husband of the seller.

Beginning of text:
مرج عرب ظاهر القدس الشريف المشتمل على غراس عنب وغير ذلك المنتقل

End of text:
وصدقها المشتري على ذلك التصديق الشرعي وأقرَّ المشتري أنه لا يستحق عند البائعة شيئا قلّ ولا جل وأشهد عليهما

Names mentioned in text:
الشيخ الأوحد تاج الدين شيخون السايس، حسن البقاعي، علي بن إبراهيم البقاعي، عمر العجمي

Places mentioned in text:
مرج عرب، القدس الشريف

Names of witnesses:
بلال بن عمر بن أبي القاسم، علي بن محمد الحجازي[115]

115 Identical to the notary witness identified in Müller, *Der Kadi und seine Zeugen*, 554: #390 (796/1394), #237 (796/1394), #290 (797/1394) (witness ID P313).

(10) #922 Sale contracts with accounts (cotton) (edited in Appendix 1b, VIII, see fig. 17 and 18)

10/a, Text #922/1 (recto), contract 1
Arabic
7 Ṣafar 776/1374
35.5/31.1 x 12.2 cm, 4 lines, 2 witness clauses, paper. The document is severely damaged at the upper end with substantial loss of text.

Summary: An individual (whose name is lost because of the material damage) buys cotton from ʿUmar b. Muḥammad b. ʿUmar al-Ḥuṣrī (?) al-ʿAllāf. The price is payable in weekly instalments at the end of the week.

Beginning of text:

[. . .] وخمسة وأربعون درهما [. . .تحل عليه] في كل أسبوع

End of text:

[الشرعي عن] وزن قطن ابتاعه وتسلمه وبه شهد عليه

Names mentioned in text (on basis of following contracts):

[الحاج عمر بن محمد بن عمر [الخضري/الحصري؟] العلاف]

Names of witnesses:

علي بن إسماعيل بن شاكر [الفقير؟]، عبد الرحمن بن محمد[. . .]

The two witness signatures were crossed out at a later date.

10/b, Text #922/2 (recto), contract 2
Arabic
7 Ṣafar 776/1374
5 lines, 2 witness clauses. There is textual loss (including the amount of the weekly instalment) because of three holes.

Summary: The cotton trader Aḥmad b. Ibrāhīm al-Ḥimṣī al-Qaṭṭān buys cotton from the trader ʿUmar b. Muḥammad b. ʿUmar al-Ḥuṣrī (?) al-ʿAllāf. The price of 198 dirhams is payable in weekly instalments at the end of the week.

Beginning of text:

[في ذمة؟] الحاج أحمد بن إبراهيم بن محمد الحمصي القطان للحاج عمر بن محمد بن عمر [الخضري/الحصري] العلاف

End of text:

قطن ابتاعه منه وتسلمه وبه شهد عليه

Names mentioned in text:

الحاج أحمد بن إبراهيم بن محمد الحمصي القطان، الحاج عمر بن محمد بن عمر [الخضري/الحصري] العلاف

Names of witnesses:

علي بن إسماعيل بن شاكر [الفقير؟]، عبد الرحمن بن محمد [. . .]

10/c, Text #922/3 (recto), contract 3
Arabic
7 Ṣafar 776/1374
6 lines, 2 witness clauses. This passage of the document is in very good condition with no lacunae.

Summary: Muḥammad b. Ḥasan al-ʿAjamī buys cotton from the trader ʿUmar b. Muḥammad b. ʿUmar al-Ḥuṣrī (?) al-ʿAllāf. The price of 211 dirhams is payable in weekly instalments of 6 dirhams at the end of the week.

Beginning of text:

في ذمة محمد بن حسن بن ياسين العجمي من الحاج عمر بن محمد بن عمر [الخضري/الحصري] العلاف من الدراهم

End of text:

ذلك وقبض العوض الشرعي من قطن ابتاعه منه وتسلم وبه شهد عليه

Names mentioned in text:

محمد بن حسن بن ياسين العجمي، الحاج عمر بن محمد بن عمر [الخضري/الحصري] العلاف

Names of witnesses:

علي بن إسماعيل بن شاكر، عبد الرحمن بن محمد [. . .]

10/d, Text #922/4 (recto), contract 4
Arabic
7 Ṣafar 776/1374
6 lines, 2 witness clauses. This passage of the document is also in very good condition with no lacunae.

Summary: Niʿma b. Bishāra al-Naṣrānī buys cotton from the trader ʿUmar b. Muḥammad b. ʿUmar al-Ḥuṣrī (?) al-ʿAllāf. The price of 218 dirhams is payable in weekly instalments of 6 dirhams at the end of the week.

Beginning of text:
في ذمة نعمة بن بشارة النصراني من [جفنا الجوز؟] للحاج عمر بن محمد بن عمر [الخضري/ الحصري؟] العلاف

End of text:
والقدرة على ذلك وقبض العوض الشرعي عن وزن قطن ابتاعه ومنه وتسلم وشهد عليه

Names mentioned in text:
نعمة بن بشارة النصراني، الحاج عمر بن محمد بن عمر [الخضري/الحصري] العلاف

Places mentioned in text:
[جفنا الجوز؟]

Names of witnesses:
علي بن إسماعيل بن شاكر [الفقير؟]، عبد الرحمن بن محمد [. . .]

The two witness signatures and the main text were crossed out at a later date.

10/e, Text #922/5 (verso), Accounts of instalments for repaying debts
Arabic
Undated (but must be after 7 Ṣafar 776/1374)
16 lines. The document is severely damaged so that the entries for the first payer are lost at the very least.

Summary: List of instalments for repaying the debts mentioned on the document's recto. However, the amount of the repayments (twenty-four dirhams) is different from the amount stipulated on the recto (six dirhams). This list is thus most probably a record of monthly payments.

Beginning of text:

قبض مما [في باطنها من؟ . . .]

End of text:

وأيضا نقدة من يد النصراني أربعة وعشرين

Names mentioned in text:

محمد العجمي، النصراني

(11) #967 Petition for invalidating a sale contract

Arabic
undated
26.3 x 12.6 cm, 14 lines, paper. There are several holes and slight water damage leading to some textual loss.

Summary: An individual writes to an authority (a judge?) asking him to declare a sale contract void.

Beginning of text:

الحمد لله [. . .] أبقاكم الله لنا وللمسلمين

End of text:

وهذا من بعض الإحسان وأجركم على الله وأنتم أكثر من هذا ومعاد السلام [. . .] الله

Names mentioned in text:

البعلبكي

(12) #923 Rent contract for baths (edited in Appendix 1b, IX, see fig. 19)

Arabic
19 Jumādā II 737/1336
34.6/27.2 x 25.5/19.1 cm, 14 lines, 3 witness clauses, paper. The document has some holes and the upper left corner is missing.

Archival note on verso:

ادعى [إجـ]ـارة الحمام [. . .] لسنة سبع وثلاثين وسبعماية

Summary: Three individuals, Shibl b. Khalaf, Sālim b. Muḥammad and Ismāʿīl b. Ḥajjī, rent the Pool of the Patriarch's baths (see Little, *Catalogue*, 136), which are close to the Church of the Holy Sepulchre. These baths are endowed for the benefit of the Ṣalāḥīya Khānqāh and the document refers to the endowment deed. The *khānqāh* is here represented by Shams al-Dīn Muḥammad al-Maqdisī. The rent contract is for one year and the renters are obliged to dispose of the ashes outside the city walls of Jerusalem every day. The daily rent is sixteen dirhams from which three dirhams are deducted so that the Sufis of the *khānqāh* have free entry to the baths. The text states that the baths are so well known that there is no need to describe the properties' boundaries. #046 is another rent contract for the same baths ten years later with the same conditions, but for a daily rent of thirteen dirhams (see Al-ʿAsalī, *Wathāʾiq maqdisīya*, I, 245).

Beginning of text:
هذا ما استأجر شبل بن خلف بن سبع وسالم بن محمد بن محرز وإسماعيل بن حجي بن إبراهيم وهم معروفين عند شهوده

End of text:
من ماله وذمته بإذنهما له بذلك ضمانا شرعيا الحمد لله وحده وصلوته على سيدنا محمد وآله وصحبه وسلم تسليما كثيرا

Names mentioned in text:
شبل بن خلف بن سبع، سالم بن محمد بن محرز، إسماعيل بن حجي بن إبراهيم، شمس الدين محمد بن أحمد بن غانم المقدسي

Places mentioned in text:
حمام البترك (حمام البطرك)، القدس الشريف، الخانقاه الصلاحية

Names of witnesses:

محمد بن أحمد [. . .]، محمود بن خلف بن محمود [السعيدي؟]، محمد بن الحريري

ʿAlāma of judge in the top left corner:

الحمد لله الحاكم [. . .]

(13) #948 Rent receipt

Arabic
Rajab 778/1376
5.4 x 8 cm, 4 lines, paper. There is one archival hole in the centre of the document.

Summary: An individual acknowledges that he received the rent for the two months of Rabīʿ II and Rajab 778 from Nāṣir al-Dīn al-Ḥamawī. There is no mention what property was rented.

Beginning of text:

الحمد لله، قُبض من المولى ناصر الدين الحموي

End of text:

أجرة جماد[ى] الآخر ورجب

Names mentioned in text:

ناصر الدين الحموي

This receipt was most likely part of the estate archive of the affluent merchant Nāṣir al-Dīn al-Ḥamawī (d. 788/1386). His estate archive plays a prominent role in the Ḥaram al-sharīf corpus with over ninety sheets, providing a rare insight into the commercial and social world of a Jerusalemite merchant of that period (see Müller, *Der Kadi und seine Zeugen*, 175–94).

II.3 Accounts, debts and receipts

see also documents (34)/#921, (10/e)/#922/5 and (41)/#947/2

(14) #890 Accounts (soap)

Arabic
undated
62.7 x 12 cm, 47 lines, paper. There is one archival hole in the upper quarter of the document on the right.

Summary: This accounting on soap sales are organized by buyer. For each buyer the accounts list the quantity bought (specified in *raṭl)* and the respective price (specified in dirhams).

Beginning of text:

المُباع من الصابون المُبارك بالدرهم الخاص

End of text:

من ذلك عند جمال الدين 140 عند الصيرفي 54

Names mentioned in text:
الحاج يوسف الورّاق، كمال الدلّال، ابن الشماعة، ابن الجماعين، خواجة، الجلودي، ابن الجوسكا، بدر العجلوني، السكاوي، سلمان جحا، ابن حجرين، الطرابي، الخطّابي، إسحاق الجلودي، الجمال، الصّيداوي، [الخِراص/ الخراصي/ الحبراصي؟]، شرف الدين، بُدير، علي بن [بُدير؟]، صالحي، قه [لجا؟]، صدقة، المرداوي، [فراس/ نبراس؟]، [ثابت؟]، خليل، أبو سلمان، عبد الرحمن، الصيرفي، حسن ابن علي المصري، حسن ابن الزغلي، صبي الموله، خليل الياسوري [الياصوري] ، ريحان، يعقوب بن غازي التركماني، حسن بن علي المغربي، محمد بن محمد بن يحيى، عثمان بن علي بن إبراهيم العجمي، البانياسي، شرف علي، عيسى الياسوري [الياصوري]، خليل بن مكي

The numerical values are written in Arabic Documentary Numerals (see Aljoumani/Hirschler, *Owning Books and Preserving Documents*, Chapter 6).

The format of the accounting is unusual. Generally, we find such accounts in the Ḥaram al-sharīf corpus in the *daftar* format (c. 18 x 28 cm, such as #583 on purchases of soap, #796 on sale of soap, #817 on sale of soap and other commodities, (35)/#968, (20)/#971 and (19)/#979).

(15) #924 Accounts (soap and wool)

Arabic
undated
25.8 x 12.6 cm, 11 lines, paper. There is one archival hole in the centre towards the top of the document.

Summary: An undated (trader's?) accounts listing quantities of soap in *raṭl* and their prices as well as wool.

Beginning of text:

حساب [. . .] من صابون، الوزن

End of text:

[أرقام قبطية]

The numerical values are written in Greek/Coptic/Rūmī/*ḥurūf al-zimām* numerals.

(16) #940 Accounts (lambs) (subsequently reused, see catalogue entry (48))

Text #940/1 (recto)
Arabic
undated
22 x 8.6 cm, 3 lines, paper

Summary: Accounting registering two payments by an individual called Ibn al-Nūrī who bought lambs *(khirāf)*. This sheet was subsequently reused to write poetry, see catalogue entry (48).

Beginning of text:

من يد ابن النوري من جمعه الخراف [في الأصل الخروف]

End of text:

نقدة ⅛½ 32، ثاني نقدة ½ 58

Names mentioned in text:

ابن النوري

The numerical values are written in Arabic Documentary Numerals (see Aljoumani/Hirschler, *Owning Books and Preserving Documents*, Chapter 6).

(17) #953 Accounts (grain?)

Text #953/1 (recto)
Arabic
undated (text only mentions 'from year nine. . .')
13.7/12.9 x 9.6 cm, 10 lines, paper. The upper end of the document was cut off leading to textual loss, in addition to slight additional textual loss at lower end because of substantial hole.

Summary: The accounting is organized by individual with a sum under each name.

Beginning of text:

[. . .] البعلبكي 20، [. . .] الأعور 18، المصري الأعمش 45، حسابه ½ 230

End of text:

الحارث [. . .] 12، أبو إسحاق 12، حسن [. . .] 12

Names mentioned in text:
البعلبكي، [. . .] الأعور، المصري الأعمش، عمر، ابن سليم، ابن شرف الدين، [. . .]، [. . .]، ابن حمدان [. . .]، أبو بكر العرادي، الحارث [. . .]، أبو إسحاق، حسن [. . .]

The numerical values are written in Arabic Documentary Numerals (see Aljoumani/Hirschler, *Owning Books and Preserving Documents,* Chapter 6).

Text #953/2 (verso)
Arabic
undated
11 lines. The lower end of the document was cut off leading to textual loss. Slight additional textual loss in first line because of substantial hole.

Summary: The owner of this accounting most likely dealt with grain and calculated in Egyptian and Florentine ('أفرورية' for 'أفلورية'?) dinars.

Beginning of text:

المحـ[. . .] الخباز [. . .] من يده ثمن [. . .] أفرورية 18

End of text:

صرف فلوس قبضت ثمن سميد

(18) #957 Accounts (wheat and barley)

Arabic
undated
23.9 x 5.5 cm, 14 lines, paper. There are some holes and some words are erased.

Summary: The owner of this list registers sums of money and amounts of wheat and barley owed to him by others.

Beginning of text:

على جماعة من جهة الوصط [الوسط] كيلجة قمح

End of text:

على محمد ابن ناصر كيلجة قمح

Names mentioned in text:

أحمد المصري زوج مريم، محمد غلام خليل، رعيان البقر، نمير من العيساوية، محمد ابن ناصر

Places mentioned in text:

العوجا

The writer uses the unit الكيلجة for measuring the products; on this term see Dozy, *Supplément*, II, 506.

(19) #979 Accounts (onions and meat)

Arabic
792/1389 to 793/1391
20.5 x 15.9/14 cm, *daftar* format sheet of paper with four pages with two columns per page. One column is missing. The document has substantial holes and ink blots.

Summary: Accounts for products (such as onions and meat) imported from al-Baqʿa (close to Hebron?). The accounting is organized by year, then by month and occasionally by day.

Beginning of text:
في الصفحة 1: [الحمد لله رب] العالمين في سنة اثنين وتسعين [وسبعماية] مشترى [سكر؟] من البقعة من [. . .]
في الصفحة 2: ما صرف 250¾، الباقي 85، إلى يوم السبت سابع عشر

End of text:
في الصفحة 3: جمعه أربع عشر ط، فضة 17
في الصفحة 4: 12، 19، 7، 6½

Names mentioned in text:
سعيد، خليل، عثمان

Places mentioned in text:
البقعة

The numerical values are written in Arabic Documentary Numerals (see Aljoumani/Hirschler, *Owning Books and Preserving Documents*, Chapter 6).

The recto of the document has page 1 (left) and page 4 (right); the verso has page 2 (right) and page 3 (left).

(20) #971 A wholesaler's accounts (wheat and honey)

Arabic
788/1386–7 and 789/1387–8
12.3/10.2 x 18.2 cm, *daftar* format sheet of paper with four pages with two columns per page. Slight damage along the folding lines. The lower half of the *daftar* is missing and the extant text has substantial lacunae because of holes.

Summary: The accounting starts in the year 788 and is organized by month. It registers the products traded in that month, including wheat and honey. It is noteworthy that the sums recorded tend to be high, often in the thousands.

Beginning of text:

في الصفحة 1: سنة 788
في الصفحة 2: شهر رجب، نقد 364، فلوس الصوفية 593
في الصفحة 4: الباقي على التاجرين في المدة الباقية بأجمعها

End of text:

في الصفحة 3: فلوس الصوفية 595، عن دخول الصوفية 1071
في الصفحة 4: سنة 89، [أي سنة 789]

The numerical values are written in Arabic Documentary Numerals (see Aljoumani/Hirschler, *Owning Books and Preserving Documents,* Chapter 6).

The recto of the document has page 1 (left) and page 4 (right); the verso has page 2 (right) and page 3 (left).

(21) #941 Accounts (lease of orchards, *kurūm)*

Arabic
undated
15.5/11.7 x 13/8.3 cm, 7 lines, paper. The bottom left corner of the document is missing, but no text was lost. The upper end of the document was trimmed with some textual loss.

Summary: This is a list registering the names of nine individuals who rented orchards and the amount of the lease (except in the case of the ninth individual). The lease goes from seven (dirhams?) to thirty-one. Neither the geographical location nor any dates are given.

Beginning of text:

محاكرة الكروم الجدد

End of text:

[. . .] وأيوب 13، أبو سعادة

Names mentioned in text:
محمد الطويل، فراج ابن إسماعيل، إبراهيم بن حسن، إسحاق ابن عثمان، عمر ابن أبو فارس، منصور ابن نصار، [. . .] وأيوب، أبو سعادة

Some of the numerical values are written in Arabic Documentary Numerals (see Aljoumani/Hirschler, *Owning Books and Preserving Documents*, Chapter 6).

(22) #932 Accounts (most likely subsequently reused, see catalogue entry (51))

Text #932/1 (recto & verso)
Arabic & Ottoman
10 Dhū al-Ḥijja 1135/1723
30 x 22 cm, 6 lines (recto) & 5 lines (verso), paper. This accounting is on a separate piece of paper and it is unclear to what extent it really formed one unit with the prayer #932/2 (see catalogue entry (51)).

Summary: Most likely accounting.

Beginning of text: illegible

End of text:

وباقيها 5 عشـ

(23) #926 Accounts book for building works on the Ḥaram al-sharīf in the years 1232–3/1817–8

Arabic
18 Shaʿbān 1232/1817 to Dhū al-Qaʿda 1233/1818
44.9 x 16.5 cm, 17 sheets (34 pages), paper. This is a bound *daftar* in good condition with occasional ink blots and damaged binding threads.

Summary: This booklet entitled *Blessed daftar containing the costs of building works (ʿimāra) on the Ḥaram al-sharīf in the years 32 and 33* contains entries for a period of seventeen months. Each entry includes the amount spent on building works and the reasons why it was spent. This is a central source for following the building works during this period, the materials used and their provenance, as well as the names of the supervisors, the traders of building materials and the craftsmen.

Beginning of text:
عن دفتر مصارف ورشة الحرم الشريف في يد كاتبه مصطفى علي أفندي ابتداه في 18 شهر شعبان المعظم سنة 1232

End of text:
بيد القلفة بوجوس تحت أجرة النحاس

Names mentioned in text:
السيد حسن سعسع معلم الطواحين، مصطفى قسطلاوي، القساطلي، أحمد سمقة، حسين طحان، المعلم إبراهيم قسطندي، الحاج سعيد، علي ابن عليم، عثمان آغا متسلم الرملة، القلفا بوغوز، الشيخ كريم، حسين رزاري، الحاج محمد الزغبي، أبو السعود، حمدان الحمد، أحمد إسماعيل، شاهين، أحمد المصري، عبد الحميد، مرزوق باورقة، أحمد حمو، عبد الله باشا، عبد الله السمان، بشير العكاري، محمد آغا، المعلم جرجس، الحاج سعيد، حسين وعلي الفضلي، صالح أفندي، محمد كردي، حسين سقلاوي، محمد آغا جاويش، صالح أفندي معمار، الدرويش حسين، جرجس نصر، يوسف الوعري، إلياس التلحمي، محمد يوسف، خليل غندور، إبراهيم بلبيسي، إبراهيم المغربي، جرجس منسا، واكيم، جرجس نصر، المعلم سمعان، مصطفى السمان، خليل قلفا، عبد الله القانوع، مصطفى شعبان، إبراهيم دورار، علي المليجة، عثمان آغا، الحاج إبراهيم المصري، عبد الكريم آغا، محمد آغا باش جاويش، الاوسطة يوسف وولده محمد وولده عمر ونسيبه محمد، صالح خليفة، إبراهيم آغا، السيد صالح النامي، إلياس صحناوي، بطرس لطفي، خليل درعطاني، ميخائل حجار، ميخائيل داراني، موسى قندلفت، يوسف ابن أبو طعمة، انطانيوس توما، نقولا روماني، يوسف شطها، خليل درعطاني، يوسف دحلان، المعلم سمعان، القلفة بوجوس

Places mentioned in text:
،الحرم الشريف، القدس، الصخرة المشرفة، الرملة، يافا، عكا، غزة، مدينة الخليل، سلوان

This *daftar* is closely connected to (24)/#927 and both have been briefly discussed by Salameh, *Renovations*.

(24) #927 Accounts book for building works on the Ḥaram al-sharīf in the year 1234/1818–9

Arabic
24 Muḥarram 1234/1818 to 28 Shaʿbān 1234/1819
22 x 16.2 cm, 7 sheets (14 pages), paper. This is a bound *daftar* in good condition with the fourth sheet and the lower part of the seventh sheet missing.

Summary: This booklet entitled *Blessed daftar in the year 34* contains entries for a period of eight months. Each entry includes the amount spent on building works and why it was spent. This is a central source for following the building works during this period, the materials used and their provenance, as well as the names of the supervisors, the traders of building materials and the craftsmen.

Beginning of text:

عن تابع المصارف الورشة

End of text:

بيد حمَّامية ستي مريم

Names mentioned in text:
عثمان آغا، محمد أفندي، أبو السعود، محمد جاويش، إبراهيم آغا، محمد آغا، المعلم إلياس قلفا، عبد الحميد أسطة، سعيد آغا، مصطفى السمان، الحاج سعيد، حسن نجار، سليمان أبو زرفة، جرجس منسا الكاتب وتابعه واكيم، حسين طنطش، حنا ناصر، إبراهيم الداوودي، عيسى عبده، ميخائيل، يعقوب نسيبة، عيسى تلحمي، إلياس تلحمي، أندوني أبو شقرة، عبد الصمد، علي محسن، علي الفضلي، جرجس نظيلي، جرجس يناكي أسطفاني، الحاج محمد قيشانجي، صالح أفندي، حسين سقلاوي، الفتياني، الشيخ عبد الله، إسماعيل شراباتي، أنطون تلحمي، يوسف مرداور، أبو محمد، أحمد عسلي، علي محسن السقلاوي، حسان عبد الكريم آغا، إلياس الفتال، إلياس السلقيني، جرجس بن سمعان، محمد الحلاق، خليل شاهين أفندي، إسماعيل أفندي، محمد قاسم، حمدان حميدان، عبد السلام تركية، السيد رحيم

Places mentioned in text:
حمام السلطان، جامع سيدنا عمر، سطوح الصخرة، صحن الحرم، القدس، الرملة، الخليل، يافا، عكا، بيت لحم، نابلس، حمام العين، حمام ستي مريم

This *daftar* is closely connected to (23)/#926 and both have been briefly discussed by Salameh, *Renovations*.

(25) #936 Accounts of expenses for religious sites in Jerusalem

Arabic
End of Muḥarram 1139/1726 to end of Ramaḍān 1139/1727
32.2 x 22.2 cm, *daftar* format sheet of paper with four pages. The top of the document and the right-hand side was trimmed, leading to textual loss.

Summary: Tabulation of weekly expenses for important religious sites in Jerusalem (among them in particular the Dome of the Rock, Aqsa Mosque, Maghāriba Mosque, Ḥanbalīya Madrasa, Qubbat Mūsā, Qubbat al-Miʿrāj, the various gates of the Ḥaram al-sharīf and ʿAfīfīya Madrasa) with amounts spent for tasks such as cleaning and lighting. The list is organized by week separating them with a long horizontal stroke. The expenses are generally registered on Tuesdays.

Beginning of text:

[بيان نهار الثلاثة 29 محرم سنة 1129] [باب] الأسباط، [باب] الرباط، [ثلثية]، كرسي سليمان، رواق الشيخ منصور

End of text:

[بيان نهار الثلاثة . . . رمضان سنة 29] الحنبلية، قبة موسى والعفيفية، ناطور ومجاورين

Places mentioned in text:

باب الأسباط، باب الرباط، كرسي سليمان، رواق الشيخ منصور، قبة السلسلة، قبة المعراج، صخرة الله المشرفة، الأقصى الشريف، الحنبلية، قبة موسى والعفيفية، جامع المغاربة، أبواب الأقصى، بابي الصخرة قبلي وشرقي، بابي الصخرة غربي وشمالي، باب السلسلة، باب المتوضى، باب القطانين، باب الحديد، باب الناظر، باب الغوانمة، باب الدويدارية، قبر سليمان، الرواق الغربي، باب الرحمة، باب حطة، بابي الصحن قبلي وشرقي بابي الصحن غربي وشمالي.

(26) #949 Authorisation for spending and subsequent accounting

Text #949/1 (recto)
Arabic
undated (most likely Ottoman period)
11.9 x 8.3 cm, 3 lines, paper

Summary: This is permission for two individuals, among them a certain ʿAbd Allāh al-Jurdānī, to spend money (for an unknown purpose) in Istanbul.

Beginning of text:

في إسلامبول، يختمو[ا] ريال قبلي هذا الضف عبد الله الجرداني

End of text:

يختمو[ا] [محبوب؟] شمال هذا الضف آل عثمان

Names mentioned in text:

عبد الله الجرداني، آل عثمان

Places mentioned in text:

إسلامبول

The term *ḍaff* means here ‘sum total’.

Text #949/2 (verso)
Arabic
undated
4 lines, paper

Summary: Accounts for the monies spent by ʿAbd Allāh al-Jurdānī, who is named on the document’s recto.

Beginning of text:

الذي إلى عبد الله الجرداني، عند الله سبحانه بموجب الكشف

End of text:

سدر 1، طلح 1، [. . .] 1، ماء 1، فاكهة 1

Names mentioned in text:

عبد الله الجرداني

(27) #962 Debt slip (butter)

Arabic
undated
25.9 x 8.7 cm, 7 lines, paper

Summary: Ibrāhīm al-Ḥammāl receives, but seemingly does not pay for, one *raṭl*, 5.5 *wūqīya* and two large glass vessels of butter.

Beginning of text:

تذكرة بوزن، القطرميز السمن، الذي أخذه إبراهيم الحمال

End of text:

والحساب يرجع إليه، رطل وخمس أواق ونصف [أ]وقية

Names mentioned in text:

إبراهيم الحمال

(28) #907 Receipt of payments

Arabic
9 Rabīʿ II 770/1368
28.1 x 10.7 cm, 6 lines, paper. The document is in good condition with some textual loss due to two large holes. In addition to these holes, the document has two small holes, but it is difficult to ascertain whether they served archival purposes.

Summary: Receipt confirming payment (of a debt?) by Ḥasan al-Rūmī and ʿUmar al-Ādamī. Such receipts typically lack contextual information and only become more meaningful when other documents by their protagonists have survived. For one such case see documents #109, #843 and #850. These are similarly concise receipts, but they were issued for Burhān al-Dīn al-Nāṣirī whose estate archive has survived with over fifty documents (discussed in Aljoumani/Hirschler, *Owning Books and Preserving Documents).*

Beginning of text:

الذي [. . .] حسن الرومي

End of text:

وعمر الآدمي

Names mentioned in text:

حسن الرومي، عمر الآدمي

The numerical values are written in Arabic Documentary Numerals (see Aljoumani/Hirschler, *Owning Books and Preserving Documents*, Chapter 6).

II.4 Estates and inheritance

(29) #901 Estate inventory *(wuqūf)*

Arabic
18 Dhū al-Qaʿda 795/1393
25.4 x 12.1 cm, 23 lines, 4 witness clauses, paper. The upper end of the document is severely damaged so that line 1 and parts of line 2 are missing. There is further slight damage between lines 18 and 20. There are four archival holes: One at the upper and one at the lower end; one on the right and one on the left.

Archival note verso on the lower half:
شمس الدين العجمي بالخاتونية ق[116] غ[117]

Summary: Estate inventories in the form of *wuqūf* (inspection) are the largest group of documents within the Ḥaram al-sharīf corpus (see Müller, *Der Kadi und seine Zeugen*, 89–94). As in many cases, the legator, here a certain Shams al-Dīn Muḥammad al-Tabrīzī[118] al-ʿAjamī, is severely ill. He resides in the Khātūnīya Madrasa in Jerusalem and must have been quite wealthy. The document lists his possessions, including what he borrowed from and lent to others (such as 3,000 dirhams lent to an individual in Damascus and copperware lent to an individual in Aleppo). The document also lists those entitled to inherit, among them his two brothers who reside in his hometown of Tabrīz. It also details the arrangements for the legal guardianship of his son, manumits two slaves and makes charitable donations.

Beginning of text:
بتاريخ ثامن عشر ذي قعدة الحر[ام سنة] خمس وتسعين وسبعماية حـ[ـصل الوقوف على رجل ضعيف يدعى شمس الدين]

End of text:
وواضع خطه من العدول المندوبين من مجلس الحكم العزيز الشافعي أجله الله تعالى بالقدس الشريف وبه شهد

Names mentioned in text:
شمس الدين محمد بن شهاب الدين أحمد بن شمس الدين محمد التوريزي، شمس الدين العجمي، خواجا شمس الدين لمشا، محمد المهدي، زين الدين عبد الرحمن بن محمد بن أحمد بن محمد التوريزي، شرف خاتون، علاء

116 ق: اختصار شهر ذي القعدة.
117 غ: اختصار الغياب، أي أن بعض مستحقي الإرث غائبون خارج القدس.

118 In original *ʿal-T-w-rīzī'*.

الدين علي التوريزي، [ناما التوريزي؟]، بشارة بن عبد الله، دولات بنت عبد الله، شمس الدين محمد بن نجود بن قاسم الأصبهاني، الشيخ فضل الله، صلاح الدين خليل بن الشيخ جمال الدين يوسف.

Places mentioned in text:

القدس الشريف، المدرسة الخاتونية بالقدس الشريف، دمشق، حلب، توريز ، زاوية الجنيد

Names of witnesses:

محمد بن [. . .]، ناصر بن سالم الحنفي،[119] علي بن حسن،[120] عبد الله بن محمد المصري[121]

On the recto in the margin of line 19 we find a note that three exemplars *(nusakh)* were made of this document.

119 Identical to the notary witness identified in Müller, *Der Kadi und seine Zeugen*, 571 who was active between the years 780 and 797 (witness ID P254). See also (31)/#978.

120 Identical to the notary witness identified in Müller, *Der Kadi und seine Zeugen*, 552 who was active between the years 793 and 797 (witness ID P277).

121 Identical to the notary witness identified in Müller, *Der Kadi und seine Zeugen*, 537 who was active between the years 793 and 797 (witness ID P560).

(30) #945 Estate inventory *(wuqūf)* (edited in Appendix 1b, X, see fig. 20)

Arabic
25 Ramaḍān [7]95/1393
10.6/8 x 9/8 cm, 9 lines, paper. There is substantial material and textual loss on the document's lower end and left-hand side.

Summary: Estate inventories in the form of *wuqūf* (inspection) are the largest group of documents within the Ḥaram al-sharīf corpus (see, Müller, *Der Kadi und seine Zeugen*, 89–94). In this case the legator is a sick woman called Quṭlūwa bt. ʿAbd Allāh. The name of her residential quarter is missing, but it is most likely the Maghāriba quarter.

Beginning of text:

الحمد لله بتاريخ الخامس والعشرين من شهر رمضان المعظم قدره سنة خمسة وتسعين

End of text:

وملوطة كتان فص لؤلؤي وشملة مطرزة وخرقة [. . .] وخرقة حمراء [. . .]

Names mentioned in text:

قطلو بنت عبد الله، الحاج عمر، شهاب الدين أحمد

Places mentioned in text:

القدس الشريف، [حارة المغاربة؟]

(31) #978 Estate inventory *(wuqūf)*

Arabic
24 Rabīʿ I [797/1395]
26 x 18.3/14 cm, 19 lines, 2 witness clauses, paper. There is damage to the right-hand side and there are holes, especially in the centre, with substantial textual loss.

Summary: Estate inventories in the form of *wuqūf* (inspection) are the largest group of documents within the Ḥaram al-sharīf corpus (on this see, Müller, *Der Kadi und seine Zeugen*, 89–94). In this case the legator, a man called Muḥammad b. Aḥmad b. Ḥasan al-Ramlī, is severely ill, but still alive. The document lists his possessions, what he borrowed from and lent to others, and those entitled to inherit.

Beginning of text:
[في تار]يخ رابع عشري شهر ربع الأول سنة سبع تسـ[ـعين وسبعمية حصـ]ـل الوقوف على رجل ضعيف
يدعى الحاج محمد بن أحمد بن حسن [الرمـ]ـلي الصبان بالقدس الشريف

End of text:
مجلس الحكم العزيز الشافعي أجله الله تعالى وأدام أيام متوليه وإقرار زوجته حامل منه وبه شهد في تاريخه أعلاه

Names mentioned in text:
محمد بن أحمد بن حسن الرملي الصبان، موسى النحاس، [. . .] الطوري صاحب المصبنة، محمد الاسكندري
النساج، الحاج أحمد [. . .]، شهاب الدين صبحي، محمد الحلبي الصبان، قمر بنت محمد، خليل بن حسن
الصواف، الجارية سعيد[ة . . .]، تقي الدين أبو بكر بن المرحوم الجناب العالي الشمسي شمس الدين محمد بن
إبراهيم الظاهري، زين الدين عبد الرحمن

Places mentioned in text:
القدس الشريف، الرملة

Names of witnesses:
ناصر بن سالم الحنفي[122]، أحمد بن [الربعي؟]

On the recto in the margin of line 18 we find a note that three exemplars (*nusakh*) were made of this document.

122 Identical to the notary witness identified in Müller, *Der Kadi und seine Zeugen*, 571 who was active between the years 780 and 797 (witness ID P254). See also (29)/#901.

(32) #939 Draft of estate inventory *(wuqūf)* (reuse stage, see catalogue entry (56))

Text #939/2 (verso)
Arabic
undated
17.7 x 13.2 cm, 15 lines, paper

Summary: This is a list of the possessions of the deceased al-Shaykh Muḥammad al-Raṭūnī including his wife's statement that al-Shaykh Muḥammad b. Saʿīd had sold his robe *(jubba)* and turban to cover the funeral costs. This Shaykh had a substantial library including two Korans (one in Kufi script), different parts of the *Muwaṭṭaʾ* by Mālik b. Anas, the *Risāla* by ʿAbd al-Karīm al-Qushayrī, *al-Taysīr fī al-ṭibb*, a part of al-Ghazālī's *Iḥyāʾ*, *al-Muntakhab* by Ibn al-Jawzī, Ibn al-Marzubān's *Faḍl al-kilāb* and the first part of a Koran commentary that carried an endowment statement for the Ṣalāḥīya Madrasa.

Beginning of text:

الذي وجد للشيخ محمد الرطوني مصحف كريم بخط كوفي كبير نصف مصحف الأربعين الطائية

End of text:

وقطرميزين بأحدهما قليل جبن والآخر قليل ربّ وزبديتين [. . .] سلطيّة وقدرة [. . .] وزبدية أيضاً سلطيّة وذراع حديد

Names mentioned in text:

محمد الرطوني، محمد بن سعيد

Places mentioned in text:

المدرسة الصلاحية

This inventory lacks the typical features of the almost 400 *wuqūf* documents that are part of the Ḥaram al-sharīf corpus: There is no date and the names of the witnesses who conducted the inspection are missing (see Müller, *Der Kadi und seine Zeugen*, 89–94). What we have here is thus an informal draft that was written in the process of settling the deceased's estate. As it is just a draft it comes at little surprise that it was written on the back of a disused sheet – the Sufi text #939/1 that was arguably found among the deceased's numerous books (see catalogue entry (56)). The inventory explicitly mentions 'loose sheets' *(awrāq khurūm)*.

(33) #897 Draft of estate inventory (reuse stage, see catalogue entry (4))

Text #897/2 (verso)
Arabic
between years 777/1375 and 789/1387
26.3 x 13.4 cm, 27 lines, paper. The document is in good condition with no parts missing.

Summary: This is a list of the items sold from the estate of Fāṭima, the wife of Burhān al-Dīn al-Nāṣirī (d. 789/1387), who lived in Jerusalem. The list also states how these items were to be distributed among the heirs: Fāṭima's mother, Burhān al-Dīn himself, their daughter Khadīja and their son Kamāl.

Beginning of text:

الذي يخص إبراهيم الناصري من المبيعات المخلفة عن زوجه فاطمة

End of text:

خارجاً عن الصداق والصداق في ذمة الزوج ثلثماية

Names mentioned in text:

الزوجة فاطمة، إبراهيم الناصري، ابنهما كمال، ابنتهما خديجة، الجدة أم فاطمة

This undated document subsequently became part of Burhān al-Dīn's estate archive. It must have been produced at some point between the birth of Kamāl in the year 777/1375 and the death of Burhān al-Dīn in the year 789/1387, as they are both alive here. This document was produced in the course of settling Fāṭima's estate and it is noteworthy that it carries no witness signatures. It was thus most likely an informal first draft that was to be followed by a more formal estate inventory at a later date. For this informal inventory the scribe of this document reused a sheet from the petition on the document's recto. He (or a paper merchant) cut off the petition's first sheet and trimmed its lower edge so that the petition's text became incomplete. This list, by contrast, is complete. The list is published and analysed in Aljoumani/Hirschler, *Owning Books and Preserving Documents*, Appendix 2.

(34) #921 Sale of inheritance (accounts)

Arabic
undated
18.6 x 11.5 cm, 13 lines (recto) & 15 lines (verso), paper

Summary: This list was written after the estate of Shihāb al-Dīn Kahmān had been sold under the supervision of Ibrāhīm b. Mīkāʾīl for 248 dirhams. To this was added the cash and silver Shihāb al-Dīn left behind (320 dirhams). The estate (or a part thereof) was allocated to an unidentified *khānqāh* to be spent on its expenses. This was probably the Ṣalāḥīya Khānqāh in Jerusalem for which we have numerous documents in the Ḥaram al-sharīf corpus, including the accounts. The document carries no witness signatures and was an informal document written in the process of settling the deceased's estate. The money was mostly spent on food (such as wheat, flour, apples, almonds, nuts, butter, saffron and honey), and also candles.

Beginning of text (recto):

ثمن [التبن؟] حاصل تحت يده منهم [. . .] الحمام ثمن نحاس

End of text (recto):

ويُنظر ما صُرف غير ذلك لوز وزعفران 10، ثمن [. . .]

Beginning of text (verso):

الشيخ إسماعيل 50، الصوفية 20

End of text (verso):

الحوائج التي أباعها بيد إبراهيم بن ميكائيل

Names mentioned in text:

شهاب الدين كهمان، إبراهيم بن ميكائيل، الشيخ إسماعيل

Places mentioned in text:

الخانقاه

The numerical values are written in Arabic Documentary Numerals (see Aljoumani/Hirschler, *Owning Books and Preserving Documents*, Chapter 6).

(35) #968 List of receivables written during process of settling an estate

Arabic
15 Dhū al-Qaʿda 789/1387
27.6 x 18.9 cm, *daftar* format sheet of paper with four pages (two of them blank) with two columns per page. There is slight damage along the folding lines and there are two archival holes in the document's upper quarter.

Summary: This is an accounting list produced during the process of settling the estate of Burhān al-Dīn al-Nāṣirī (d. 789/1387). Burhān al-Dīn's estate had been auctioned off and a more detailed sale booklet had been written, which is also preserved in the Ḥaram al-sharīf corpus (#061, #180 and #532). With the present document the *amīn al-ḥukum*, responsible for settling the estate, and his men wrote a more concise list in which they recorded the names of the buyers, the sum each of them owed and the sum total of all outstanding payments.

Beginning of text:
جميع ما أبيع من تركة المرحوم الناصري بتاريخ خامس عشر ذي القعدة ذي القعدة [مكرر] الحرام سنة تسع ثمانين وسبعماية

End of text:
ابن يونس ½ 12، حسابه 9242

The numerical values are written in Arabic Documentary Numerals (see Aljoumani/Hirschler, *Owning Books and Preserving Documents*, Chapter 6). This document is edited and discussed in Aljoumani/Hirschler, *Owning Books and Preserving Documents*, Chapter 8.

(36) #944 Decision on monthly obligatory maintenance payment *(farḍ)*

Arabic
18 Ramaḍān (probably late 700s/1300s)
26.5 x 9 cm, 11 lines, 1 witness clause, paper. The left-hand side of the document was trimmed and substantial parts of the text were thus lost.

Summary: This is the decision (by a judge?) concerning the amount of the monthly obligatory maintenance payment to which the guardian of two half-orphans is entitled. These two girls were the daughters of the deceased Ismāʿīl b. Khalīl.

Beginning of text:

بسم الله الرحمن الرحيم فرض سيدنا ومولانا العبد الفـ[ـقير. . .]

End of text:

الأخذ والوصول إلى ما لهما [. . .]

Names mentioned in text:

إسماعيل بن خليل

Places mentioned in text:

القدس الشريف

Names of witnesses:

عبد الرحمن بن محمد [الحبراني؟][123]

This document belongs to the large corpus of estate-related documents within the Ḥaram al-sharīf corpus, the vast majority of which date to the late 700s/1300s. The only other decisions on the amount of the *farḍ* in the corpus are two documents that date to 789/1387 and 790/1388 (#052 and #111).

123 Identical to the notary witness identified in Müller, *Der Kadi und seine Zeugen*, 539 as ʿAbd al-Munʿim b. Muḥammad al-Anṣārī, who was active between the years 793 and 797 (witness ID P100).

II.5 Endowments

(37) #931 Endowment for a *madrasa*

Arabic
undated
29/20.9 x 21.9 cm, 8 lines, paper. The lower part of the document is cut off with substantial textual loss (including the witness signatures that must have been there). The upper right corner is damaged with textual loss to the *ʿalāma*. The extant main text is is barely legible as many words are effaced.

Summary: Endowment for a *madrasa* with the delimitation of the boundaries of the endowed property.

Beginning of text:

[. . .] بقنطرة وحجر أبلق [. . .]

End of text:

وذراع من الطريق الآخذ إلى طاحون

Names mentioned in text: The name of the endowment's supervisor is mentioned, but not legible.

Places mentioned in text:

الطريق الآخذ إلى الطاحون

ʿAlāma of judge in the top right corner:
وقف مدرسة [. . .] [. . .مـ]ـسقفات وأحكار و[دور؟] . . .[شيخ] الإسلام بركة الأنام [. . .] [النـ]ـاظر بالمدرسة [. . .]
المذكوري [المذكورة]

The *ʿalāma* resembles those of Ottoman-period documents that renew old documents. On the verso of the document is an illegible seal.

(38) #970 Endowment for the Ḥaramayn

Arabic
undated
13.1/10.9 x 12.8 cm, 2 lines, paper. Only two lines of this document are extant.

Summary of content: This is the remnant of a document concerning the endowment of a property for the benefit of the endowments in (most likely) Jerusalem and Hebron.

Beginning of text:

[أ]وقا[ف. . .] ساحل آغروس وغيره [. . .] على

End of text:

الحرمين المكرمين شرفهما الله تعالى [. . .] على ما شُرح فيه

Places mentioned in text:

ساحل آغروس

(39) #937 Petition for appointment of supervisor and the *muftī's* endorsement

Text #937/1 (recto)
Arabic
before 1141/1728 (on the basis of the *muftī's* death date, see verso)
21.7 x 21.7 cm, 4 lines, paper. The document's lower end and left edge were trimmed leading to substantial textual loss.

Summary: ʿAbd al-Razzāq petitions to be appointed as supervisor *(nāẓir)* in an endowment in Jerusalem.

Beginning of text:
بالمجلس الشرعي المحرر المرعي أجَلَّهُ | الله | تعالى لدى مولانا وسيدنا مفخر قضاة الإسلام

End of text:
ومحفل الدين المنيف مفخر الخطباء الفخام [...] الكرام عبد الرزاق [...]

Names mentioned in text:
عبد الرزاق [...]

ʿAlāma of judge in the top right corner.

Text #937/2 (recto)
Arabic
undated
11 lines

Summary: Muḥammad b. ʿAbd al-Raḥīm al-Ḥusaynī Ibn Abī al-Luṭf, the *muftī* of Jerusalem, endorses the petition and states that the petitioner is well qualified for this position.[124]

Beginning of text:
الحمد لله وحده، وبعد فما حواه [مطاوي؟]، هذا الصك المزبور [...] به، من أهلية المذكور لإقامته، ناظراً على ذلك أمرٌ لا شبهة فيه

124 For Muḥammad al-Ḥusaynī see the detailed biography in Barakat, *Tārīkh al-qaḍāʾ*, 352–68.

End of text:

وأنا الحقـ[ـير الفقير]، [إلى] لطف مولاه القدير محمـ[ـد بن]، [عبد] الرحيم الحسيني [. . .]، أبي اللطف حفَّهم الله باللطـ[ـف]، المفتي بالقدس الشريف و[الحرم]، المنيف

Names mentioned in text:

محمد بن عبد الرحيم الحسيني ابن أبي اللطف

Places mentioned in text:

القدس الشريف

Below the endorsement is the *muftī's* seal.

(40) #951 Petition for position in *madrasa* in Cairo

Arabic
undated
3 x 13.7 cm, 2 lines, paper. The document was cut at the lower end so that only the first two lines are extant.

Summary of content: This might be a petition for a position in the Ḥijāzīya Madrasa in Cairo. To the left of the main text we find a note in a different hand stating that 'the appointment is approved' [التولية مقبول].

Beginning of text:

الشيخي التقوي بالمدرسة الحجازية

End of text:

الصالحي نفع الله به بالقاهرة المحروسة

Names mentioned in text:

التقوي الصالحي

Places mentioned in text:

المدرسة الحجازية بالقاهرة

(41) #947 Travel permit for endowment business and accounts

Text #947/1 (recto)
Arabic
undated (probably early 8th/14th century)
9.1 x 6.2 cm, 7 lines, paper. Only the top right corner of this document is extant.

Summary: This document grants at least three individuals permission to travel. They were most likely granted permission to go to the village of Bayt Dajan where properties were endowed for the benefit of an institution (the Ḥaram al-sharīf?) in Jerusalem.

Beginning of text:

الحمد لله، أذنتُ لبدر الدين بن نور [الدين . . .] وشهاب الدين ابن حامـ[ـد . . .] وأذنتُ لهم أن يسافـ[ـروا]

End of text:

فلاحين بيت دجن [. . .] طلبوها الفلاحين من [. . .] اللذين بشرط الواقف [. . .]

Names mentioned in text:

بدر الدين بن نور [الدين . . .]، شهاب الدين ابن حامـ[ـد]

Places mentioned in text:

بيت دجن

Text #947/2 (verso)
undated (probably early 8th/14th century)
4 lines, paper

Summary: This is a mere series of numbers without any text with their sum total at the end.

Beginning of text:

[. . .]، 30، 25، 20، 16، 12، 36

End of text:

441

The list of numbers on the verso might belong to the recto in the sense that the individuals who were sent to Bayt Dajan wrote here a draft version of products or income linked to the endowment. That the endowment warranted the dispatch of at least three individuals to sort out business with peasants indicates that it must have been of considerable size. This makes it likely that this document is part of the Ḥaram al-sharīf sub-corpus within the Ḥaram al-sharīf corpus. There are numerous documents related to the endowments of the Ḥaram al-sharīf and they are typically concerned with villages (#265: Bayt Ūnya, #697: ʿAyn, #703 and #712: Nūbā). The documents in this sub-corpus typically date to the early $8^{th}/14^{th}$ century (#712 dates to 705/1306; #332 to 706/1306; #265 to 706/1307; #697 and #703 to 707/1307; #596 to 707/1308). In consequence, the document (41)/#947 might date from these years as well.

The numerical values are written in Arabic Documentary Numerals (see Aljoumani/Hirschler, *Owning Books and Preserving Documents*, Chapter 6).

II.6 Letters

(42) #889 Letter of introduction for a *murābiṭ*

Arabic
undated
17.8 x 11 cm, 15 lines, paper

Summary: Letter of introduction for a *'murābiṭ'* whose name is not mentioned. The letter is addressed to al-Ḥajj Maḥmūd al-Shakhmī (?) and the writer sends his regards to several individuals, all of whom are linked to what we read as 'Zāwiyat al-Burāk'. No such *zāwiya* is known from Jerusalem or the wider Bilād al-sham. As the text was written in Maghribī script and uses the term *murābiṭ*, a term rarely employed in the Ḥaram al-sharīf corpus, there might be a link to the Zāwiyat al-Burāk in modern-day Libya.

Beginning of text:

الحمد لله وحده ولا يدوم إلا ملكه [. . .] السيد الحاج محمود الشخمي

End of text:

والحاج حسن وصاحبه الحاج أحمد المتوكلي والسلام

Names mentioned in text:

الحاج محمود الشخمي، الحاج أحمد الشخمي، الحاج إبراهيم أدرو، الحاج حسن، الحاج أحمد المتوكلي

Places mentioned in text:

زاوية البراك

(43) #899 A merchant's letter concerning leather

Arabic
undated
27/25.9 x 9.8 cm, 20 lines, paper. The document is damaged at its upper end and the first line has suffered some textual loss. The document has several holes and the hole between lines 4 and 5 might be of archival nature.

Summary: This is a letter referring to the sale of leather *(julūd)*. The writer *('al-akh Muḥammad')* asks the addressee, who lives in Jerusalem, to inspect the quality of the merchandise and to reply promptly. If the merchandise is of good quality, the writer is to come to Jerusalem to conclude the deal.

Beginning of text:
[بسـ]ـم الله [. . .] سلام الله تعالى ورحمته وبركاته وأزكى تحياته على الأخ العزيز الموفق الرشيد

End of text:
وعلى جميع المعارف والأصحاب كل واحد باسمه والحمد لله وحده وصلى الله على سيدنا محمد

Names mentioned in text:
الأخ محمد، الأخ عبد الرحمن، الأخ مجير الدين

Places mentioned in text:
القدس

The name of the sender is written in the right margin:
من عند الأخ محمد

(44) #925 A father's letter to his daughter and his son-in-law's financial guarantee

Text #925/1 (recto & verso)
Arabic
undated
26.5 x 11.8 cm, 25 lines (recto) & 9 lines (verso), paper. There is material damage to the top without textual loss.

Summary: A father writes to tell his daughter that he has run out of money on his journey. He has failed to secure any loans and even his companions are refusing to pay his way without a legal guarantee *(wikāla sharʿīya)*. He thus asks his daughter to convince her husband to act as guarantor so that he can complete his journey.

Beginning of text:

بسم الله الرحمن الرحيم إلى حضرة البنت العزيزة [حُسْن؟] والابن العزيز حرسهم الله تعالى والذي أعرفكم لا عرَّفكم الله مكروه أننا على جملت السلام

End of text:

وإن سيَّرو شي سيّروه مع حاملت الكتاب وبنت عمي تسلم تسلم عليكم وصيتكم في حاملت الكتاب والحمد لله وحده.

Names mentioned in text:

عمر، ابن الفارس، الشيخ علي، محمد، ابن الزركشية

Text #925/2 (verso)
2 lines. The first line is not legible on account of material damage.

Summary: This is most likely the financial guarantee, as sought by the writer of the letter on the recto. The money was seemingly to be handed over to one of the writer's travel companions, Nāṣir al-Dīn.

Beginning of text: missing
End of text:

إلى ابن الموكاني تسلم إلى يد ناصر الدين [...]

Names mentioned in text:

ابن الموكاني، ناصر الدين

(45) #935 An unidentified letter

Arabic
undated
21.9/17.5 x 20.2/11 cm, 4 lines, paper. Another document must have become attached to this document leaving traces of ink on #935 that render it illegible. A letter was written in Arabic in the margins, but it is so badly damaged that it is also mostly illegible.

Summary: The content remains unclear to us, except for the following:

Beginning of text:

بعد إهداء أزكى التحيات وأنماها وإتحاف أطيب التسليمات

End of text:

لتكميل شرائط اتحاد الانتسا[ب؟ . . .]

II.7 Poetry

(46) #930 Religious Persian poetry from Ottoman Aleppo

Persian & Arabic
1210/1795–96
31.2 x 18 cm, 13 lines, paper. This is a folio that became detached from a manuscript. The ink has faded in places. A vertical chain line and lines framing the text in *nastaʿlīq* script, which is arranged in two columns, are visible. There are lacunae in lines 9 and 13.

Summary: Religious poetry mentioning Prophet Mūsā written by Sayyid Muḥammad Qudsī al-Rahhāwī al-Naqshabandī the *naqīb* of Aleppo in 1210.

Beginning of text:

هو يا نبي الله يا موسى الكليم

End of text (before date):

نمقه الفقير السيد محمد قدسي الرهاوي النقشبندي النقيب بمدينة حلب الشهباء [. . .] سنة 1210

Names mentioned in text:

محمد قدسي الرهاوي النقشبندي

Places mentioned in text:

حلب

(47) #961 A *qaṣīda* in dialectical Arabic

Arabic
undated
19.6 x 14.3 cm, 17 lines (recto) & 7 lines (verso), paper. There is slight damage on the right side.

Summary: A *qaṣīda* in dialectical Arabic in response to a missive that reached the writer from the Banū Fāris.

Beginning of text (recto):

أول قولنا نمدح محمد رسول الله له علخد شاما

End of text (recto):

أريد أعلمك يا بو محمد تر[ا] إسماعيل جارح في كلاما

Beginning of text (verso):

تر[ا] إسماعيل تربات المناصب ولا مثله حين زرق الوشاما

End of text (verso):

وتدعين الفناء من بعد عز غريب الدار وصفا رق غلاما

Names mentioned in text:

بني فارس، أبو محمد، أبو إسماعيل، إسماعيل

The verso has 6 further faint lines that seem to be a draft for a letter.

(48) #940 Poetry (reuse stage, see catalogue entry (16))

Text #940/2 (verso)
Arabic
undated
22 x 8.6 cm, 2 lines

Summary: These 2 lines of poetry are written on the back of accounting registering two payments (see catalogue entry (16)). The script on both sides looks very similar. It is thus likely that the writer of the accounts reused the verso of this accounts to write these two lines.

Beginning of text:

يقول الحزين ابن قاسم

End of text:

وبه ألمٌ قد عايا الطبيب دواءه

Names mentioned in text:

ابن قاسم

II.8 Prayers

(49) #952 *Du'ā* (invocation) prayer

Arabic
undated
18.3/16.9 x 10 cm, 18 lines (recto) & 7 lines (verso), paper

Summary: Prayers and blessings for the Prophet Muḥammad in Maghribī script.

Beginning of text (recto):

اللهم صلي على سيدنا [و] مولـ[ا]نا محمد

End of text (recto):

وبارك عليه وعلى آله وصحبه أجمعين

Beginning of text (verso):

وعلى جميع البياء [الأنبياء] والمرسلين

End of text (verso):

عدد ما كان وعدد مايكون وعدد، ما هو كون في علمك إلى يوم الدين

(50) #956 *Duʿā* prayer

Arabic
undated
15.3/11.2 x 15/11.3 cm, 11 lines (recto) & 6 lines (verso), paper. The lower right corner is damaged leading to some textual loss.

Summary: *Duʿā* prayer for *faraj* and *raḥma.*

Beginning of text (recto):

فنسئل [فنسأل] الله بجاه المصطفى وآله وصحبه والخلفاء أن يتوفنا على الإسلام

End of text (recto):

في ظلمات القبور بجاه سيد الود العدنان [ولد عدنان]

Beginning of text (verso):

ألا يا لطيف يا لطيف [. . .] اللطف فأنت الطيف منك

End of text (verso):

بلطف أنه لطيف لطيف لطفه دائم اللطف

(51) #932 *Duʿā* prayer (most likely reuse stage, see catalogue entry (22))

Text #932/2
Arabic
undated
30 x 22 cm, 10 lines, paper. This sheet is torn and has several holes. It is unclear to what extent it really formed one unit with the accounts of 932/1 (see catalogue entry (22)).

Summary: A certain Muḥammad b. Z-r-w-f (?) writes a *duʿā* prayer in Maghribī script for his own benefit and that of his mother.

Beginning of text:

بسم الله الرحمن الرحيم وصلى الله على سيدنا

End of text: illegible
Names mentioned in text:

محمد بن [زروف؟]

The writer most likely reused an old document/sheet for writing his prayer. He starts in the middle of the sheet and carefully avoids the part that was torn off (text (22)/#932/1).

(52) #965 Instructions to write amulet prayers

Arabic
undated
13.9/13.2 x 9.6 cm, 16 lines, paper

Summary: The text contains instructions to write two prayers to be worn as amulets, one for marriage and the second to stop grain rotting.

Beginning of text:

باب للبنت البايرة يُكتب ويُعلق في عنقها

End of text:

لم يُسوَّس ولم يعفّن قط ألم ترا [ترَ]، كيف فعل ربك بأصحاب الفيل إلا [إلى] آخرها تم

II.9 Other documents

(53) #933 Unidentified legal document, most likely judicial certification *(ishhād)*

Arabic
undated
15.2/12.6 x 21.9 cm, 8 lines, paper. The lower part of the document has been cut off. It is damaged at the top left corner and the extant text is poorly legible as many words are effaced.

The content remains unclear to us, except:

(line 5)

المعتمد الفقير إلى الله سبحانه الشيخ الإمام العالم العلامة قاضي القضاة

(line 7)

الأحكام الشرعية بالقدس وما معه [...] على نفسه الكريمة

Places mentioned in text:

القدس

(54) #976 Unidentified legal document

Arabic
28 Jumādā II 753/1352
22.1/21 x 27.5 cm, 13 lines, 10 witness clauses, paper. The upper part of the document with the main text is lost. The extant part only has the witness statements.

Beginning of text:
ذلك في ثامن عشرين جمادى الآخر من سنة ثلاث وخمسين وسبعماية كتبه محمد بن أبي بكر الشافعي

End of text:
كذلك أشهدني على نفسه الكريمة أدام الله أيامه فشهدت عليه بما نسب إليه أعلاه يوسف بن حسن بن إبراهيم كتبه عنه ماجد بن خضر

Names of witnesses:
محمد بن أبي بكر الشافعي، محمد بن عبد العزيز الحجاجي، محمود بن خليل بن محمود، خليل بن يوسف بن حسن، عبد الله بن خضر الحنفي، محمد بن أحمد الشافعي، هبة الله بن حميد بن سراج الحسيني، ناصر بن سالم بن ناصر الحنفي، يوسف بن حسن بن إبراهيم، ماجد بن خضر

(55) #954 Sheet from a Koran commentary

Arabic
undated
20.1/16.5 x 13/10.8 cm, 24 lines (recto) & 24 lines (verso), paper. The lower right corner is damaged with substantial loss and the extant text is of poor legibility as many words are effaced.

Summary: This is a discussion of various Koran commentaries (such as *'Ajā'ib al-'irfān fī tafsīr ījāz al-bayān fī al-tarjama 'an al-qur'ān* by Ibn al-'Arabī, d. 637/1240), but we have not been able to identify the text.

Beginning of text (recto):
[من إيجاز] البيان في الترجمة عن القرآن للشيخ محي الدين ابن العربي تبين أنه في

End of text (recto):
النسبة إليه صحيحة وإن كان المرحومون قد [. . .] والرحمة [. . .]

Beginning of text (verso):
[. . .] معنى نعبد نتذلل يُقال أرض معبدة أي مذللة

End of text (verso):
[. . .مما ذكرناه لا في فروع . . . وإن ظهر في شرعنا من فروع شرع من قبلنا؟]

Names mentioned in text:
ابن العربي، أبو حنيفة، الشافعي

(56) #939 Page of Sufi text (subsequently reused, see catalogue entry (32))

Text #939/1 (recto)
Arabic
undated
17.7 x 13.2 cm, 18 lines, paper. There is slight textual loss at the lower end because of a hole.

Summary: Beginning of *Faṣl al-murāqaba*. This was most likely a loose sheet from a book that had belonged to the library of the deceased al-Shaykh Muḥammad al-Raṭūnī, whose estate inventory we find on the verso (see catalogue entry (32)).

Beginning of text:

فصل المراقبة، قبلُ ينبغي للسالك أن يجتهد في المداومة على الحياء من الله تعالى فإن ذلك عين الأدب

End of text:

قال رسول الله صلى الله [عليه] وسلم خالفوا اليهود فإنهم لا يصلون في نعالهم [. . .] ولا أخفافهم

Names mentioned in text:

سهل بن عبد الله التستري

III Ottoman-language documents concerning Jerusalem and surroundings

(57) #929 *Berat* from Sultan Mehmed IV

Ottoman
16 Dhū al-Ḥijja 1060/1650
32.4/23.3 x 21.8 cm, 8 lines, paper. The top and the lower parts of the document are missing.
The verso has a *defterdâr kuyûdâtı* meaning that this official letter of investiture, *berat,* was also copied and kept in the office of the *defterdâr* (head of finance bureau).

Summary: *Berat* renewing a previous *berat* for Mevlana Shaykh Yūsuf b. Shaykh Raḍī al-Dīn for his position as a preacher in the Aqsa Mosque. The *berat* was issued upon Shaykh Yūsuf's request. His daily wage is fifteen *para.*

Beginning of text:
Taht-ı âlî baht üzre cülûs-ı hümâyûn-ı saâdet-makrûnum vâki' olmağla umûmen tecdîd-i berevât fermân-ı şerîfim olmağın

End of text: . . . *alup mutasarrıf olup devâm-ı ömr ü devletim ed'iyesine muvâzıb ola. Şöyle bileler alâmet-i şerîfe itimad kılalar*

Names mentioned in the text:
مولانا الشيخ يوسف بن الشيخ رضي الدين، محمد بن إبراهيم (الرابع)

Places mentioned in the text:
القدس الشريف، المسجد الأقصى

https://doi.org/10.1515/9783111330242-004

(58) #928 *Berat* from Sultan Ahmed III

Ottoman
undated (before 1143/1730)
32.5/30.1 x 16 cm, 2 lines, paper. Only the *tughra*, the Sultan's calligraphic insignia, and the first two lines of the main text are extant.

Summary: Official letter of investiture *(berat)* by Ahmed III (d. 1149/1736) concerning Shaykh Isḥāq b. Ṣāliḥ al-Laṭīfī's (?) land grant *(timār)* which is linked to the endowed properties of the Sultan's chief consort (*Haseki*).

Beginning of text: [. . .] vâki' merhume ve mağfiretün leha Haseki Sultân tâbet serâhânın

Names mentioned in the text:
شيخ إسحق ابن صالح اللطيفي، أحمد الثالث، خاصكى سلطان

(59) #934 *Berat* from Sultan Ahmed III

Ottoman
undated (before 1143/1730)
32.5/26.5 x 22.1/15.7 cm, 8 lines, paper. The document has suffered water damage that has almost completely erased the text. In addition, it has substantial holes in the top left and the lower right corners. The lower part of this official letter of investiture, *berat,* is entirely lost. Only traces of the *tughra* are extant.

The verso has a *defterdâr kuyûdâtı* meaning that the *berat* was also copied and kept in the office of the *defterdâr*.

(60) #887 Letter requesting a *berat* for the imam of Silwād

Ottoman
Jumādā I 1332/1914
75.4 x 47.9 cm, 7 lines, paper

There is an archival note on the verso with an authenticating seal and two stamps for 20 *qirsh* and 50 *qirsh*. The stamps are sealed with two different seals.

Summary: This is a letter from Muḥammad Kāmil al-Ḥusaynī, Deputy Judge of the Sharia Court in Jerusalem in 1914. It deals with the appointment of Shaykh Muḥammad b. Shaykh ʿAbd al-Fattāḥ Efendi as imam in the mosque of Silwād in the administrative district *(nahiye)* of ʿAbawīn (close to Ramallah). The letter is addressed to an authority in Istanbul (no specifics are given but this is probably either the Evkâf Nezareti or the Maarif Nezareti) requesting that official letter of investiture *(berat)* be issued. It also states that the person has previously been subjected to an examination before the Commission of the Court.

Beginning of text: *Der-i devlet-mekîn'e arz-ı dâî-i kemîneleridir ki*

End of text: … *uhdesine tevcîh ve yedine bir kıt'a berât-ı şerîf-i âlişân sadaka ve ihsan buyurulmak istirhamiyle pâye-i serîr-i şevket-musîr-i âlâ'ya.*

Names mentioned in text:

محمد كامل الحسيني، محمد بن عبد الفتاح

Places mentioned in text:

سلواد، عبوين

ʿAlāma of judge in bottom left corner with judge's stamp:
العبد الداعي بدوام الدولة العلية العثمانية مفتي السيد محمد كامل الحسيني وكيل القاضي بالقدس الشريف

(61) #972 Two private letters

Text #972/1
Ottoman
undated
5.3 x 7 cm, 3 lines, paper. The letter has been trimmed so that most of its text was lost.

Beginning of text: *Sultânım hazretleri [. . .] Devlet u ikbâl-i ebedî ve übbehet-i iclâl-i sermedî ile*

End of text: . . . *bende-i kadîm ve çâker-i mesnedîleridir ki hak derkâr ve payidâr olan teveccühât-ı seniyye*

Text #972/2
Ottoman
undated
4 lines, paper. The letter has been trimmed so that most of its text was lost.

Beginning of text: *Sultânım hazretleri [. . .] Hudâvend-i gayûr zât-ı saaadetleriyle dahî mesrûr ve umûr-ı hayriyyelerinde*

End of text: . . . *duânâmemiz tahrîr ve nâdî-i saadetlerine ba's u tesyîr kılındı. İnşaallahu teâlâ ledâ şerefu'l-vüsûl ma'lûm ve [. . .]*

(62) #903 *Du'ā* prayer

Ottoman
27 Sha'bān 1237/1822
21/16.5 x 31.7 cm, 6 lines, paper. The upper part has a large hole so that the first line is not fully legible.

Summary: Invocation for returning to the Aqsa Mosque in colloquial language. The document identifies some features of the Aqsa Mosque such as its proximity to other religious landmarks.

Beginning of text: *Elvedâ yâ sahratullah ya gelem ya gelmeyem Mescid-i Aksâsın. Vallahi ya gelem ya gelmeyem. Şimdi yüz kısmına*

End of text: . . . *olur mu bükrâ dîvân-ı Hak'dan. Elvedâ yâ sahratullah ya gelem ya gelmeyem*

Places mentioned in text:

المسجد الأقصى، صخرة الله

IV Persian and Persianate documents concerning Transcaucasia, Anatolia and Northwestern Iran (including Georgian, Armenian and Arabic documents)

IV.1 Documents belonging to the dossier of Amīr Ādūjī's family

(63) #891 Archival list of deeds

Persian
undated (probably before 731/1331)
51.2/52 x 11.06 cm, 20 lines, paper. There are lacunae in several places with parts torn at the top right-hand corner and the bottom.

Summary: An archival list describing a collection of legal deeds. It is entitled 'List of Deeds of the Fourth Bag, the White Bag' (*tafṣīl-i ḥujjat-hā-yi kīsa-yi chahārum, kīsa-yi sifīd).*[125] The entries in the list reproduce archival notes that are found on the verso of Ḥaram deeds involving Amīr Ādūjī b. Yāzilī (d. c. 740/1331) (see #857, #867, #870, #871, #873, #881 and #916). It is likely that this list belonged to him. The use of bags (Per. *kīsa*) to preserve fiscal documents is known from Ilkhanid Mongol accounting manuals. On this and for an edition of the list and a study of its relationship to the family archive of Amīr Ādūjī, see Bhalloo and Watabe, *A Fourteenth-Century Persian Archival List from al-Ḥaram al-Sharīf in Jerusalem* (in preparation for submission to *Der Islam*).

The 55 entries on the list are arranged in three vertical columns. So that each line contains three entries. Since the bottom of the document is torn, it is likely that the list was longer and some entries are now lost. Each entry begins with the Persian term *ḥujjat* (Ar. *ḥujja*), of which the final letter *tā'* is extended. Most entries concern individual deeds. Several entries, however, mention more than one deed and in this case appear below the plural *ḥujjat-hā* (entries 1, 14, 55).[126] In this case the letter *hā'* of the Persian pluralization suffix is extended. Directly below the term *ḥujjat*, the

---

125 I am indebted to Ryoko Watabe for her help in deciphering the Persian term *kīsa* (bag) in this title based on her research on the Ilkhanid Mongol accounting manual, *al-Murshid fī l-ḥisāb*. The Arabic term *tafṣīl* is used in New Persian lists from 12th to 13th century Khurāsān, see docs. 53, 54, 61, 63 in Mīrzā Khwāja Muḥammad and Nabī Sāqī (eds.) *Barg-hā-yī az yak faṣl yā asnād-i tārīkhī-yi ghūr* (Kābul: Intishārāt-i Sa'īd, 1388 sh./2010), 93–105.

126 The numbering of the entries is from right to left for each line.

https://doi.org/10.1515/9783111330242-005

entries usually provide the toponym of the lands, usually a village, referred to in the original deed (entry 4, 41). Persian clauses such as *az aʿmāl-i* (from the district or province of) (entry 50) or *dar bāb-i* (about) (entry 47) are used in some entries to provide more details about the location of the land or to summarize the content of the deed. There are also entries which specify the names of individuals involved in the transfer or purchase of the lands mentioned in the original deed (entry 7, 37, 55). In contrast to these longer entries, some entries are short and only specify whether the document is a sale deed (entry 19) or an endowment deed (entry 3). Sometimes the term *maktūb* is used instead of *ḥujjat* for deed or document (entry 26). If the deed is not in Arabic or Persian and is in Armenian, for example, this is specified (entry 26). The number of exemplars or related deeds preserved in the bag is also mentioned in the entry using terms such as *dū bāra* (two exemplars) (entry 1) or *dū ʿadad* (two deeds) (entry 26, 55), for example entry 55: deeds of the underground water canal of the Sufi lodge that was purchased from Arak (?) ʿUmar, two deeds.

Beginning of text:

تفصیل حجتها [ی] کیسه چهارم کیسه سفید

End of text (entry 55):

حجتها [ی] کریز خانقاه کی از [ارک؟] عمر خریده شد، دو عدد

(64) #896 Purchase contract for half a mine

Persian
Muḥarram 705/1305
67.5 x 13 cm, 28 lines, 3 witness clauses in Arabic, 1 witness clause in Persian, paper. There are lacunae in the text of the judicial attestation of the judge at the top left-hand corner of the document.

Summary: The document describes the purchase by Amīr Ādūjī b. Yāzilī of half a mine/quarry (*kān*) known as K-l-l-siyā (?) from Shams al-Dīn (?) Muḥammad Abī l-Faḍl al-Sīnjānī (?) for 60 dinars. The main text (28 lines) is preceded by a five-line Arabic judicial attestation. A two-line additional note below the third witness clause confirms the receipt by the seller of the purchase sum from Ḥasan b. ʿAlī. In another two-line additional note below the first one, the seller confirms that the document contains his acknowledgement.

Beginning of text:
اين ذكر محتوايست در بيان آنک خريد ملک الأمرا و الملوك مقرب الحضرة افتخار الخواص أمير آدوجى بن يازلي زيد اقباله

End of text:
بر اين جمله گواه گرفتند كسانى كى انساب و اسامى خود نوشته اند

Names mentioned in text:
أمير آدوجى بن يازلي، شمس [الدين؟] محمد أبي الفضل [السينجاني؟]، غريب سعده، محمود أحمد، حاجي مطرب، نصرة [الدين؟] أمير چوپان، [؟] ، أمير [بكوداد؟]، حسن بن علي

Places mentioned in text:
[كللسيا؟]

Names of witnesses:
تمور بن [. . .] طغا جار، محمد شاه بن خليل [. . .]، خواجه صالح ابن عز الدين [اردساى؟]، خواجه محمد بن عز الدين بن [. . .]

Judicial attestation of the judge on the top-left corner of the document:
[صححت؟] [المبايعة؟] جرى عندي وحكمت بصحته وأقضيته و [نفذته؟] وكتبه [. . .] و [أنا القاضي؟] [. . .] [عبده؟] محمد بن محمد [البخاري؟] [. . .]

(65) #909 Sale contract of an underground water canal

65/a, Text #909 (recto), sale contract
Persian
8 Dhū al-Ḥijja 747/1347
61.5 x 15.8 cm, 20 lines, 7 witness clauses in Persian, 1 witness clause in Arabic, paper. There is textual loss due to lacunae in lines 1–7 and 10–15.

Summary: The recto records the sale of an underground water canal (*kahrīz*) known as Kahrīz-i Khwāja ʿAzīz (line 4, verso) for 450 dinars. The parties to the sale are difficult to decipher due to lacunae; however, some, if not all, of the persons mentioned on the recto were also involved in the court proceedings described on the verso of the document. The scribe of both the recto and verso is Abū Saʿīd al-Marwānī.

Beginning of text:

[. . .] در [محادس؟] [. . .] دام دولته و غفر أسلافه

End of text:

و از مجلس شرع مطهر متعرف شدند حقی [. . .] بایع مذکور و با [أولاد ؟] و با کسی دعوی کند دروغ و باطل
و افك و طغیان باشد

Names mentioned in text:

أبو سعيد المرواني، حاجي عزيز، [قره؟] بن [كوكداس؟]

Names of witnesses:

اتا بک بن [مسامر؟]، حاجي أحمد بن شاه [. . .]، علاء الدين تاج [. . .] القصاری، [سمهر؟] بن علی،
شیخ عبد الله بن محمد شاه، داود بن میکائیل، حبش بن [توکای؟]

The scribe uses *kahrīz* (line 14) instead of *kāriz* (from Middle Persian *kārēz*). The document has a *ṣaḥḥa al-waṣl* note on the right-hand margin at the sheet joints. There is an additional one-line note below the witness clauses where Qurra (?) b. Kukādās (?) confirms the ownership of the canal by Ḥājjī ʿAzīz.

65/b, Text #909 (verso), judicial decision
Persian
18 Ramaḍān 748/1347
17 lines, 1 witness clause in Persian

There is textual loss due to lacunae in lines 1–3, and 8–10, and in the judicial attestation of the judge.

Summary: The verso confirms, probably by a judicial decision, eight months after the conclusion of the sale described on the recto, the rights of Amīr Barāt (?) to 3 ½ *dāng* (*dāng* = one sixth part of any estate) and of Shaykh Muḥammad and Shaykh ʿĀdī, sons (*abnāʾ*) of the deceased Amīr Kurd (b. Amīr Ādūjī?) to 2 ½ *dāng* of the canal.

Beginning of text:

[. . .] أكابر مقرب الملوك و السلاطين [. . .] دام دولته و غفر أسلافه [. . .] تمامت [. . .] كهريز بيرون
آورده آيد معروف و مشهور است بر كهريز خواجه عزيز [مخلده؟] أميرزادگان معظم

End of text:

و گذاشت اين معانى بحضور جماعت أسامي و ألقاب [و] أنساب [كى] در آخر مكتوب ثبت كرده شود

Names mentioned in text:

شيخ محمد، شيخ عادي، أمير [برات؟]، أمير كرد ، [. . .] بن عبد الكريم [. . .]، أبو سعيد المرواني

Names of witnesses:

أمير شاه بن حسن

The main text is preceded by a four-line judicial attestation by a judge named [. . .] bin ʿAbd al-Karīm [. . .]. There is a three-line additional note on liability (*ḍamān*) below the witness clause which mentions the share of 3 ½ *dāng* of the canal by Amīr Barāt (?) and 2 ½ *dāng* by Shaykh Muḥammad and Shaykh ʿĀdī. There are two undeciphered marks above the witness clause. If the Amīr Kurd mentioned in this document is the son of Amīr Ādūjī then the document belongs to the dossier of Amīr Ādūjī's family.

(66) #916 Deed of acknowledgement (*iqrār*) about the ownership of the village of Aghūrs

Persian
5 Ṣafar 705/1305
32.1 x 10.9 cm, 7 lines, 14 witness clauses in Persian, 1 witness clause in Arabic, paper. This is the document's bottom fragment, the top part is missing. There are lacunae in lines 1 and 2.

Archival note on verso:

حجت جماعت من رؤسای مکرود درباب اغورس

Summary: The recto records the acknowledgement and witness testimonies of a group of village chiefs (*ru'asā'*) from Makrūd concerning the ownership of the village of Aghūrs (var. Aghūrth) by Amīr Ādūjī b. Yāzilī. There is an undeciphered witness clause or scribal signature after the date of the main text of the *iqrār*.

Beginning of text:

جماعتی [. . .] یوسف [. . .] جماعتی [. . .] آدوجی آقا درباب دیه اغورس حق و ملك وی است

End of text:

و بدو تعلق دارد و بهیچ کسی را در باب دیه اغورس دعوی نیست [و] نباشد بگواهی جماعتی کی حاضر بوده
است حجت دادیم در

Names mentioned in text:

آدوجی آقا

Places mentioned in text:

مکرود، اغورس

Names of witnesses:

[فاجورا؟]، [طابا؟]، محمد ابن بوبکر،[بوعاچی؟]، [اوروچ؟]، عثمان بن حسن، محمد شاه [. . .]، قتلغبك، چريك، شمس الدين محمد شاه، اسماعيل بن محمد، [الاكواز؟]، [ييرمز يدى؟]، علي بن عثمان، مير حسن بن أحمد

Amīr Ādūjī bought the village of Aghūrs (var. Aghūrth) in the district of Zangezur of Arrān on 30 Ramaḍān 700/8 September 1301 for 400 gold dinars from Shams al-Dawla wa-al-Dīn Maḥmūd Shāh b. al-Marḥūm Muḥammad b. al-Saʿīd (#868 and #869, see Little, *A Catalogue*, 383). It is possible that this village is situated in Zangezur (Armenian: Զանգեզուր), a historical and geographical region in Eastern

Armenia on the slopes of the Zangezur Mountains which largely corresponds to the Syunik Province of the Republic of Armenia. Arārān is also mentioned in (83)/#915 (line 5). Entry 4 in the archival list (63)/#891 refers to the deed (probably sale deed) of Aghūrs. The location of Makrūd in relation to Aghūrs is unclear. If Makrūd is located close to Aghūrs in the region of Zangezur, then it is unlikely that it corresponds to the village of the same name (Mak Rūd) in Māzandarān Province, Iran. The archival note on the verso is reproduced as entry 47 in the archival list of deeds, see (63)/#891. Entry 49 also refers to a deed containing testimony from the village chiefs of Makrūd about the peasants of Makrūd.

(67) #911 Transfer of *iqṭāʿ* (benefice) (edited in Appendix 1a, I, see fig. 6 and 7)

Persian
Middle of Ramaḍān 711/1312
30.2/31.5 x 13.5 cm, 13 lines, 1 witness clause in Arabic (?), 1 witness clause in Persian, 1 witness clause in Georgian (recto) & 3 witness clauses in Persian, 1 witness clause in Turkic, 1 witness clause in Mongolian (verso), paper. The top of the document is missing.

Summary: A document issued by Zakariyā. He was one of the sons of the *wazīr* and *ṣāḥib-dīwān* (in charge of state finance) of the early Ilkhanid period, Shams al-Dīn Muḥammad b. Muḥammad Juwaynī, who was executed in 1285 (see Gronke, *Derwische im Vorhof der Macht*, 307; Rajabzadeh, *Jovayni Family*). According to an earlier document (#856) dated 13 Rabīʿ II 710/9 September 1310, Zakariyā transfers the village of Arīghī located in the district of Kilākūn (between Berdaa, Azerbaijan and Ardabīl, Iran), assigned to him as a benefice (*iqṭāʿ*) in an imperial decree (*yarlīgh*), to Amīr Ādūjī and his descendants. In the present document, issued in the following year, Zakariyā confirms the transfer.

Beginning of text:
اين خط من کی زکريا بن محمد جوينی ام دادم بخدمت [بارم؟] أمير معظم آدوجي آقا کی اقطاع ديه اريغي کی از حکم بمن تعلق دارد

End of text:

و اين ذکر بر سبيل [ا. . .] داده شود

Names mentioned in text:

آدوجي آقا، زکريا بن محمد جوينی

Places mentioned in text:

اريغي

Names of witnesses (recto):

زکريا[127]، [. . .][128]، جمال [؟] الملک

127 Autograph witness clause of Zakariyā probably based on the Arabic clause *bi-khaṭṭihi* (in his own hand).
128 Georgian witness clause მართალია (*martalia*), 'it is true, correct'. There is no name. It is possible that it is an autograph witness clause of Zakariyā. See also footnote 127.

Names of witnesses (verso):

[توبي] بن حسن، [. . .] بن محمد، [. . .]

Turkic witness clause (verso):
b(u)bitig MMN? čänggä? tanuq biz = *We, MMN?* and *Čänggä?* are witness(es) (to) this document.

Mongolian witness clause (verso):
quča burur? gere bui̯ = *Quča-Burur* (?) is witness.

On Zakariyā b. Shams al-Dīn Muḥammad b. Muḥammad Ṣāḥib Dīwān Juwaynī, see the introduction to this catalogue and the Ḥaram al-sharīf documents #867, #876 and (97)/#885/#920. The first two documents, #867, #876, and the present document (67)/#911 contain the distinctive autograph witness clause of Zakariyā (see Figure 21). The village of Arīghī is mentioned twice in the archival list (63)/#891: entry 24, document (*maktūb*) concerning Arīghī from Shams al-Dīn (?) Zakariyā, and entry 27, deed (*ḥujjat*) of the village of Arīghī from Zakariyā.

(68) #910 Deed of acknowledgement (*iqrār*) concerning a debt

Persian
Middle of Ṣafar 692/1293
39.6 x 13.7 cm, 14 lines, 5 witness clauses in Persian, paper. The top of the document is missing.

Summary: A debtor acknowledges receipt of the sum of 200 gold dinars from a group of creditors and says it was repaid with funds provided to him and his sons by (Amīr) Ādūjī (b. Yāzilī). The debtor, who with his family later joined the household of Ādūjī's son, claims to have a document proving receipt of the funds used to pay off the debt and says that no one has made any further claims against him. The scribe of the document is ʿAlī b. ʿUthmān.

Beginning of text:

[. . .] بوده ام از جماعت أمير شاه [تماس؟] و [بلياق؟] و [قمري؟] و قبجاق و [نصراني؟] مبلغ دويست دينار زر قرض گرفته بوده ام چون آدوجی اين مبلغ دويست دينار را در حق من و فرزندان من بداد مرا از دست قرض در آن رهانيد

End of text:

هيچ كس را درين ميان كار من دعوى و مطالبتى نباشد جواب و عهده بر من باشد بحضور جماعتى حاضر بوده اند

Names mentioned in text:

آدوجی، أمير شاه [تماس؟] و [بلياق؟] و [قمري؟] و [قيحاق؟] و [نصراني؟]

Names of witnesses:

اسماعيل أحمد [. . .]، درويش بن شير بيك، ستاي بن [واحوق؟]، رجب بن حسن، لاجن [شيوسوجى؟]

There is an undeciphered mark at the bottom left-hand corner of the document. This is the earliest dated document of the Ādūjī dossier.

(69) #914 Deed of acknowledgement (*iqrār)* concerning mortgage of property

Persian
Shawwāl 705/1306
31.9/34 x 13 cm, 16 lines, 15 witness clauses in Persian, 1 witness clause in Turkic (recto) & 1 witness clause in Persian (verso), paper. The top of the document is missing.

Summary: The document concerns a certain Maḥmūd who declares that he gave a particular property to Amīr Ādūjī b. Yāzilī in exchange for the sum of 400 dinars according to Ilkhanid Mongol law (*bi-ḥukm-i yāsā*). Any claim made by anyone else to the said property is void and Maḥmūd has the right of response if anyone attempts to make a claim.

Beginning of text:
أمیر آدوجی دادیم [برضاء] محمود [. . .] او تا بعد الیوم بنده او باشد چنانک بندگان دیگر اگر خواهد فروشد و بخشد

End of text:
و اگر کسی سخنی گوید با ید محمود دعوی دارد جواب و عهده بر ما باشد و [خمیس؟] و برادران او [اعتراوسن؟] و ایسن و [عیسی؟] و [خلیل] برین جمله گواه گشتند

Names mentioned in text:
أمیر آدوجی، محمود، [خمیس؟]، [اعتراوسن؟]، [عیسی؟]، [ضلیك؟]

Names of witnesses (recto):
[. . .]، [حاروق؟]، کرداباجي، مجد الدين [مخلس؟]، پیر محمد جماقلو، اباداد، حسینک أمیر [. . .]، [ارمنج بن کوانی؟]، [بادکر؟] بن أمیر الله خواجه، خواجه موسی، [کوجنکی؟]، هندو، علي میر [. . .]، [اسعملش؟]، [بدو أحسنجی؟]

Turkic witness clause (recto):
bu bitig-gä män / toqdämür tanuq = I, Toq-dämür, am witness to this document.

Names of witnesses (verso):
قتلغ بوغا

(70) #942/#898 Marriage contract for a deferred dowry (edited in Appendix 1a, II, see fig. 8 and 9)

Persian and Arabic
3 Muḥarram 769/1367
(#942) 17.1/20.2 x 16.7 cm, 7 lines, paper. This is the document's top fragment with lacunae in the judicial attestation and in lines 3 to 5 and 7.
(#898) 34.7 x 16.7 cm, 15 lines, 1 witness clause in Persian, 4 witness clauses in Arabic, paper. This is the document's bottom fragment with lacunae in line 1 and one archival hole on the left between lines 3 and 4.

Summary: These two fragments constitute the marriage contract of the daughter of Amīr Kurd b. Amīr Ādūjī. The marriage is between Khurram Shāh Khānum and Amīr Shaykhī b. Amīr Khwāja ʿAlī b. Amīr Abū Bakr. The deferred *ṣadāq* and *mahr* is 16,000 dinars. The deed is authenticated by the judge Ḥājjī Yaʿqūb b. Yūsuf.

Beginning of text:

(#942)

هو، الحمد الله خالق النور والظلام ومكوّن الشهور و العوّام و مدبّر الليالي و الأيّام و مصوّر [الأجثات؟] في الأرحام الذي

(#898)

السعيد الشهيد ملاذ الأمرا في عصره افتخار الأنصار [...] مخدوم العشاير في زمانه الواصل إلى رحمت ربّه وغفرانه أمير خواجة علي بن الأمير [الماضي؟][الأمير؟]

End of text:

(#942)

در عقد نكاح افتد أمير موطنين ولي الأهالي [...] العظام زبدة الأعاظم نتيجة الامراء الأكارم مشير الخوافين الملحوظ بنظر عنايب السلاطين أمير شيخي بن الأمير المغفور مقدم العساكر في اوانه

(#898)

و حقى واجب و ثابت فلها أن تطالبها منه متى شأت و تأخذ منه اذا أرادت

Names mentioned in text:

(#942)

حاجي يعقوب بن يوسف، أمير شيخي بن الأمير المغفور [...]

(#898)

خرَّمشاه خاتون بنت الأمير كرد، [. . .] أمير خواجة علي بن الأمير أبي بكر

Names of witnesses:

(#898)

بدر الدين بن عمر خواجه، حاجي الخازن بن بواروق، أحمد بن ميكائيل النخجواني، بكتاش بن غازي الألباوت، غازان بن شادي الألباوت، مسيحي بن جواد علي

Judicial attestation on the top-left corner:

(#942)

ثبت [. . .] عندي و حكمت بصحته الشرعية المرعية كتبه [ال]عبد الضعيف حاجي يعقوب بن يوسف

This document switches between the use of Persian and Arabic for different parts. The scribe, Aḥmad b. Mīkāʾīl al-Nakhjawānī, mentions his name at the end of the main text of the deed. This practice can also be seen in (65) #909, (68) #910, (81) #900 and (82) #975/#893.

IV.2 Documents from Anatolia (Kayseri and Sīwās)

(71) #913/#892 Draft of an Ilkhanid decree (edited in Appendix 1a, III, see fig. 10 and 11)

Persian
undated
(#913) 52.5 x 16 cm, 6 lines, paper. This is the document's top fragment.
(#892) 59.7/65 x 16.4 cm, 6 lines, paper. This is the document's bottom fragment with lacunae in line 1.

Summary: #913 is the top fragment of an administrative decree issued by an *amīr* or *wazīr* under the authority of the Ilkhanid ruler Abū Saʿīd Bahādur Khān (r. 1315–16). It is addressed to the local rulers of Qayṣarīya (Kayseri) in Anatolia and mentions an unidentified, uncultivated garden (*bāgh*) and the salaries of peasants. It is possible that #913 is the beginning of #892, which is the bottom fragment of a similar decree issued in the context of a dispute.

Beginning of text:

(#913)

الله المستعان، أبو سعید بهادر خان یرلیغندین بتقاول و حکام قیصریه بدانند کی [مرآد آمد و] [نمود] کی از
اجر تعهد از فلاحه

(#892)

خود دعوی میکرده اند کی هیچ آفریده را [. . .] در أمری کی بر قید أمر أمر شریعت در [حکمی؟] و تعلقی
سازد و اگر در این باب سخنی داشته باشند

End of text:

(#913)

تلاش بوده است و آنجا یکباره باغ [. . .] است و مر کسی بر این [. . .]

(#892)

برین جمله روند و اعتماد نمایند

Names mentioned in text:

(#913)

أبو سعید بهادر خان

Both #913 and #892 are fragments from an unfinished draft copy of the same or two separate decrees. #892 is undated, unsealed and contains no *'uthbita'* registration notes, or Mongolian or Turkic dorsal notes in in Uyghur script. #913 does not have the clause with the name of the issuing *amīr*, which ends with *sūzī* (my command). For these elements in decrees issued in the name of Abū Saʿīd Bahādur Khān, see Urkunde VIII, plates 36–40; Urkunde IX, plates 41–47, in Herrmann, *Persische Urkunden der Mongolenzeit*, 90–96, 97–101.

(72) #918 Tax receipt issued in Sīwās

Persian
24 Ramaḍān 681/1283
23.1 x 17.8 cm, 6 & 5 lines, paper. This is the document's bottom fragment, the top is missing.

Summary: This document was issued by the royal treasury (*khizāna-yi ʿāmira*) at the instigation of a certain Kamāl al-Dīn Yūsuf bin Qutlūbak. It mentions the receipt of 15,000 units of *qaraṭāsh* (?) and *aʿẓamā* (?) from lands in the district of Sīwās (Sivas) (*az aʿmāl-i maḥrūsa-yi sīwās*, line 5) in central Anatolia. The main text ends with a formulaic clause suggesting the missing top part contained an authenticating signature (*tawqīʿ*).

Beginning of text:
رسید بخزانه عامره عمره الله تعالی [. . .] کمال الدین یوسف بن قتلوبک بن [. . .] ادام الله تمکینه از بهاء دیوان

End of text:
اعتماد بر توقیع أعلی أعلاه الله تعالی کتب الأمر النافذ الأعلی أنفذه الله و أمضاه و الحمد لله و الصلاة علی محمد و آله أجمعین

Names mentioned in text:
کمال الدین یوسف بن قتلوبک

Places mentioned in text:
سیواس

For a complete example of this type of administrative document including the *tawqīʿ* with the formula *ṣuḥiḥa* (it was verified) in large black *naskh*-script letters on the top right-hand corner of the sheet see #661 dated 1 Muḥarram 658/25 December 1259. #661 also mentions one thousand units of *qaraṭāsh* (?) and *aʿẓamā* (?) and it is not clear whether these are the names of specific taxes or refer to toponyms. For an edition and study of these two receipts see Bhalloo and Yajima, *Two Anatolian Tax Receipts from al-Ḥaram al-Sharīf in Jerusalem dated 658/1259 and 681/1283* (in preparation for submission to *Annales Islamologiques*).

(73) #919 Loan agreement issued in Sīwās

Arabic
Rabīʿ II 742/1341
22.4 x 12.4 cm, 14 lines, 6 witness clauses, paper. This is the document's bottom fragment, the top is missing. There is material damage and textual loss at the top of the document.

Summary: An officer in the region of Sīwās (Sivas) in central Anatolia takes out a debt of 4,200 dirhams from the estate of an unidentifiable individual for the duration of one year.

Beginning of text:

[. . .] بيد المدعو الحاج [. . .] من ثمن تركة [. . .]

End of text:

أربعة آلاف ومايتي درهم، أتم الأمر حامداً مصليا مسلما نصفها 2100 درهم

Names mentioned in text:

القاضي أحمد

Places mentioned in text:

ولاية سيواس

Names of witnesses:

عثمان الشافعي، عثمان [. . .]، أبو بكر بن محمد [. . .]، أحمد بن [. . .]، [. . .] بن عبد الله، عكاشة بن [بيرم؟]

(74) #888 Judicial certification *(ishhād)* on the invalidity of a collateral agreement (*rahn*) and three related deeds of acknowledgement *(iqrār)*

Arabic and Persian
42.2 x 15.5. cm, paper. The recto contains the text of an *ishhād* in Arabic (text 1) and an *iqrār* in Persian (text 2). The verso contains the text of a deed of acknowledgement in Persian (text 3) and an additional deed of acknowledgement in Persian not written in the usual *iqrār* form (text 4). The upper part of the document is trimmed, resulting in textual loss at the beginning of text 1 and 3. Possible remains of an archival hole are visible at the top of the document.

Text #888/1 (recto), judicial certification (*ishhād*)
Arabic
late Jumādā II 715/1315, 10 lines, 6 witness clauses in Arabic

Summary: Shujāʿ al-Dīn Ramaḍān, ʿIzz al-Dawla Amīr Yūsuf b. Nāṣir al-Dawla b. Naṣrullāh and Nūr al-Dawla Sūrayk (?) b. Ṣāfī al-Dawla b. Abī al-Ghanāʾim appear before a judge in the judicial court (*majlis al-ḥukm*) of Qayṣarīya (Kayseri) in central Anatolia. Shujāʿ al-Dīn presents a collateral agreement (*rahn*) dated fourteen years earlier (i.e. 701/1301) through which ʿIzz al-Dawla, acting as the legal representative of his father, borrowed the sum of 1,200 dirhams from Sābiq al-Dīn Abū Bakr b. Amīr al-Ḥasan al-Ḥaydarī (?). The security given for the loan was the shared half of the village of lower (*al-sufl*) Sībkūsh (?) in the district of Nasūdān (?) (the reading and vocalisation of both toponyms is uncertain). Since it was determined, however, that the ownership of the village was shared (*mushāʿan*) between several people, the judge annuls the collateral agreement and transfers possession of the village to its rightful owners, ʿImād al-Dawla wa-al-Dīn b. Abī al-Faraj b. Dāwūd b. Yaʿqūb and Nūr al-Dawla Sūrayk(?).

Beginning of text:
هذا ذكر ما حضر بمجلس الحكم [بدار ؟] الفتح قيصرية [. . .] المدعو بشجاع الدين رمضان [. . .] وعز الدولة أمير يوسف بن ناصر الدولة نصر الله

End of text:
وهو الصدر المعظم عماد الدولة و الدين بن أبي الفرج بن داود بن يعقوب ونور الدولة سوريك المذكور وبذلك وقع الإشهاد

Names mentioned in text:

شجاع الدين رمضان، عز الدولة أمير يوسف بن ناصر الدولة نصر الله، نور الدولة سوريك بن صفي الدولة بن أبي الغنائم، سابق الدين بن أبي بكر بن أمير الحسن الحنبلي، عماد الدولة و الدين أبي الفرج بن داود بن يعقوب.

Places mentioned in text:

قيصرية، قرية [سيبكوش؟] السفل من توابع [نسودان؟]

Names of witnesses:

أمجد بن يوسف القيصري، الحسين بن الحسن الخطيب أعانه الله بتوفيقه أحمد بن رسول القيصري، يونس بن أبي الفتح المنصوري، يوسف بن نصر الله، چوبان محمد الأمير [. . .] أحسن الله عواقبه، [. . .] بن أبى الفتح المنصوري أحسن الله [. . .]

Text #888/2 (recto), Deed of acknowledgement *(iqrār)*
Persian
11 (?) Jumādā II 715/1315, 9 lines, 4 witness clauses in Persian

Summary: An acknowledgement made by a certain Hūmān b. Kambay (?) inhabitant (*az muqīmān*) of the village of Nasūdān (?) pledging to pay administrative tax (*wajh-i māl wa mutawajjihāt; mutawajjihāt-i maqṭaʿ-i dīwānī)* of 200 units (*ʿadad*) to ʿImād al-Dawla.

Beginning of text:

اقرار كردم و معترف شدم و گواه بر خود كردم بتنى درست و عقل [. . .] بى اكراهى و اجبارى من كى هومان بن كمباى ام

End of text:

نوشته داده شد بوكالت يوسف تا وقت حاجت عرض افتد بگواهى جماعتى كى حاضر بودند

Names mentioned in text:

هومان بن كمباى، عماد الدولة و الدين، يوسف

Places mentioned in text:

ديه [نسودان؟]

Names of witnesses:

مير شاه بن علي، كاتب أحمد بن يوسف ، عوض حمد [. . .] بن [أمير؟] أحمد، أمير أحمد بن علي

The Persian text refers to the village (*dīh*) of Nasūdān (?). In Arabic text 1, however, Nasūdān (?) is the name of the district (*ṭawābʿi*), while the name of the village (*qarya)* is lower Sībkūsh (?).

Text #888/3 (verso), Deed of acknowledgement *(iqrār)*
Persian
28 Jumādā II 715/1315, 14 lines, 9 witness clauses in Persian

Summary: An acknowledgement made by someone (the name is missing as the top part of the text is trimmed) who confirms that he and his ancestors were among the old cultivators of the village of Nasūdān (?). The acknowledgement proceeds to give an account of the possession of the village mentioning that the village was empty for some time and its cultivators were scattered.

Beginning of text:

او خالی [سپاه؟] است اقرار درست بی اکراه و اجبار [کرد که؟] أبا عن جد [از] رعیت قدیم دیه مذکور است و پیش از این کی مدتی دیه [نسودان؟] خالی شده بود

End of text:

بگواهی جماعتی کی ذکر می شود

Names mentioned in text:

Places mentioned in text:

[نسودان؟]

Names of witnesses:

علي بن كاتب، حاجي علي معروف چوپان [. . .]، [. . .] علی برادر مذکور، کمبا یونس بن أمیر شیر بن گرجی، أمیر أحمد میرباشی قیصریه، نظام بن چوپان قیصری المعررف بشجاع، علي شحنه دیه مذکور، عبد الله بن عیسی، قتلغبك بن عیسی

Text #888/4 (verso), Deed of acknowledgement *(iqrār)* (?)
Persian
undated, 8 lines

Summary: A certain Qūydān (?) confirms giving ʿImād al-Dīn (probably the same as ʿImād al-Dawla, see Text #888/1 and #888/2) a written copy of the present document as proof that he agrees to pay arrears (?) of eleven years' worth of taxes, termed *ʿushr-i mustaghallāt*, and two units of two undeciphered items.

Beginning of text:

من کی قویدان ام این مکتوب را بر سبیل حجت [بخدمت؟] أمیر ستوده [طاشالقا؟] عماد الدین دادم مبنی برآنک

End of text:

حق خود را [براستی؟] [برسانم؟] عشر مستغلات و دو عدد [دخای؟] و [کندو؟] [برسانم؟]

Names mentioned in text:

[قویدان؟]، عماد الدین

Places mentioned in text:

[نسودان؟]

IV.3 Further documents

IV.3.1 Decrees and receipts

(75) #904 Decree assigning lands

Persian
27 Ṣafar 740/1339
41.1 x 11.4 cm, 9 lines, paper. This is the bottom fragment of the document; the top is missing. Lines 1–3 are illegible owing to lacunae. Line 1 has been recently repaired using sellotape. Horizontal folding lines are visible. There is a hole in the bottom left-hand corner of the document. The date begins with the Arabic preposition *fī* written in the stylized manner used in Mongol decrees with the *yā'* extended backwards round parts of the text. A small letter *qāf* (?) (see (29)/#901) and the numeral 2 are visible next to the letter *fā'* of *fī*. This is possibly an archival note.

Summary: An administrative decree mentioning the assignment of land and its revenues to a certain Muqīm b. Shāh based on a previous order issued by someone of higher rank.

Beginning of text:
[. . .] از اعمال آنجا بدو تعلق دارد [. . .] دستخط [. . .] در این باب دستخط أشرف ارزانی فرموده بدان سبب
این حکم فرموده این مکتوب در قلم آمد تا بر موجب دستخط أشرف

End of text:

مقیم بن شاه مال و مواجب مالکی انرا متصرف گردد درین باب [تقضی؟] نماید

Names mentioned in text:

مقیم بن شاه

(76) #906 Decree on collection of revenues (edited in Appendix 1a, IV, see fig. 12)

Persian
Ṣafar 740/1339
36.4 x 11.7 cm, 10 lines, paper. This is the document's bottom fragment, the top is missing. A square black seal is visible on the last line of text containing the date.

Summary: The decree is issued by a certain Shaykh ʿAlī who assigns someone with the collection of revenues from the peasants in a place, as this person had done in the past. The decree was issued in order that no doubt remains on this point.

Beginning of text:
بدو افتد کی رعایا را مجتمع گرداند و محصولات باقی را بمواجبی که پیش از این در سابق الأیام معهود متصرف شود [درین. . .]

End of text:
مطالبتی نماید و مدخل ستد و آنچ قاضی سامی شده باشد چون [بدین جانب رسیده است و معدی کرد؟] باز گرداند [برین جمله] اعتماد نماید برساله شیخ علي

Names mentioned in text:
شیخ علي

In Ilkhanid Mongol Iran, one could judge the level of a document's importance based on the colour and size of the seal. This decree is sealed using the square black seal (*qārā ṭamghā*) used by lower nobility officials, *amīr*s. On this seal see Yasuhiro Yokkaichi, "On the Qara Tamgha (Black Seal) of the Ilkhanate: Its Meaning, Image, and Semiosis" (unpublished paper in Japanese). For other examples, see Hermann, *Persische Urkunden*, Urkunden IX, XIV, XVI and XVII.

The seal has the following inscription in *naskh*:
توکلت علی الله [. . .] سوزی [باد؟]

(77) #969 Decree on payment of revenues and receipt

Persian
9 Rabīʿ I 748/1347
29 x 14.3 cm, 9 lines, paper. This is the document's top fragment, the bottom is missing. There are lacunae in places including several large holes at regular intervals on the paper, which is also damp stained.

Summary: The recto contains an administrative decree which opens with the clause *az ḥukm-i zīr (?) shawad*, which is reminiscent of similar administrative decrees from Ardabīl (see Herrmann, *Persische Urkunden der Mongolenzeit*, Urkunde XI, plate 51). It orders a certain Sarfarāz (also mentioned in (79)/#980) to pay annual revenues in kind to someone. The payment includes twenty female horses (*mādiyān*) and fourteen sheep (*gūsfand*). The verso consists of an administrative receipt which mentions wheat and barley.

Beginning of text (recto):

[هو الله الحي؟] از حکم زیر شود أمراء [...] بدانند کی سرفراز [با این کی؟] هر سال [...] بیست سر
مادیان چهارده سر گوسفند را و حق موجب را بر موجب [...] کی در دست دارند تمامت را جمع کرده
بخدمت [...] معظم

End of text (recto):

مطالع کندگان برین جمله باید اعتماد نمایند

Beginning of text (verso):

آنچه کی در عهده گرفته است اسمش [اینجا؟] مالکانه [مینمایم] و مواجبی بمقدار سیصد و پنجاه [...] گرفتیم
و غیره

End of text (verso):

جو شیس [من؟] رسید خاتون را

(78) #959 Unidentified decree

Persian
3 Ramaḍān 746/1346
19 x 16.5 cm, 4 lines, paper. This is the document's middle part and the document's top and bottom parts are missing.

Summary: Fragment of an administrative decree.

Beginning of text:

تا بغور رسیده حکمی [. . .] برین ذکر نمود کی بر رعیت قدیم موضوع مذکور

(79) #980 Unidentified decree

Persian
10 Dhū al-Qaʿda 745/1345
40.5 x 15.7 cm, 6 lines, paper. This is the document's bottom fragment, the top part of the document is missing. There are tears along horizontal folding lines with lacunae in lines 1 and 3.

Registration note:

أثبت و له الحمد

Summary: An administrative decree mentioning a certain Sarfarāz (line 3) (also mentioned in (77)/#969) as owner of the village of Aq Kūy and Shaykh Ḥasan (line 4). There is an inter-linear *uthbita* registration note between lines 3 and 4.

Beginning of text:

بتقاول و حكام و نواب و متصرفان [طرر؟] [آقاج؟] بدانند كى بر قرار

End of text:

درين باب تقصير ننمايد برين جمله روند اعتماد نمايند

Names mentioned in text:

شيخ حسن

(80) #955 Receipt for a share of grain

Persian
undated
17.5 x 11.2 cm, 12 lines, paper. The document is in good material condition and horizontal fold lines are visible.

Summary: The recto records the receipt of a share (*ḥiṣṣa*) assigned to *amīr* Aḥmad of quantities of wheat (*gandum*), barley (*jaw*) and *gulūl*. A line in the shape of a speech bubble is drawn around parts of the text. The verso has the note: *ḥiṣṣa*.

Beginning of text (recto):

حصه أمير أحمد از گندم پانزده من [. . .] از جو نوذده من [. . .] گلول سه من [. . .]

End of text (recto):

أمير أحمد داده شد [. . .] گندم چهل من جو بيست من رسيد

Names mentioned in text (recto):

أمير أحمد

(verso):

حصه [. . .]

For a similar 'speech bubble' type receipt see the verso of #858. The meaning of *gulūl* or *kulūl* also mentioned in (89)/#963 is uncertain. It could refer to a type of black grain known as *qarā-gulūla*.

IV.3.2 Sale and lease

(81) #900 Sale contract for six *dāng* of a village

Persian
Shawwāl 715/1316
62.4/65.3 x 15.2 cm, 16 lines, 8 witness clauses in Persian, paper. This is the document's bottom fragment made up of two sheets of paper glued together. The top part of the document is missing. There are lacunae in the first line, a large tear in the third line and damp stains on the left-hand margin.

Summary: The document records the sale probably via a deed of acknowledgement (*iqrār*) of six *dāng* of a village (*dāng* = one sixth part of any estate) for 2,000 gold dinars at the value currently in use in the town of Tabrīz (line 4) by a group of four sellers to a buyer.

Beginning of text:
شیش دانگ از دیه مذکور را کی نصفه باشد سه دانگ بمبلغ دو هزار دینار ز[ر] رائج الوقت في المدينة تبريز
حماه الله من الآفات و العقوبات کی نصف المبلغ باشد

End of text:
و از حقوق و املاک [مشتری مذکور و مذکوران؟] در ذمت گرفتند کی جواب مدعیان کنند عند المخاصامة

Names mentioned in text:

محمود بن محمد شاه السمرقندی

Places mentioned in text:

تبریز

Names of witnesses:
[...]، [سوبک؟] شاه بن [...]، [با تمشر؟] بن [بايدار؟]، [عبدلشاه؟] بن [...] ، نور شاه بن [قارباعدي؟]
[...] [کتبه؟] [...] بن الثابت، [بکلیک؟] بن محم الثابت، [متکلي؟] بن عبد الله الثابت

The scribe of the document is Maḥmūd b. Muḥammad Shāh al-Samarqandī. The purchase amount is prominent as the words are spaced out and a larger script size is used compared with the rest of the text. There is an additional note *ḥarrahahu muḥarrir dar (?) aṣl* (written by the scribe in the original), which appears on the right-hand margin where the two sheets of papers are glued together. Four witness clauses which use a similar construction, *īn iqrār iqrār-i man ast* (this is my acknowledgement), probably belong to the four sellers.

(82) #975/#893 Sale contract of two *dāng* of the village of Azād (edited in Appendix 1a, V, see fig. 13 and 14.)

Persian
10 Dhū al-Qaʿda 723/1323
(#975) 26/28.2 x 13.1 cm, 6 lines, paper. This is the document's top fragment with lacunae in lines 3 and 6 and in the judicial attestation of the judge. Possible remains of an archival hole are visible at the top centre of the sheet.
(#893) 72 x 13.3 cm, 20 lines, 1 witness clause in Arabic, 9 witness clauses in Persian, paper. This is the document's bottom fragment consisting of two sheets of paper glued together. Possible remains of an archival hole are visible below the witness clauses in the bottom quarter of the second sheet of paper.

Summary: In this sale contract, Shaykh Zankī (Zangī) and Shaykh Qārān sell 2 *dāng* (*dāng* = one sixth part of any estate) of the village of lower (*zīrīn*) Azād, which they inherited from their deceased father, for the sum of 140 dinars to Khwāja Mīr Jumla Tīmūr Būghā (mentioned in line 10 and in the five-line additional note in #893). The scribe of the deed, who also acts as one of the witnesses, is Muḥammad b. Ḥusayn al-ʿAlawī (#893). The first line of the main text is preceded by a six-line judicial attestation in Arabic by the judge ʿAlī b. Muḥammad al-Bukhārī (#975).

Beginning of text:

(#975)
غرض تحریر این کلمات و تقریر این عقد شرعی آن است که فروختند شیخ زنکی و شیخ قاران [. . .]

(#893)
رائج شهر [روکسر؟]زر سفید معاملات وقت مضروب و مسکوک که نیمه این مبلغ باشد تاکید را هفتاد دینار

End of text:

(#975)
المرحوم نکودنی دو دانگ از دیه ازاد زرین که حق ایشان بود موروثی [. . .] قره با چهار حد [. . .] دینار
[. . .] رائج

(#893)
و این مکتوب در قلم امد تا وقت حاجت معرض افتد

Names mentioned in text:

(#975)

علي بن محمد البخاري، المرحوم نكودنى

(#893)

شيخ زنكى، شيخ قاران، محمد بن حسين العلوى، خواجه مير جمله تمربغا

Places mentioned in text:

(#893)

ازاد، [روكسر؟]، [قوشون؟]، [كوزه بک؟]، [يركبرو؟]، [زبارت ارتوغ؟]

Names of witnesses:

(#893)

اسلان بن [گران؟] أمير، اسماعيل ابن ملك شاه، اخى صلاح الدين صالح ابن مرحوم عز الدين يوسف، خواجه
،موسى بن ابراهيم، ابراهيم ولى بن يوسف، محمود مؤذن، شبيخ بابا بن [مه كان؟]، [پيره؟] غازى ابن سليمان
قتلغبغا ابن عمر، شادى بن [زكه نبى؟]

Judicial attestation by the judge at the top-left corner:

(#975)

هو، ثبت عندي مضمون هذه الحجة الشرعية المخلّد في هذه المعاملة المرعية كتبه علي بن محمد البخاري

Azād is possibly the present-day village of Azād in West Azerbaijan province, Iran. The purchase sum is expressed in lines 2–3 as half the amount (#893). The document contains three additional notes. The first note directly below the main text confirms that Shaykh Zankī, acting as the authorized proxy (*wakīl*) of Shaykh Qārān, sold one *dāng* of the village belonging to the latter to the buyer. This is witnessed by Aslān b. Girān (?) Amīr and Ismāʿīl b. Malik Shāh (#893). The second note, below the witness clauses, confirms that 140 dinars, the purchase sum, was received in full by the sellers Shaykh Zankī and Shaykh Qārān from the buyer Khwāja Mīr Jumla Tīmūr Būghā (#893). It is not clear whether this is the same Tīmūr Būghā mentioned in (84)/#886. The final note in Arabic, *al-waṣl*, is visible at a right angle to the main text on the right-hand margin where the two sheets of paper are glued together (#893). Longer *al-waṣl* marginal notes such as *al-waṣl ṣaḥīh* followed by the name of the person who wrote the note appear in the documents from Ardabīl see Gronke, *Arabische und persische Privaturkunden*, 181, 352 and (65a)/#909.

(83) #915 Sale contract of half a *dāng* of a village

Persian
undated
29.5 x 16. 5 cm, 8 lines (recto) & 7 lines (verso), paper. This is the document's middle fragment; the top and bottom parts are missing.

Summary: The recto describes the sale of half a *dāng* of the village of Khāghuraysh-i Kūchal (?) in the district of Kasrtāsh (?) to Amīr Barāt (?) b. al-Amīr al-Maghfūr Tīmūr Būghā b. Jingāj (?). The land was sold by: the sons of Sayf al-Dīn Amīr b. al-Marḥūm Shaykh Arslān b. Jamāl Qutlughbak, his two nephews (*barādar-zāda*) Kamāl b. Tūbak and ʿImād al-Dīn ʿĀrif b. al-Marḥūm Qutlughā (?) [. . .] and their paternal uncle (*ʿamm-i īshān*) Muʾayyad b. Amīr Arslān Jamāl b. Qutlughbak. The verso is possibly part of an administrative decree as it contains a long list of honorifics and titles ([. . .] *pādishāh-i banī ādamī wa sulṭān-i salāṭīn-i ʿarab wa ʿajam* [. . .]) referring to a ruler.

Beginning of text (recto):
این ذکریست مشتمل و ناطق در بیان آنک بفروخت ملکزادگان خلف الأمراء سیف الدین أمیر ابن المرحوم شیخ ارسلان بن جمال بن قتلغبک طاب ثراه

End of text (recto):
حد چهارم [. . .] بدین چهار حد و حدود با توابع

Beginning of text (verso):
[. . .] آفریدگار شاه اهل روزگار [. . .] خلد عظمته در[. . .] احکام مطاعین [. . .] سالها بی نهایت [. . .] بی غایت مستند او باد [. . .] در جمیع احوال ناصر و جامی و معالی فتح و ظفر

End of text (verso):
در جمیع مرادات و مطالب مجد و [. . .] بارگاه علیا [. . .] مطلق پادشاه [. . .]

Names mentioned in text:
(recto)
سیف الدین أمیر ابن المرحوم شیخ ارسلان بن جمال بن قتلغبک ، کمال الدین ابن توبک، عماد الدین عارف ابن المرحوم قتلغا [. . .]، مؤید ابن أمیر ارسلان جمال بن قتلغبک، أمیر [برات؟] بن الأمیر المغفور تمور بغا

Places mentioned in text:
(recto)
[خاغریش کوچل؟]، [کسرطاش؟]

The Amīr Barāt referred to in this document is possibly the man with the same name mentioned in (65/b)/#909. It is also unclear whether his father, Tīmūr Būghā b. Jingāj, is the same Khwāja Mīr Jumla Timur Bughā mentioned in (82)/#975 and #893, or the Timūr Bughā appearing in (84)/#886. The spelling of the names in each case is slightly different.

(84) #886 Sale contract (lands)

Arabic
23 Rajab 745/1344
56.4/48.5 x 23.5 cm, 22 lines, paper. The right and upper margins of the document are damaged, the first half of lines 7 to 9 is lost. There is one archival hole in the upper quarter of the document.

Summary: Sayf al-Dīn Khiḍr, Muḥammad b. Ibrāhīm and Muḥammad's brother acknowledge that they sell lands *('aqārāt)* to Tīmūr Būghā. It is not clear whether this is the same Tīmūr Būghā mentioned in (82)/#975 and #893 and (83)/#915. Sayf al-Dīn also acts as the legal representative of his mother and siblings. No further details of the lands are identifiable on account of the document's material damage. The price is paid with a black horse (valued at 1,000 dinars) and woollen cloth (valued at 300 dinars).

Beginning of text:
[. . .] الحجة الشرعية [. . .] عما أقرَّ سيف الدين خضر بن الحاج محمد بن أحمد

End of text:
أنهم قبضوا منه جميع الفرس الأسود المقوَّم بألف درهم وثوب لي جيد من الصوف [. . .] المقوّم بثلثماية درهم عوضا عن جميع الموهوب المحدد والمذكور فيه وأشهد على ذلك الجماعة الحاضرين المذكورين آخره

Names mentioned in text:
سيف الدين خضر بن محمد بن أحمد، خرّم خاتون بنت الحاج [. . .]، بكتاش بن محمد بن أحمد، مصطفى بن محمد بن أحمد، محمد بن إبراهيم بن محمد، موسى السقا، إبراهيم [الزوجني؟]، نصرت زوجة عثمان، تاج النساء بنت الخطيب، تيمور بوغا، هبة الله بن محمود بن محمد الخوارزمي

Names of witnesses:
شمس الدين محمد بن حسن [. . .]، كريم الدين حاجي بك بن كمال [. . .]، جمال الدين محمد بن أحمد بن عبد القادر، ومحرره علاء الدين [الطبري؟]، محمد بن إبراهيم [البرنيسي؟]، مصطفى بن إسحق [البرنيسي؟]، إلياس بن عمر، يحيى بن أشرف، خواجة عمر البزاز، أبو بكر بن معد، حاجي عبد الله، ولد سعد الدين جلبي، إسحاق بن يوسف، حسن بن يوسف ابن حسام الدين [الحافظ جده؟]، [. . .]

Judicial attestation by the judge on the top-left corner:
[. . .] بما نسب إليهما أصالة ووكالة واخذهما بذلك كتبه هبة الله بن محمود بن محمد الخوارزمي الحاكم

(85) #958 Sale contract (lands)

Persian
undated
12.2/13.5 x 16.8 cm, 9 lines, paper. This is the document's middle fragment, the top and bottom parts are missing. There are lacunae in lines 1 and 9.

Summary: The document records a sale contract of lands and the receipt of the purchase sum and transfer of the object of sale.

Beginning of text:

[. . .] رسید و دست خریده از بهای این مبیع بری و آزاد گشت و مبیع مذکور را بخریده مذکور تسلیم کرد و
تسلیم [. . .] بلا مانع و مزاهم و این عقد بیع بعد از دقت کی خریده مذکور و وکلا و معتمدان او

End of text:

از زمینها آبادان و خراب و کوه و صحراء و بیشه و اساب خانها و منازل و درختان میوه دار و غیر [. . .]

The document has a *ṣaḥḥa al-waṣl* note on the bottom right-hand margin.

(86) #960 Settlement contract (including horses and wool)

Persian
undated
12.6 x 15.7 cm, 7 lines, paper. This is the document's middle fragment, the top and bottom parts are missing. There are lacunae in lines 1 and 7.

Summary: This is a document on the purchase of several items, including a brown horse (*madiyan-i kahar*), wool (*ṣūf*) and a black horse (*asb-i siyāh*), by a certain Amīr Altunā (?) Bek via a settlement (*muṣālaḥa kard*) for 60 dinars.

Beginning of text:

أمير التنا بک دام اقباله مصالحه کرده یک سر مادیان کهر و مبلغ شصت

End of text:

و اگر دعوی شرعی [. . .] بدارد و ذمت أو را بجای داده است و بعد از این [. . .]

Names mentioned in text:

أمير التنا بک

(87) #905 Lease contract (cultivation of lands)

Persian
Jumādā II 746/1345
25.9 x 15.9 cm, 9 lines, 10 witness clauses in Persian (recto) & 11 witness clauses in Persian, 2 witness clauses in Arabic (verso), paper. This is the document's bottom fragment, the top is trimmed.

Summary: The recto records a lease contract for the cultivation of a parcel of land; it mentions the lessee (line 6) and the annual payment of half a Dinar (line 1). One of the witnesses, Sujunk (?) b. Kurd Amīr, mentions he is the scribe of the contract *(shāhiduhu kātibuhu)*. The verso contains additional witness clauses.

Beginning of text:
کی هر سال نیم دینار [اداء؟] کرده شود و اجارت [محتاج؟] [شرعي؟] وشرائط ارکان مشتمل بر ایجاب و
قبول و [عزر؟] و غلت و مواجب مذکور امانت و دیانت بجای آورد

End of text:
و این ذکر برین معنی در قلم آمد بحضور جماعتی اسامی و القابی کی در آخر این حجت ثبت کرده شد

Names of witnesses (recto):
[سوجنک؟] بن کرد أمیر، أحمد بن کرد أمیر، [دیلنجی؟] بن محمد، شادی بن [جادل؟]، مولا تمور بن
[بویکسای؟] حاجي بن [سووبدک؟]، تغلق بن چریکتیمور، قتلغ [. . .] بن أمین الدین، خواجه بن اسماعیل،
حیدر بن [. . .] شاه

Names of witnesses (verso):
گرجی بک بن کرد أمیر، [. . .] خواجه بن اغل، [. . .] شاه بن قتلغ خواجه، ولي الدین بن أمیر بک، تاتر بک
بن اسماعیل، [. . .] بن [. . .]، قتلغبک بن [اکو؟]، ملکشاه بن [سوبدک؟]، خضر بن [البوسجی؟]،
[أورد؟] شاه بن [فخامي؟]، [. . .] خواجه بن اسماعیل، توبکشاه بن علي، [اروچ؟] بن چریکتمور.

(88) #938 Payment receipt (*iqrār*)

Persian
700 (?)/1300–1301
14.5/16.8 x 12.3 cm, 6 lines, 9 witness clauses in Persian, paper. This is the document's bottom fragment, the top is missing.

Summary: An unidentified individual confirms paying all beneficiaries their salaries or rights (?) relating to several villages including Aq Kūy, ʿUmar Kūy and ʿUthmān Kūy. There were no further claims concerning the matter.

Beginning of text:
[. . .] ام ولد شیخ این حجت دادم [. . .] و[. . .] و مکتوب خاتون

End of text:
هر کی مأجور [. . .] [حق؟] بخشیدم و قطع کردم عوض من ستدم دیگر هر جواب قطع کردم بگواهی جماعتی که حاضر بودند

Places mentioned in the text:
اق کوی، عمر کوی، عثمان کوی

Names of witnesses:
علي باشاه ابن نساب، چنکیز مؤید، محمد بن [. . .]، [جعفر؟] حسن بن [. . .]، حیدر بن حاجي [التا؟]، محمد بکر بن النجک، [جعفر؟] بن اروج بک، حمد بن [شباب؟]، حاجي بک بن موسی [. . .]

IV.3.3 Inventories

(89) #963 Inventory of expenditure

Persian
undated
21.8 x 12 cm, 15 lines (recto) & 12 lines (verso), paper. This is the document's top fragment, the bottom is missing. There are lacunae in the bottom half of the document.

Summary: Records the expenditure of the household of the great lady (*khātūn-i muʿaẓẓama*). The entries of the list are divided into four columns which continue onto the verso. The entries mention quantities of grain, barley (*jaw*), wheat (*gandum*) and *gulūl* (see (80)/#955) under the names of individual recipients.

Beginning of text (recto):

[. . .] خرج خانه خاتون معظمه

End of text (recto):

رسید [. . .]

Beginning of text (verso):

گندم دوازده من

End of text (verso):

رسید [. . .]

(90) #977 Estate inventory

Persian
undated
27.6/33 x 12.3 cm, 11 lines, 5 witness clauses in Persian, paper. This is the document's bottom fragment, the top is missing. Material damage on the top left-hand corner has caused lacunae in lines 1 to 3 and lines 5 to 6.

Summary: The document appears to be an estate inventory (?) of a deceased individual authenticated by several witnesses, one of whom is the scribe. The inventory lists numerous items such as slaves (*yak sar ghulām*), carpets (*qālī*) and wool (*ṣūf*).

Beginning of text:

مفخر المدعیان مرحوم مغفور [. . .] مانده از [. . .] نزد گواهان

End of text:

همه خاتون را رسید بگواهی جماعتی که حاضر بودنده

Names of witnesses:

خواجه حسن بن حاجب، خلیل بن بو بکر، [. . .] شاه محمد، دانشمند بن الیاس، [. . .] [أحمد؟] [حسین؟]
بن [. . .]

IV.3.4 Other legal documents

(91) #894 Deed of acknowledgement (*iqrār*)

Persian
721/1321–22
25.5/31 x 20.3 cm, 7 lines, 5 witness clauses in Persian, 3 witness clauses in Arabic, paper. This is the document's bottom fragment, the top is missing. There are lacunae in several places and damp stains on the right-hand margin.

Summary: Based on one of the witness clauses it is possible to work out that the document records the acknowledgement of a certain Būlād b. Muḥammad Ḥusayn in a dispute. The latter also agreed to act as a respondent in case of any counter claim.

Beginning of text:

[. . .] حکمی مالکانه کی خواهد از داشتن و فروختن

End of text:

باشد و جماعتی حاضران را بر اقرار خود گواه گرفتند کی بوقت حاجت گواهی دهند

Names of witnesses:

[. . .] بن [. . .]، [. . .] محمد، [. . .] بن حسین، [بولاد؟] بن محمد حسین، [. . .] بن [. . .]، [. . .] محمد،
[. . .]، ابراهیم بن یوسف [. . .]، [أحمد؟] بن [. . .]، عبد الله بن سلیمان

(92) #912 Witness clauses on the issuance of a judicial decision

Persian/Arabic
undated
47 x 21.5 cm, 10 witness clauses in Persian, 4 witness clauses in Arabic, paper. This is the document's bottom fragment with only the section containing the witness clauses.

Summary: The witness clauses attest to the issuance of a judicial decision (*ḥukm*) by a judge named Shāfī b. Muḥammad Shāh al-Nakhjawānī. Both the Arabic and Persian witness clauses use the term *sijill* to refer to the document. The *nisba* '*Nakhjawānī*' of the judge and '*Baylaqānī*' of several witnesses suggests the document was produced in the region of Nakhchivan or Beylagan in southern Azerbaijan. One of the witnesses is the muezzin of the congregational mosque of Beylagan.

Names mentioned in text:
مولانا شافعي بن محمد شاه النخجواني

Names of witnesses:
[. . .]، محمود بن حسن بن بوبكر بيلقاني، محمد بن خطّاب، محمد بن حمزه صفّار بيلقاني، حسين بن حسن المؤذن بجامع بيلقان، حاجي بن خواجه محمود [كدوا؟]، محمد بن علي [بري؟]، [مرهم؟] حاجي إلياس، حسين بن نوشيران، محمد جمال بن محمود أبوالقاسم، نجم الدين أبو بكر نواده كمال بيلقاني، علي شاه بن أبو بكر محمود بن محمود بن أحمد بن محمود [الخالداري؟]، [سرخام؟] بن [. . .] [الديواني؟]

On the use of the term *sijill* for court records containing the decision of the *qāḍī* (see Bhalloo, *Pre-Mongol New Persian Legal Document*).

(93) #895 Unidentified legal document (probably *iqrār)*

Persian
End of Jumādā II 716/1316
19.5 x 15.7 cm, 3 lines, 6 Persian witness clauses, 1 Turkic witness clause, paper. This is the document's bottom fragment, the top is missing.

Summary: The surviving text, probably of a deed of acknowledgement (*iqrār)*, suggests a particular claim (*daʿwā*) made by someone was void (*bāṭil bāshad*) based on the recorded witness testimony.

Beginning of text:

هر دعوی کی [ازق؟] بکند باطل باشد از [. . .] مذکور

End of text:

بگواهی جماعتی کی ذکر می شود

Names of witnesses:

یوسف بن محمد، [. . .] عبده [. . .]، [اغلجه؟] بن [قرعاجی؟]، درویش بن طغای، علي بن مصطفی، خواجه باروجی

Turkic witness clause:
buu bitig / män ačbuq(a)? bitidim = I, Ačbuqa?, wrote this document.

One of the witnesses, Yūsuf b. Muḥammad, uses a *ṭughrā'* type signature.

(94) #917 Unidentified legal document (subsequently reused, see catalogue entry (97))

Text #917/1 (recto)
probably Persian
undated
20.2 x 16.9 cm, 10 lines, paper. The top part of the document was trimmed with traces of a line of writing still visible. There is possibly one archival hole in the lower half.

Summary: The text of the actual document is lost and all that remains are the signatures of the witness so that this document's content and language is unknown. However, the style of the witness clauses of this document are very close to those in other Persianate documents. The document was subsequently reused to write God's names and a *du'ā* prayer (see catalogue entry (99)).

Names of witnesses:
المولا باعلي فقيه ابن حاجي فقيه بن حسين فقيه، محمد بن حاجي محمود بن إبراهيم، شيخ حسن بن محمد بن حاجي فقيه، أبو المرجا بن علي بن أبو المرجا، الشيخ [. . .]، عين الدين [. . .] بن حسين بن أحمد، أبو رشاه بن أحمد، موسى بن [. . .]، [. . .]، صدر الدين بن محمود بن [. . .]، الحافظ أبو بكر الخليلي

(95) #902 Unidentified Armenian legal document

Armenian
undated
37.5 x 12.7 cm, 4 witness clauses in Armenian & 2 witness clauses in Persian (verso), paper

Summary: The recto has a long text in Armenian, probably written by a certain Jalal, probably about borrowing or lending money. The lower part of the verso contains signatures of four witnesses in Armenian: one Aristakes, one Georg son of Bakht, one Karmraykel (i.e. in Georgian Gamrekeli?) and one Snoy(?).

(96) #885/#920 Georgian/Armenian/Persian document

Georgian/Armenian/Persian
June 1294
36.8/35.3 x 24.6 cm (#885), 37.2/44 x 25 cm (#920), paper

Summary: Two fragments (#885 and #920) of the same document containing Georgian, Armenian, and Persian text. Both fragments are missing the upper and lower ends. Comparing the lines of the torn parts of the sheet shows that one fragment is a continuation of the other. The first five lines of the document (#885), although the text is not complete, contain important information about the authors of the document and the place and date of its creation. This is a kind of protocol at the end of the legal document. According to the Georgian text, the name of the copyist is Telobeg, son of Zomo (*zomos ʒisa qelita telobegisita*). He is the scribe of Shahansha (*šahanšas mcịgnobrisa*). This suggests a north-western Armenian provenance of the document. The witness signatures that can be identified on the document are those of: Davit VIII (r. 1273-1311), King of Georgia, *xošaki mqargrʒeli* (Khoshaki Mkhargrdzeli), wife of the Ilkhanid finance minister Ṣāḥib Dīwān Shams al-Dīn Juwaynī (d. 1284), Zakariyā (son of *xošaki* and Shams al-Din Juwaynī) who signs in Persian in Arabic script (*guwāhī-yi zakariyā b. ṣāḥib dīwān*) and at least three other individuals, Natel, Kravai (a woman) and Grigol. On Zakariyā son of Ṣāḥib Dīwān Shams al-Dīn Juwaynī, see also Ḥaram docs. #876, #911 and the introduction.

IV.3.5 Prayer

(97) #917 God's names and *duʿā* prayer (reuse stage, see catalogue entry (94))
Text #917/2 (verso)

Arabic
undated
20.2 x 16.9 cm, 9 lines, paper

Summary: List of thirty-one of God's beautiful names and a *duʿā* prayer.

Beginning of text:

الآخر، الظاهر، الباطن، الوالي، المتعالي، البر، التواب

End of text:

نويت أصلي فرض الصلوة هذا الصبح اثني ركعاة مستقبل القبلة لله تعالى الله أكبر

The statement 'Zakī Sharaf al-Dīn wrote [this]' is at the bottom of the page turned by 180 degrees. This note is most likely linked to the document on the sheet's recto (see catalogue entry (94)), not to its reuse stage.

Appendix 1a: Edition of five Persian documents (Zahir Bhalloo)

I Edition of (67), Jerusalem, al-Ḥaram al-sharīf, Islamic Museum, #911

Transfer of *iqṭāʿ*, 711/1312

Text (recto)

1- اين خط من كى زكريا بن محمد جوينى [ام]
2- دادم بخدمت [بارم؟][129] أمير معظم آدوجي آقا
3- كى اقطاع ديه اريغي كى از حكم [يرليغ جهانگشاى] بمن تعلق
4- دارد بغير تعين وجوه قيچاچان[130] آنچ نصيب منست
5- آن را [ببارم؟] أمير معظم آدوجى آقا* دادم كى
6- | * و فرزندان او بطن بعد بطن و نسلن بعد نسلن[131] |
7- سال بسال اين وجوه را خدمت او صرف مى
8- كند و من كه كاتب ام متوجه اقطاع را
9- از خاصه خود سال بسال ميدهم هيچ افريده را
10- گرفتن اقطاعى كى بمن تعلق دارد [نباشد] بدين كارى
11- [و] براتى و حوالتي نگشت و نباشد[132] و اين ذكر بر سبيل اظهار
12- داده شود كتبه في الواسط شهر الله اعظم رمضان المعظم
13- سنة احدى عشر و سبعمايه

Witness clauses (recto)

1- [Autograph witness clause of Zakariyā?[133]]
2- [Georgian witness clause] მართალია (*martalia*), 'it is true'.
3- [اين؟] حكم [محتواى؟] [شهادت؟] زكريا است بيده مرا گواه گرفت [. . .] جمال [؟] الملک

129 The meaning of this honorific, which also appears in line 5 before the name of Ādūjī, is unclear.

130 This word can either be read as *qaychākhān*, referring to the name of an individual, or referring to a group *qaychāchān*. In the latter case, it is possibly a misspelling of *qachāchiyān* (the tailors). If so, it is not clear why tailors are mentioned here, they may be workers in the court workshops.

131 Ar. نسلًا بعد نسلٍ. The reading after *ādūjī āqā* (line 5) is inter-linear (line 6).

132 *nakunand wa nabāshand* is another possible reading.

133 This could be read as the Arabic clause *bi-khaṭṭihi* (in his own hand), suggesting the document was written by Zakariyā himself and not a scribe. See also the the third witness clause which confirms the document is in the handwiriting of Zakariyā.

https://doi.org/10.1515/9783111330242-006

(verso)

4 [Turkic witness clause] *b(u)bitig MMN? čänggä? tanuq biz* = We, MMN? and Čänggä?, are witness(es) (to) this document.
5 [Mongolian witness clause] *quča burur? gere buị* = Quča-Burur (?) is witness.
6 بر اقرار صاحب اعظم شمس الدين زكريا گواهى دهم [العبد؟] سعد الدين بن محمد [. . .]
7 بشهادة [. . .] [. . .]
8 بگواهى توبى بن حسن

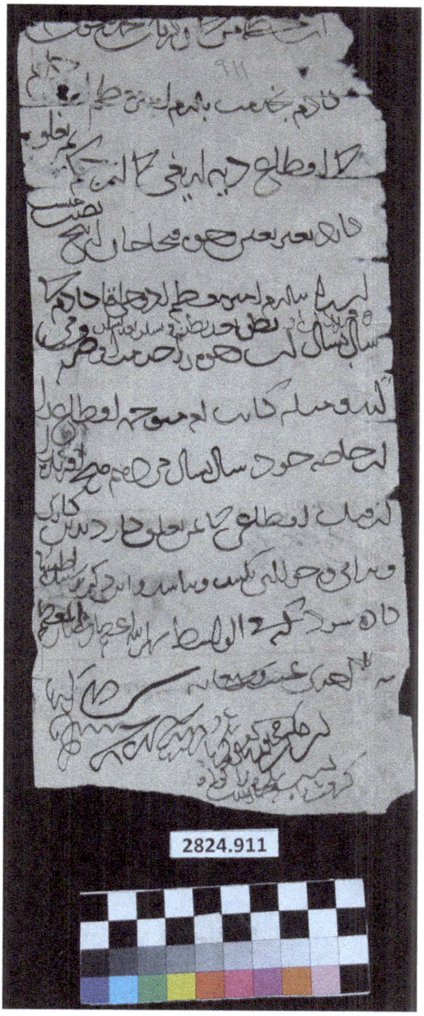

Fig. 6: Ia (67)/#911v Transfer of *iqṭāʿ*, 711/1312, © Mohammad H. Ghosheh.

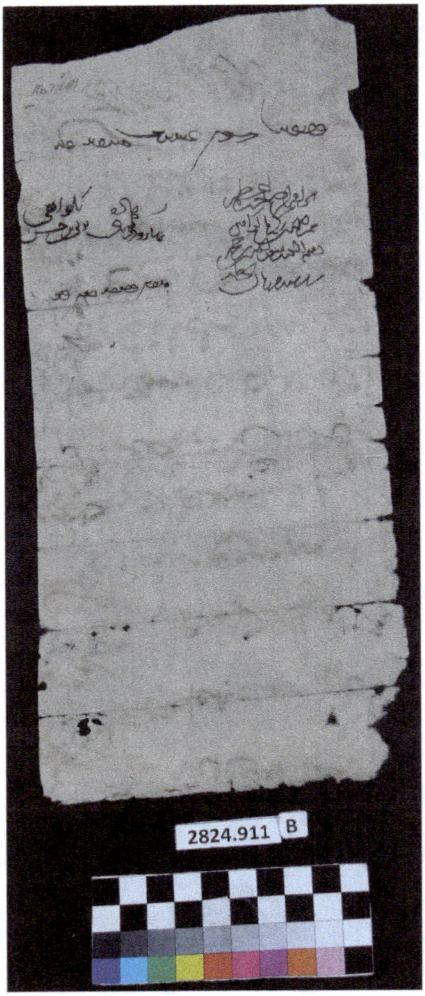

Fig. 7: Ib (67)/#911r Witness clauses, © Mohammad H. Ghosheh.

II Edition of (70), Jerusalem, al-Ḥaram al-sharīf, Islamic Museum, #898 and #942

Marriage contract for a deferred dowry, 769/1367

Text (recto)

Judicial attestation by the judge

#942

1- ثبت عندي [بيدي؟] وحكمت

2- بصحته الشرعية المرعية

3- كتبه [ال]عبد الضعيف حاجي يعقوب

4- بن يوسف

Main text

1- هو

2- الحمد الله خالق النور والظلام ومكوّن الشهور و العوّام و مدبّر الليالي و الأيام و مصور [الأجثات][134] في الأرحام الذي

3- جعل النكاح مميزا بين الحلال الحرام ذالك الله الملك العلام و الصلوة و السلام على سيدنا محمد

4- خير الأنام و على آله و أصحابه الكرام و بعد سبب [تحرير اين كلمات؟] [مستطير؟] انست كى

5- در عقد نكاح افتد أمير موطنين ولي الأهالي [. . .] العظام زبدة الأعاظم

6- نتيجة الامراء الأكارم مشير الخوافين الملحوظ بنظر عنايب السلاطين أمير شيخي بن الأمير المغفور

7- [. . .] مقدم العساكر في اوانه

#898

1- السعيد الشهيد ملاذ الأمرا فى عصره افتخار الأنصار [. . .]

2- مخدوم العشاير في زمانه الواصل إلى رحمت ربه وغفرانه أمير خواجة علي بن الأمير [الماضي؟] [الأمير؟]

3- أبو بكر ادام الله دولته خاتون معظمه مكرمه سيدة المخدرات و الخواتين تاج النساء في العالمين

4- عصمت الدنيا و الدين صفوة الاسلام و المسلمين خرمشاه خاتون بنت الأمير الكبير السعيد الشهيد ملجاء الضعفاء

5- ناظم مصالح الكافة في زمانه باسط أقسام الرأفة في أوانه الأمير كرد بن الأمير الماضي أمير ادوجى

6- دامت عصمتها و زيدت رفعتها را بايجاب و قبول شرعي در حضور شهود و عدول مشتمل بر ساير شرايط

7- و اركان شرعى بصداق و مهر مؤجل مبلغ شانزده هزار دينار

8- زر رايج فضّى عبارت هر يك دينار از نيم مثقال نقره صاغ مضروب و مسكوك كى نيمه باشد تحقيق را

9- هشت هزار دينار بمساس و وقاع در ذمت خاطب مذكور حاج خواجه مستقر گشت ديني لازم

10- و حقى واجب و ثابت فلها أن تطالبها منه متى شأت و تأخذ منه اذا ارادت

11- و قد جرى ذالك في ثالث شهر المبارك المحرم الحرام سنة

12- تسع و ستين و سبعمايه و الحمد لله رب العالمين و الصلوة على محمد و آله أجمعين

13- حرره الضعيف

134 The scribe has used the singular form: الجثة.

14- أحمد بن میکائیل النخجوانی
15- أصلح الله شأنه

Witness clauses

1- شهد بذالك بدر الدين بن عمر خواجه
2- شهد بذالك حاجي الخازن بولدوق
3- اقرار من است مسيحي بن جواد علي بخطه
4- شهد بذالك بكتاش بن شادي الالباوت
5- شهد بذالك غازان بن شادي الالباوت

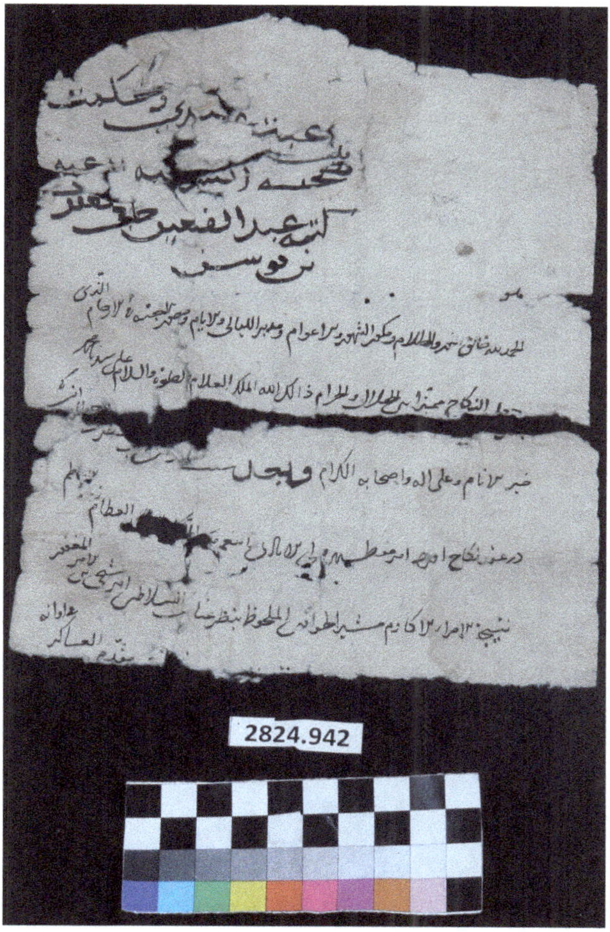

Fig. 8: IIa (70)/#942 Marriage contract for a deferred dowry, 769/1367 (top), © Mohammad H. Ghosheh.

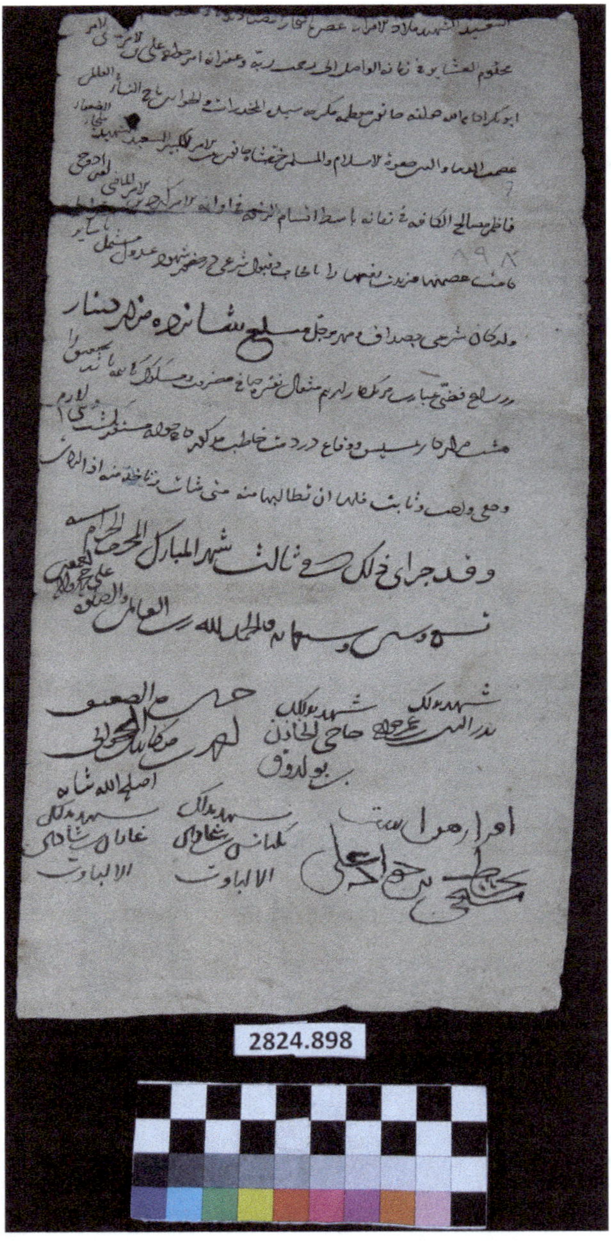

Fig. 9: IIb (70)/#898 Marriage contract for a deferred dowry, 769/1367 (bottom), © Mohammad H. Ghosheh.

III Edition of (71), Jerusalem, al-Ḥaram al-sharīf, Islamic Museum, #913 and #892
Ilkhanid decree, undated

Text (recto)

#913

1- الله المُستعان
2- أبو سعيد بهادر خان يرليغندن
3- بتتقاول و حكام قيصريه بدانند كى
4- مرآد آمد و نمود كى از أجر تعهد از فلاحه
5- تلاش بوده است و آنجا يكباره [بكناره؟] باغ [داشته؟] است و هر كسى بر اين [. . .]

#892

1- [. . .] خود دعوى ميكرده [. . .]
2- كى هيچ آفريده را [. . .] در أمرى كى بر قيد أمر شريعت
3- مدخلى و تعلقى نسازد و اگر در اين باب سخنى داشته باشند
4- بسراى شرع حاضر شده بقطع رسانند و خيرت [سازند؟]
5- [كى؟] در مذكور حيفى نرود و كسى بنا حق و [شوربازى؟]
6- نرساند برين جمله روند و اعتماد نمايند

Fig. 10: IIIa (71)/#913 Draft of Ilkhanid decree, undated (top), © Mohammad H. Ghosheh.

Fig. 11: IIIb (71)/#892 Draft of Ilkhanid decree, undated (bottom), © Mohammad H. Ghosheh.

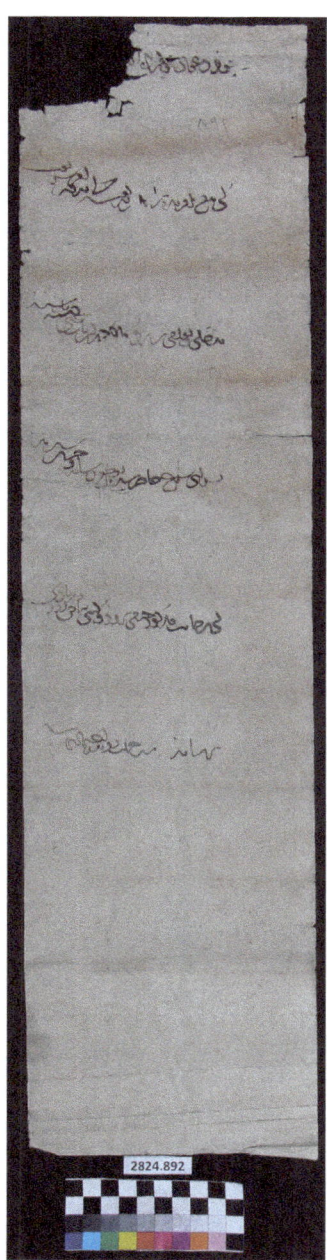

IV Edition of (76), Jerusalem, al-Ḥaram al-sharīf, Islamic Museum, #906

Decree on collection of revenues, 740/1339

Text

1- [. . .]

2- بدو افتد کی رعایا را مجتمع گرداند و محصولات باقی را

3- بمواجبی کی پیش از این در سابق الأیام معهوده متصرف شود [درین وقت؟]

4- [. . .] کی انجایگاه رفته است و مزاحم می شود بدین سبب

5- این مکتوب در قلم امد کی قطعا و [سهلا] انجایگاه مزاحم می شود و في ما بعد

6- مطالبتی نماید و مدخل ستد و انچ [سامی ماضی]

7- شده باشد چون [بدین جانب نرسیده است و او حیف و معدی آمد؟]

8- باز گرداند [برین جمله] اعتماد نماید برساله شیخ علي

9- [کتب في . . .] من صفر ختم بالخیر والظفر لسنة أربعین و سبعمایه

10- یا رب أختم بالخیر [. . .]

Seal

توکلت علی الله [. . .] سوزی [باد؟]

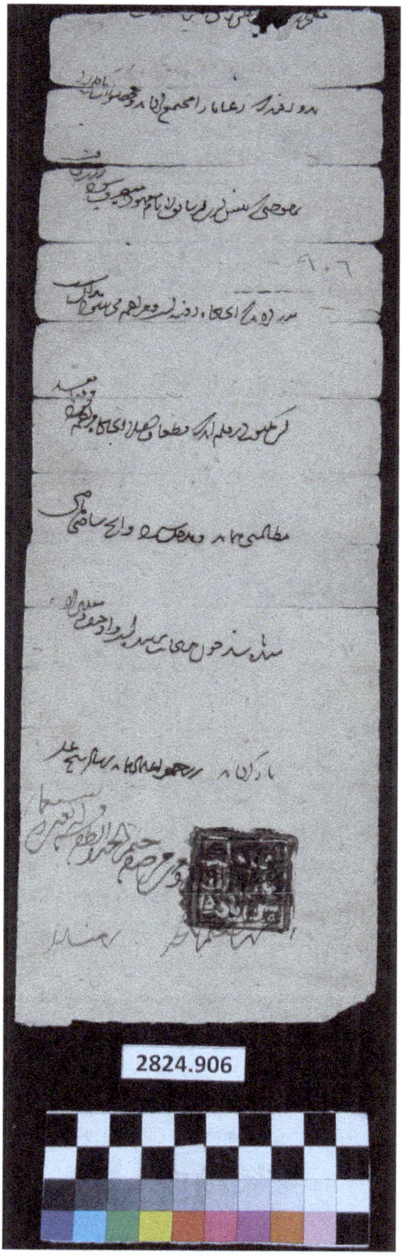

Fig. 12: IV (76)/#906 Decree on collection of revenues, 740/1339, © Mohammad H. Ghosheh.

V Edition of (82), Jerusalem, al-Ḥaram al-sharīf, Islamic Museum, #975 and #893

Sale contract of two *dāng* of the village of Azād, 723/1323

Text (recto)

Judicial attestation by the judge

#975

1- هو

2- ثبت عندي

3- مضمون هذه الحجة الشرعية [المخلّد؟] في هذه

4- [المعاملة؟][135] المرعية كتبه علي بن محمد

5- البخاري

Main text

1- غرض تحرير اين كلمات و تقرير اين [مقالات؟][136] شرعى

2- آنست كه فروختند شيخ زنكى و شيخ قاران [ابنان][137]

3- [مرحوم أمير] [. . .] كبير

4- المرحوم نكوداى دو دانگ از ديه ازاد زيرين كه حق

5- ايشان بود موروثى [. . .] قره با چهار حد

6- [. . .] دينار [. . .] رائج

#893

1- شهر [روكسر؟] زر سفيد معاملات وقت مضروب

2- و مسكوک كه نيمه اين مبلغ باشد تاكيد را

3- هفتاد دينار و اين مبلغ بتمام و كمال بريشان

4- رسيد حد أول با [قوشون؟] و حد دوم با سنگ

5- بزرگ متصل [كوزه بک؟] و حد سيم با [يركوير؟] و

6- و حد چهارم با [زيارت؟] ارتوغ فروختنى درست

7- شرعى و بايعان مذكوران اقرار كردند كه اين

8- دو دانگ از ديه ازاد با جايگاه اسباب و آب

9- و باغ و درخت و زمين آبى و ديمى وهر چه

10- داخل ويست حق و ملك أمير تمربغاست

11- و ما را هيچ حقى و دعوى در اين دو دانگ ديه

12- نماند بعد اليوم هر كه از اقاريب و عشاير

13- برادران ايشان دعوى كند دروغ و نامسموع

135 The scribe has recorded the word المرعية in line 4 and the missing word المعاملة appears at the start of line 5.

136 عقد is another plausible reading.

137 The scribe has written ابنتان.

14- باشد و عهده و درک بریشان باشد و این
15- مکتوب در قلم امد تا وقت حاجت معرض
16- افتد و ذالك جری في عاشر ذ[ی] القعدة
17- سنة ثلاث و عشرین و سبعمائه
18- شاهده و کاتبه
19- محمد بن حسین
20- العلوي

Additional notes

1- و شیخ زنکی بوکالت شیخ قاران فروخت یک دانگ نصیب وی را بگواهی اسلان بن [گران؟] أمیر و بگواهی اسماعیل ابن ملك شاه
2- و این مبلغ صد و چهار دینار که در بطن این مکتوبست از دست خواجه میر جمله تمربغا رسید بدست شیخ زنکی و شیخ قاران
3-

Witness clauses

1- بگواهی اخی صلاح الدین صالح ابن مرحوم عز الدین یوسف و کتبه بامره
2- بگواهی خواجه موسی بن ابراهیم و کتبه بامرهب
3- گواهی ابراهیم ولی بن یوسف و کتبه باذنه
4- بگواهی محمود مؤذن و کتبه بامره
5- بگواهی شییخ بابا بن [مه کان؟] و کتبه بامره
6- [پیره؟] غازی ابن سلیمان
7- قتلغبغا ابن عمر و کتبه بامره
8- شادی بن [زکه نبی؟]

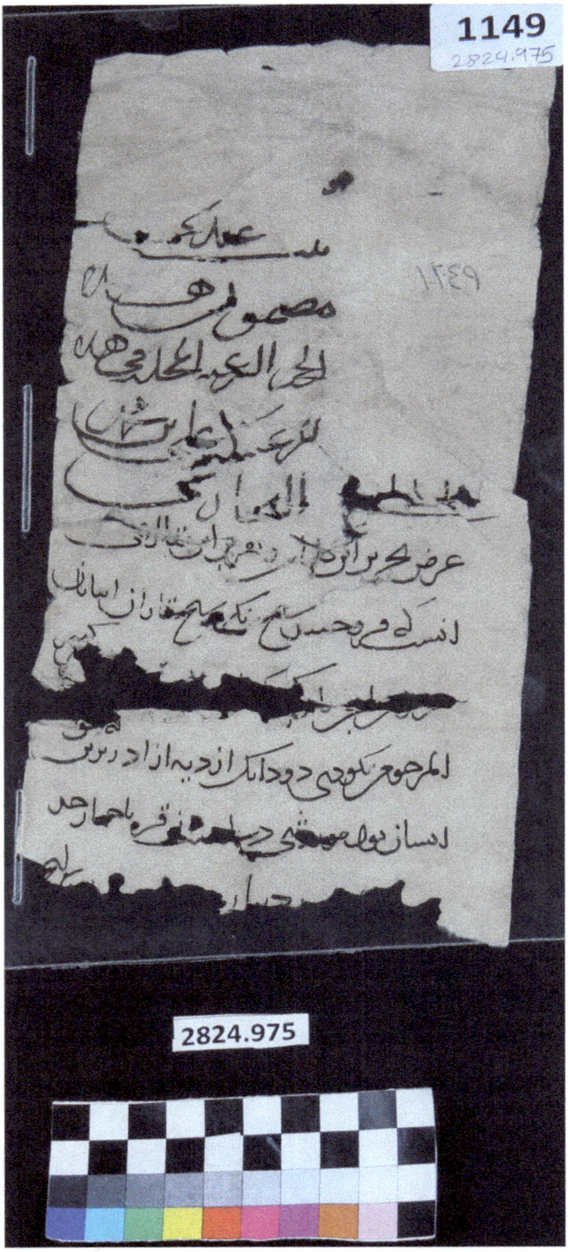

Fig. 13: Va (82)/#975 Sale contract of two *dāng* of the village of Azād, 723/1323 (top), © Mohammad H. Ghosheh.

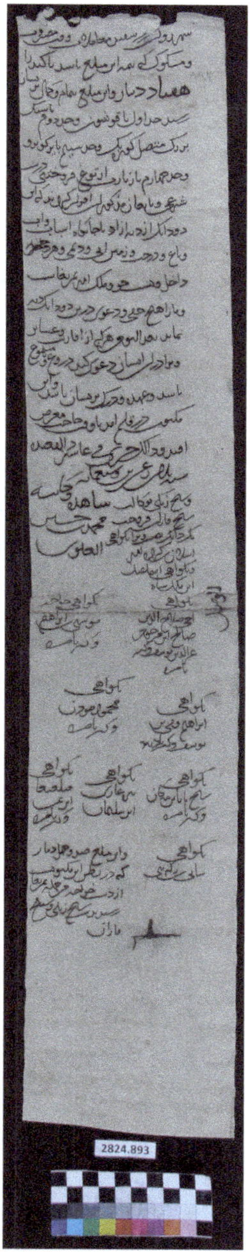

Fig. 14: Vb (82)/#893 Sale contract of two *dāng* of the village of Azād, 723/1323 (bottom), © Mohammad H. Ghosheh.

Appendix 1b: Edition of five Arabic documents (Said Aljoumani)

VI Edition of (3), Jerusalem, al-Ḥaram al-sharīf, Islamic Museum, #966
Report on a Sultanic decree and a judge's order concerning the confiscation of an (officer's?) estate, 797/1395

1- بسم الله الرحمن الرحيم

2- بتاريخ العشر الأول من شهر رمضان المعظم قدره سنة خمس وتسعين وسبعماية ورد مربع شريف ملكي ظاهري خلَّد الله ملكه وأدام اقتداره ومثال

3- كريم من المقر العالي المولوي ~~القضائي~~[138] الصاحبي أبو الفرج مدبر الممالك الإسلامية بالأبواب الشريفة أسبغ الله ظلاله على يد الأمير الكبير الغازي العالي

4- علاء الدين ألطنبغا البريدي بالأبواب الشريفة أعزه الله تعالى على المجلس العالي المولي الناصري نائب الغيبة يومئذ بالقدس الشريف أعز الله تعالى نصره من مضمون

5- المربع الشريف بعد البسملة الشريفة والعلامة الشريفة والعلائم على العادة والرحمة على العادة أن ينعم على المجلس السامي الأجلي الكبيري سيف الدين جقمق الدوادار الظاهري

6- أعزه الله تعالى بما خلفه خضر المتوفى بالقدس الشريف المُلك والموجود بحكم أنه منطاشي وعاصي إعانة له على الخدمة الشريفة حسب الأمر الشريف شرَّفه الله تعالى وعظَّمه

7- يوم شموله بالخط الشريف بعد الخط الشريف شرفه الله تعالى وعظمه إن شاء الله تعالى مؤرخ ~~الحادي~~[139] ثاني عشر رجب الفرد سنة خمس وتسعين وسبعماية ومن مضمون المثال المشار إليه أعلاه بعد

8- البسملة الشريفة ~~والرحمة على العادة ويوضح لعلم المجلس العالي~~[140] بعد اليد الكريمة العالية المولوية الأميرية الكريمة [. . .]

9- وحقق مرجوها وينهى بعد بث شوقه وولائه ووده [. . .]

10- بضبط تركة خضر التركماني وفيه [. . .]

11- الألفي علاء الدين [ألطنبغا]

138 مضروب عليها في الأصل.
139 مضروب عليها في الأصل.
140 مضروب عليها في الأصل.

https://doi.org/10.1515/9783111330242-007

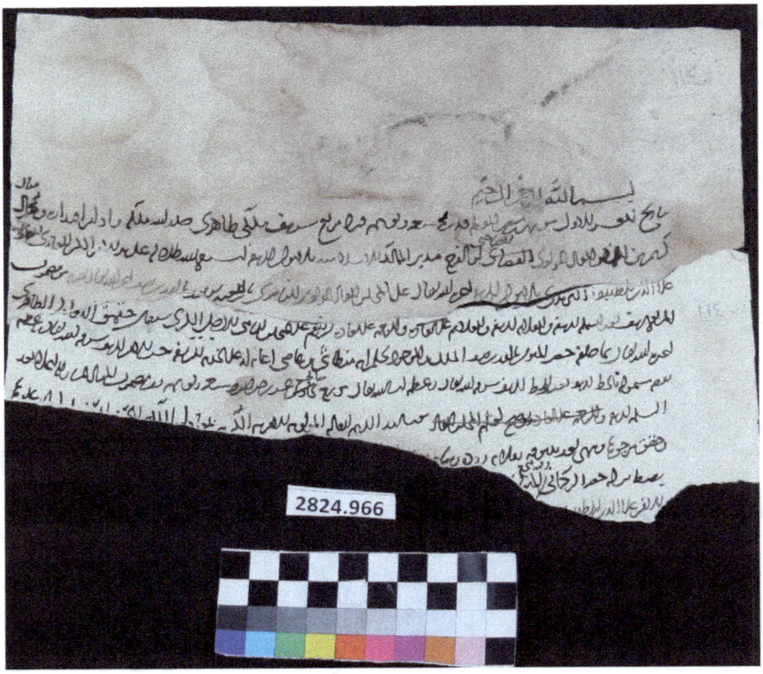
بسم الله الرحمن الرحيم

2824.966

Fig. 15: VI (3)/#966 Report on a Sultanic decree and a judge's order, 797/1395, © Mohammad H. Ghosheh.

VII Edition of (8) Jerusalem, al-Ḥaram al-sharīf, Islamic Museum, #946
Muṭālaʿa with instructions for judge regarding the visit of an officer, most likely late 700s/1300s

1- بسم الله الرحمن الرحيم
2- الشرفي المملوك
3- يقبل الأرض وينهي بعد شوقه وثنائه وإخلاصه في وده ودعائه أن الماثل بها محمد الدماميني
4- المجلس السامي الشيخي الإمامي العالمي العاملي الأوحدي الشارعي البرهاني إبراهيم العراقي أدام
5- الله وجوده من أعز أصحاب المملوك وإخوانه وممن له على المملوك حقوق كثيرة وله خدمة
6- واتصال بأكابر الدولة الشريفة وقد توجه إلى القدس الشريف برسم الزيارة ولا غنى له
7- عن ملاحظة مولانا قاضي القضاة وعنايته والمملوك يسأل إحسان مولانا قاضي القضاة
8- مضاعفة الوصية به والعناية والملاحظة ويكون نظره عليه ويحسن إليه ويعامله

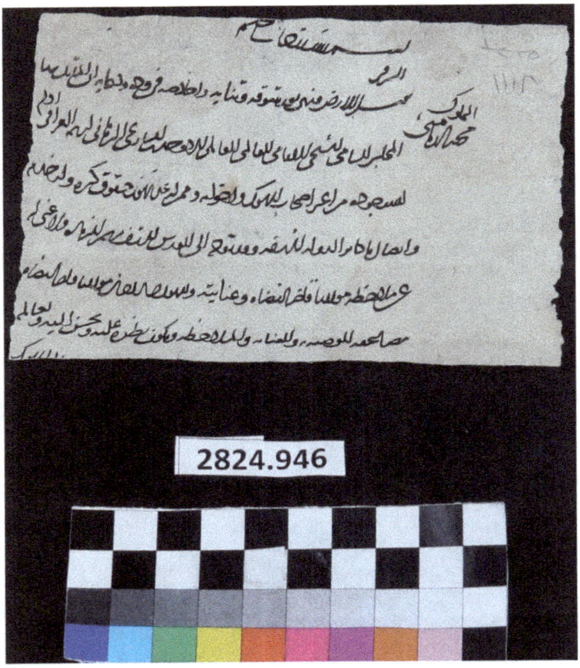

Fig. 16: VII (8)/#946 *Muṭālaʿa*, most likely late 700s/1300s, © Mohammad H. Ghosheh.

VIII Edition of (10), Jerusalem, al-Ḥaram al-sharīf, Islamic Museum, #922

Sale contracts with accounts (cotton), 776/1374

#922 (recto)

[1] 1- [...] وخمسة وأربعون درهما
2- [... تحل عليه] في كل أسبوع
3- [...] أو بالملاءة والقدرة على ذلك وقبض العوض
4- [الشرعي عن] وزن قطن ابتاعه وتسلمه وبه شهد عليه في سابع شهر صفر سنة ستة [وسبعين وسبعماية]
5- ~~شهد على ذلك~~[141] ~~أشهد على ذلك~~
6- ~~علي بن إسماعيل بن شاكر [الفقير؟]~~ ~~كتبه عبد الرحمن بن محمد [...]~~

[2] 1- [في ذمة؟] الحاج أحمد بن إبراهيم بن محمد الحمصي القطان للحاج عمر بن محمد بن عمر [الخضري/ الحصري] العلاف
2- من الدراهم الفضة الجيدة المتعامل به يومئذ ماية درهم وثمانية وتسعون درهما
3- نصفها تسعة وتسعون درهما تحل عليه في سلخ كل أسبوع من يوم تاريخه
4- خمس [...] درهم أو بالملاءة والقدرة على ذلك وقبض العوض [الشرعي عن]
5- قطن ابتاعه منه وتسلمه وبه شهد عليه في سابع شهر صفر من سنة ست وسبعين وسبعماية
6- شهد عليه بذلك أشهد عليه بذلك
7- علي بن إسماعيل بن شاكر [الفقير؟] كتبه عبد الرحمن بن محمد [...]

[3] 1- في ذمة محمد بن حسن بن ياسين العجمي من الحاج عمر بن محمد بن عمر [الخضري/الحصري] العلاف من
2- الدراهم الفضة الجيدة المتعامل بها يومئذ مايتي درهم وإحدى عشر درهما
3- ونصف درهم نصفها ماية درهم وخمسة الدراهم ونصف وربع درهم تحل
4- عند مضي سلخ كل أسبوع من يوم تاريخه ستة الدراهم أو بالملاءة والقدرة على
5- ذلك وقبض العوض الشرعي عن قطن ابتاعه منه وتسلمه وبه شهد عليه في سابع شهر صفر
6- سنة ست وسبعين وسبعماية
7- شهد عليه بذلك أشهد عليه بذلك
8- علي بن إسماعيل بن شاكر كتبه عبد الرحمن بن محمد [...]

[4] 1- في ذمة نعمة بن بشارة النصراني من [جفنا الجوز؟] للحاج عمر بن محمد بن عمر
2- [الخضري/ الحصري؟] العلاف من الدراهم الفضة الجيدة المتعامل بها يومئذ مايتي درهم
3- وثمان عشر درهم ونصف درهم نصفها ماية درهم وتسع الدراهم
4- وربع تحل عليه في سلخ كل أسبوع من يوم تاريخه ست الدراهم أو بالملاءة
5- والقدرة على ذلك وقبض العوض الشرعي عن وزن قطن ابتاعه ومنه وتسلمه
6- وشهد عليه في سابع شهر صفر سنة ست وسبعين وسبعماية
7- ~~شهد على ذلك~~[142] ~~شهد على ذلك~~
8- ~~علي بن إسماعيل بن شاكر [الفقير؟]~~ ~~كتبه عبد الرحمن بن محمد بن [...]~~

---

141 مضروب عليها في الأصل.
142 مضروب عليها في الأصل.

#922 (verso)

1- قبض مما [في باطنها من؟ . . .]
2- [. . .]
3- [. . .]
4- [. . .]
5- [. . .]
6- قبض مما في باطنها من [. . .]
7- اثنين عشرين ونقدة[143] اثنين عشرين
8- قبض مما في باطنها نقدة أربع عشرين من محمد العجمي
9- ونقدة أربعة عشرين ونقدة أربعة عشرين ونقدة أربعة عشرين
10- ونقد[ة] أربعة عشرين ونقدة أربعة عشرين أربعة عشرين
11- قبض مما في باطنها نقدة من يد محمد العجمي
12- أربعة وعشرين
13- قبض مما في باطنها نقدة أربعة عشرين من النصراني
14- ونقدة أربعة عشرين ونقدة أربعة عشرين ونقدة أربعة |وعشرين|
15- ونقدة أربعة عشرين ونقدة أربعة عشرين
16- ونقدة أربعة عشرين
17- وأيضا نقدة من يد النصراني
18- أربعة وعشرين

143 نَقَدَهُ مالاً: أعطاه إيَّاه، نَقَدَهُ مبلغاً من المال. فالنَّقدَة: دفعةٌ من المال.

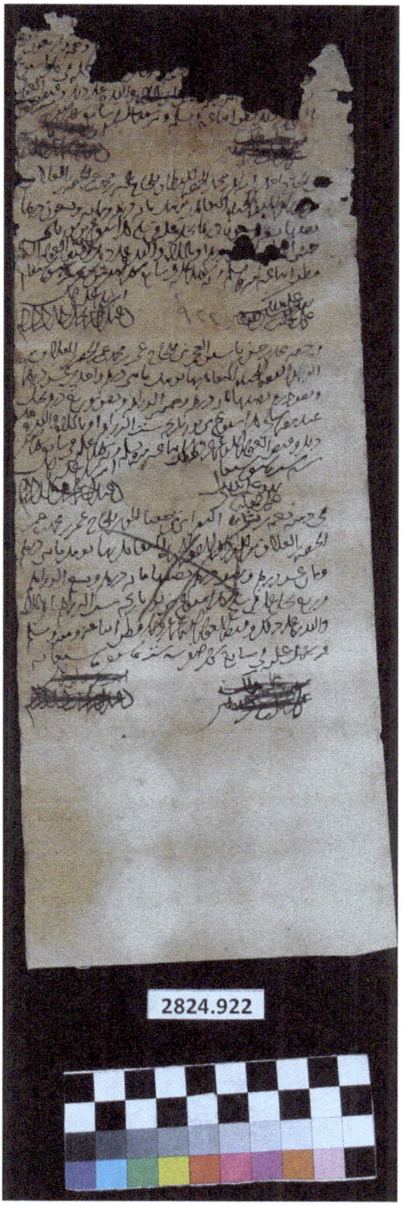

Fig. 17: VIIIa (10)/#922r Sale contracts (cotton), 776/1374, © Mohammad H. Ghosheh.

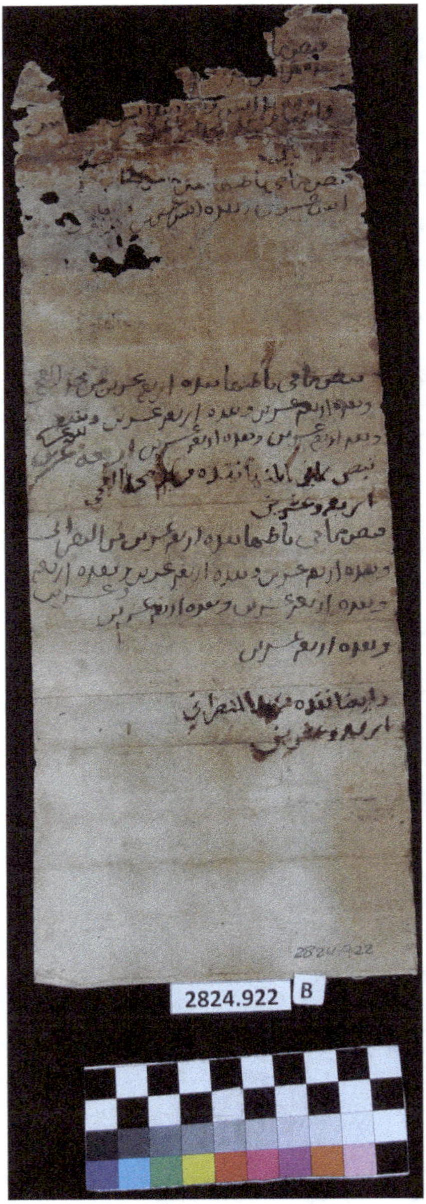

Fig. 18: VIIIb (10)/#922v Sale contract and accounts (cotton), 776/1374, © Mohammad H. Ghosheh.

IX Edition of (12), Jerusalem, al-Ḥaram al-sharīf, Islamic Museum, #923

Rent contract for baths, 737/1336

#923 (recto)

-1 الحمد لله الحكم [. . .]

-2 بسم الله الرحمن الرحيم

-3 هذا ما استأجر شبل بن خلف بن سبع وسالم بن محمد بن محرز وإسماعيل بن حجي بن إبراهيم وهم معروفين عند شهوده

-4 من الشيخ الصالح الورع شمس الدين محمد بن الشيخ الصالح المرحوم أحمد بن الشيخ [الزاهد؟] غانم المقدسي نفع الله به

-5 جميع بيوت الحمام المعروف بالبترك الوقف المؤبد والحبس المحرم الجارية أجوره ومنافعه على مصالح الخانقاه

-6 الصلاحية بالقدس الشريف وعلى السادة المشايخ الصوفية المقيمين والواردين حسب ما نُصَّ وشُرح

-7 في كتاب وقف ذلك المتقدم التاريخ وهذه الحمام بالقدس الشريف بالقرب من القمامة وهي معروفة مشهورة شهرةً تُغني

-8 عن تحديدها كل ذلك كله إجارة صحيحة لازمة شرعية مدة سنة كاملة أولها تاسع عشر جمادى الآخر سنة تاريخه

-9 بأجرة مبلغها لكل يوم يمضي من الأيام ستة عشر درهم فضة يقدم المستأجرين المذكورين [للمؤجِر][144] المذكور في كل يوم ثلاثة عشر درهم

-10 فضة ويُعتمد له ثلاثة دراهم أجرة دخول الصوفية المعروفين منهم في كل يوم وتسلموا المأجور من الآجر

-11 بعد النظر والمعرفة والمعاقدة الشرعية [ويستحق؟] المأجور من المستأجرين [نزح [ماء] البرك][145] وعليهم رفعه إلى الحمام بغير رجوع

-12 على المؤجِر والمؤجَر عليهم وإقرا[ر] المستأجرين أنهم يحملوا رماد الحمام المذكور إلى ظاهر البلد من وجه حق شرعي لهم

-13 فأشهدوا عليهم بذلك تاسع عشر جمادى الآخر سنة سبع وثلاثين وسبع ماية وكل واحد من المستأجرين ضمَّان وجعل ما على صاحبه من الأجر

-14 من ماله وذمته بإذنهما له بذلك ضمانا شرعيا الحمد لله وحده وصلوته على سيدنا محمد وآله وصحبه وسلم تسليما كثيرا

-15	أشهد عليهم بمضمونه	أشهد على كل من المؤجِر والمستأجرين	شـ[ـهد] على المستأجرين والمؤجر بما به
-16	كتبه [. . .] بن أحمد [. . .] في تاريخه	بما نسب إليهم في تاريخه	محمد بن الحريري
-17		وكتبه محمود بن خلف بن محمود	[شهد عندي بذلك؟]
-18		السعيدي	

144 استدراكا من الوثيقة 46

145 استدراكا من الوثيقة 46.

#923 (verso)

1- ادعى
2- [إجـ]ـارة الحمام
3- [...] لسنة سبع وثلاثين وسبعماية

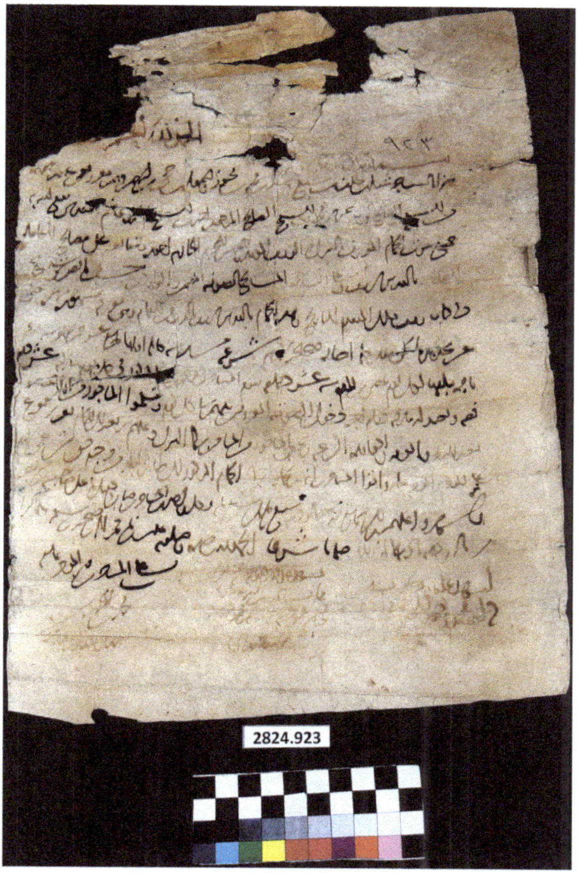

Fig. 19: IX (12)/#923 Rent contract for baths, 737/1336, © Mohammad H. Ghosheh.

X Edition of (30) Jerusalem, al-Ḥaram al-sharīf, Islamic Museum, #945

Estate inventory (*wuqūf*), 795/1393

1- الحمد لله

2- بتاريخ الخامس والعشرين من شهر رمضان المعظم قدره سنة خمسة وتسعين وسبعمية

3- وقف من يضع خطه آخره من الشهود المندوبين من مجلس الحكم العزيز

4- الشافعي بالقدس الشريف أدامه الله تعالى على امرأة ضعيفة بحارة [المغاربة؟]

5- بالقدس الشريف تسمى الحاجة قطلو بنت عبد الله عتاقة الحاج عمر [بن]

6- شهاب الدين أحمد [البا. . .يني] المقيم بالقدس الشريف والذي [أقر أنّ الذي؟]

7- تملكه ثياب بدنها قميصين أحدهما طرح |كتان| والثاني أزرق

8- وملوطة كتان فص لؤلؤي وشملة مطرزة وخرقة [. . .]

9- وخرقة حمراء [صـ. . .] ومشاية جديد[ة]

Fig. 20: X (30)/#945 Estate inventory *(wuqūf)*, 795/1393, © Mohammad H. Ghosheh.

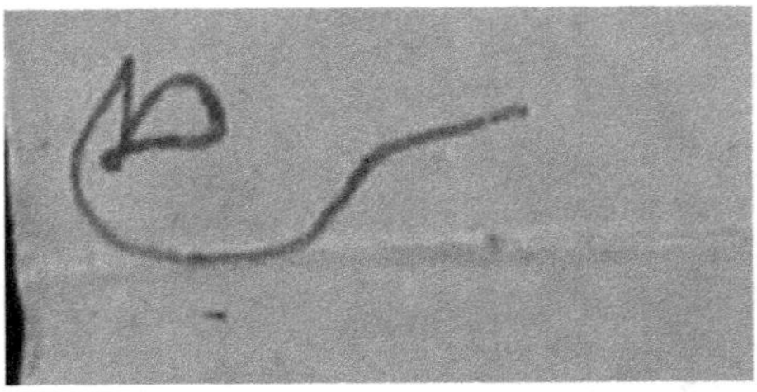

Fig. 21: XI/#867 Autograph witness clause of Zakariyā, son of Shams al-Dīn Juwaynī, © Mohammad H. Ghosheh.

Appendix 2: List of edited Ḥaram al-sharīf documents

This appendix lists all edited Ḥaram al-sharīf documents published until 2022. It is based on Christian Müller's list of editions until 2011 found in his *Kadi und seine Zeugen* (pp. 576–82) and the list of Aljoumani/Hirschler, *Owning Books* (pp. 354–61). Many of these editions can be found in digital format in the Munich *Arabic Papyrology Database* (text only) and the Paris *Comparing Arabic Legal Documents* platform (image and text, often with emendations).[146] *Comparing Arabic Legal Documents* has now also started online-only editions (see below #333). In the following list 'em.' stands for 'emendations'.

#001: Al-ʿAsalī, *Wathāʾiq maqdisīya* I, 189–91 (em. Diem, *Philologisches*, 28–32).
#002: Al-ʿAsalī, *Wathāʾiq maqdisīya* I, 199–200 (em. Diem, *Philologisches*, 36).
#003: Al-ʿAsalī, *Wathāʾiq maqdisīya* I, 195–6 (em. Diem, *Philologisches*, 32–4).
#004: Al-ʿAsalī, *Wathāʾiq maqdisīya* I, 197–8 (em. Diem, *Philologisches*, 34–5).
#005: Frenkel, *Relationship*, 107.
#006: Al-ʿAsalī, *Wathāʾiq maqdisīya* I, 183–5 (em. Diem, *Philologisches*, 25–8); Ghawānma, *Tārīkh niyābat Bayt al-Maqdis*, 193.
#007: Al-ʿAsalī, *Wathāʾiq maqdisīya* I, 203–5 (em. Diem, *Philologisches*, 38–40).
#008: Al-ʿAsalī, *Wathāʾiq maqdisīya* I, 181–2; Ṣāliḥīya, *Min wathāʾiq*, 41–6 (em. Diem, *Philologisches*, 23–5).
#009: Little, *Five Petitions*, 381–8.
#010: Al-ʿAsalī, *Wathāʾiq maqdisīya* I, 212–4 (em. Diem, *Philologisches*, 46–8).
#012: Al-ʿAsalī, *Wathāʾiq maqdisīya* I, 208 (em. Diem, *Philologisches*, 40–2).
#013: Al-ʿAsalī, *Wathāʾiq maqdisīya* I, 209–11 (em. Diem, *Philologisches*, 42–46).
#014: Al-ʿAsalī, *Wathāʾiq maqdisīya* I, 201–2 (em. Diem, *Philologisches*, 37–8).
#016: Aljoumani/Hirschler, *Owning Books and Preserving Documents,* Appendix 2.
#020: Ghawānma, *Tārīkh niyābat Bayt al-Maqdis*, 194; Ṣāliḥīya, *Min wathāʾiq*, 48–56.
#022: Al-ʿAsalī, *Wathāʾiq maqdisīya* I, 241–2.
#025: Little, *Five Petitions*, 351–7.
#026: Al-ʿAsalī, *Wathāʾiq maqdisīya* I, 206.
#028: Al-ʿAsalī, *Wathāʾiq maqdisīya* I, 227–30.
#030: Müller, *Crimes without Criminals*, 146–52; Al-ʿAsalī, *Wathāʾiq maqdisīya* II, 132–4.

146 https://www.apd.gwi.uni-muenchen.de/apd/project1c.jsp; https://cald.irht.cnrs.fr, accessed 30 November 2021.

https://doi.org/10.1515/9783111330242-008

#031: *see* #032 and #650.
#032: Al-ʿAsalī, *Wathāʾiq maqdisīya* I, 221–3.
#034: Al-ʿAsalī, *Wathāʾiq maqdisīya* I, 177–80 (em. Diem, *Philologisches*, 21–3).
#035: Al-ʿAsalī, *Wathāʾiq maqdisīya* I, 276 (recto only).
#036: Al-ʿAsalī, *Wathāʾiq maqdisīya* I, 237–8 (em. Diem, *Philologisches*, 55–7).
#039: Müller, *Écrire pour établir la preuve*, 86–93.
#043: Ghawānma, *Tārīkh niyābat Bayt al-Maqdis*, 195.
#046: Al-ʿAsalī, *Wathāʾiq maqdisīya* I, 245–7.
#047: Al-ʿAsalī, *Wathāʾiq maqdisīya* I, 254–7.
#048: Al-ʿAsalī, *Wathāʾiq maqdisīya* I, 258.
#049: Richards, *Primary Education*, 228–9.
#052: Aljoumani/Hirschler, *Owning Books and Preserving Documents,* Appendix 2.
#059: Richards, *Mamlūk Barīd*, 208–9.
#060: Hagedorn, *Domestic Slavery*, 218–9.
#061: Aljoumani/Hirschler, *Owning Books and Preserving Documents*, Chapter 7.
#067: Al-ʿAsalī, *Wathāʾiq maqdisīya* II, 168 (em. Diem, *Philologisches*, 63–4).
#068: Diem, *Philologisches*, 16–9.
#074: Al-ʿAsalī, *Wathāʾiq maqdisīya* I, 274–5 (em. Diem, *Philologisches*, 57–9).
#075: Müller, *Crimes without Criminals*, 152–5.
#082: Lutfi, *Al-Quds al-Mamlûkiyya*, 37–8.
#106: Aljoumani/Hirschler, *Owning Books and Preserving Documents,* Appendix 2.
#108: Lutfi, *Six Fourteenth Century Iqrārs*, 267–9 (em. Lutfi/Little, *Iqrārs from Al-Quds*, 327–8).
#109: Aljoumani/Hirschler, *Owning Books and Preserving Documents,* Appendix 2.
#111: Aljoumani/Hirschler, *Owning Books and Preserving Documents,* Appendix 2.
#115: Aljoumani/Hirschler, *Owning Books and Preserving Documents,* Appendix 2.
#118: Aljoumani/Hirschler, *Owning Books and Preserving Documents,* Appendix 2.
#133: Little, *Documents Related to the Estates of a Merchant*, 97–111.
#163: Al-ʿAsalī, *Wathāʾiq maqdisīya* I, 267–8; Ṣāliḥīya, *Min wathāʾiq*, 84–8.
#178: Muḥammad, *Ijrāʾāt jard al-mawārīth al-ḥashrīya*, 83–6.
#180: *see* #061.
#181: Müller, *Constats d'héritages*, 308–313.
#182: Al-ʿAsalī, *Wathāʾiq maqdisīya* I, 279 (left column only).
#183: Al-ʿAsalī, *Wathāʾiq maqdisīya* II, 107.
#184: Al-ʿAsalī, *Wathāʾiq maqdisīya* II, 109; Lutfi, *Six Fourteenth Century Iqrārs*, 262–6 (em. Lutfi/Little, *Iqrārs from Al-Quds*, 326–7).
#186: Al-ʿAsalī, *Wathāʾiq maqdisīya* II, 92.
#188: Aljoumani/Hirschler, *Owning Books and Preserving Documents,* Appendix 2.
#192: Al-ʿAsalī, *Wathāʾiq maqdisīya* II, 105.
#197: Al-ʿAsalī, *Wathāʾiq maqdisīya* II, 42.

#198: Al-ʿAsalī, *Wathāʾiq maqdisīya* II, 89.
#199: Al-ʿAsalī, *Wathāʾiq maqdisīya* II, 87.
#200: Al-ʿAsalī, *Wathāʾiq maqdisīya* II, 78.
#201: Al-ʿAsalī, *Wathāʾiq maqdisīya* II, 90.
#202: Al-ʿAsalī, *Wathāʾiq maqdisīya* II, 97–8.
#203: Al-ʿAsalī, *Wathāʾiq maqdisīya* II, 169.
#205: Al-ʿAsalī, *Wathāʾiq maqdisīya* II, 113; Lutfi, *Six Fourteenth Century Iqrārs*, 269–73 (em. Lutfi/Little, *Iqrārs from Al-Quds*, 328–9).
#206: Al-ʿAsalī, *Wathāʾiq maqdisīya* II, 103.
#209: Al-ʿAsalī, *Wathāʾiq maqdisīya* II, 120 (recto only).
#211: Al-ʿAsalī, *Wathāʾiq maqdisīya* II, 83–5.
#214: Diem, *Philologisches*, 11–5.
#215: Little, *Five Petitions*, 359–65.
#220: Ṣāliḥīya, *Min wathāʾiq*, 98–102.
#223: Al-ʿAsalī, *Wathāʾiq maqdisīya* II, 70; cf. Richards, *Qasāma in Mamlūk Society*, 282–4.
#229: Al-ʿAsalī, *Wathāʾiq maqdisīya* I, 231–2.
#232: Al-ʿAsalī, *Wathāʾiq maqdisīya* I, 215–6 (em. Diem, *Philologisches*, 49–51).
#265: Al-ʿAsalī, *Wathāʾiq maqdisīya* II, 72; cf. Richards, *Qasāma in Mamlūk Society*, 274–6.
#269: Lutfi, *Al-Quds al-Mamlûkiyya*, 46–8.
#272: Richards, *Mamlūk Barīd*, 208.
#278: Al-ʿAsalī, *Wathāʾiq maqdisīya* I, 217–8 (em. Diem, *Philologisches*, 51–4).
#287: Al-ʿAsalī, *Wathāʾiq maqdisīya* II, 111; Lutfi, *Six Fourteenth Century Iqrārs*, 273–7 (em. Lutfi/Little, *Iqrārs from Al-Quds*, 329).
#288: Al-ʿAsalī, *Wathāʾiq maqdisīya* II, 135.
#289: Al-ʿAsalī, *Wathāʾiq maqdisīya* II, 116; Lutfi, *Six Fourteenth Century Iqrārs*, 258–62 (em. Lutfi/Little, *Iqrārs from Al-Quds*, 326).
#292: Al-ʿAsalī, *Wathāʾiq maqdisīya* II, 76.
#293: Richards, *Qasāma in Mamlūk Society*, 259–61.
#298: Al-ʿAsalī, *Wathāʾiq maqdisīya* II, 149–50; Little, *Six Fourteenth Century Purchase Deeds*, 325–33.
#301: Al-ʿAsalī, *Wathāʾiq maqdisīya* II, 37–9.
#302: Abdul-Rahman, *Arabic Marriage Contract*, 125–34.
#303: Frenkel, *Relationship*, 108.
#305: Little, *Five Petitions*, 372–9.
#307: Al-ʿAsalī, *Wathāʾiq maqdisīya* II, 165–6 (em. Diem, *Philologisches*, 59–62).
#309: Muḥammad, *Marsūm al-Sulṭān al-Ashraf Īnāl*, 165–7.
#310: Little, *Five Petitions*, 365–72.
#311: Al-ʿAsalī, *Wathāʾiq maqdisīya* I, 187–8.

#312: Al-ʿAsalī, *Wathāʾiq maqdisīya* II, 101.
#313: Aljoumani/Hirschler, *Owning Books and Preserving Documents,* Appendix 2.
#315: Al-ʿAsalī, *Wathāʾiq maqdisīya* II, 118 (recto only); Lutfi, *Six Fourteenth Century Iqrārs*, 278–87 (em. Lutfi/Little, *Iqrārs from Al-Quds*, 329).
#316: Al-ʿAsalī, *Wathāʾiq maqdisīya* II, 147; Little, *Six Fourteenth Century Purchase Deeds*, 317–21.
#326/1: Ṣāliḥīya, *Min wathāʾiq*, 58–69.
#330: ʿAbd al-Raḥmān, *al-Taʿāmulāt al-qaḍāʾīya.*
#331: Al-ʿAsalī, *Wathāʾiq maqdisīya* II, 59–60.
#332: Muḥammad, *Idārat amwāl awqāf al-Ḥaram*, 266–9.
#333: Müller, *Document JerH_333 on endowed villages.*
#334: Al-ʿAsalī, *Wathāʾiq maqdisīya* II, 22–3.
#335: Al-ʿAsalī, *Wathāʾiq maqdisīya* I, 270–2; Ṣāliḥīya, *Min wathāʾiq*, 90–7; *see* Little, *Ḥaram Documents related to the Jews*, 243–57.
#336: Al-ʿAsalī, *Wathāʾiq maqdisīya* I, 280–1; Ṣāliḥīya, *Min wathāʾiq*, 70–5.
#346: Al-ʿAsalī, *Wathāʾiq maqdisīya* II, 99.
#348: Al-ʿAsalī, *Wathāʾiq maqdisīya* I, 259.
#355: Little, *Documents Related to the Estates of a Merchant*, 126–69.
#367: Al-ʿAsalī, *Wathāʾiq maqdisīya* I, 248–50.
#373: Müller, *Crimes without Criminals*, 157–9.
#374: Richards, *Mamlūk Barīd*, 208–9.
#376: Al-ʿAsalī, *Wathāʾiq maqdisīya* I, 265–6.
#382: Al-ʿAsalī, *Wathāʾiq maqdisīya* I, 252–3; Little, *Six Fourteenth Century Purchase Deeds*, 313–7.
#395: Al-ʿAsalī, *Wathāʾiq maqdisīya* I, 263–4.
#412: Lutfi, *Al-Quds al-Mamlûkiyya*, 44–5.
#436: Müller, *Écrire pour établir la preuve*, 94–7.
#441: Müller, *Écrire pour établir la preuve*, 94–7.
#445: Hagedorn, *Domestic Slavery*, 222–3.
#458: Al-ʿAsalī, *Wathāʾiq maqdisīya* II, 115.
#459: Al-ʿAsalī, *Wathāʾiq maqdisīya* II, 95.
#460: Al-ʿAsalī, *Wathāʾiq maqdisīya* II, 46.
#461: Al-ʿAsalī, *Wathāʾiq maqdisīya* II, 44.
#467: Al-ʿAsalī, *Wathāʾiq maqdisīya* II, 40.
#469: Lutfi, *Al-Quds al-Mamlûkiyya*, 49–50.
#487: Muḥammad, *Ijrāʾāt jard al-mawārīth al-ḥashrīya*, 80–2.
#488: Al-ʿAsalī, *Wathāʾiq maqdisīya* II, 68; Richards, *Qasāma in Mamlūk Society*, 265–7.
#490: Al-ʿAsalī, *Wathāʾiq maqdisīya* II, 140.
#494: Ṣāliḥīya, *Min wathāʾiq*, 109–14.

#495: Hagedorn, *Domestic Slavery*, 220–1.
#501: Al-ʿAsalī, *Wathāʾiq maqdisīya* I, 273.
#503: Ṣāliḥīya, *Min wathāʾiq*, 104–7.
#508: Aljoumani/Hirschler, *Owning Books and Preserving Documents*, Appendix 2.
#509: Aljoumani/Hirschler, *Owning Books and Preserving Documents*, Appendix 2.
#531: Muḥammad, *Ijrāʾāt jard al-mawārīth al-ḥashrīya*, 99–102.
#532: *see* #061.
#535: Richards, *Mamlūk Barīd*, 208–9.
#554: Little, *Ḥaram Documents related to the Jews*, 233–43.
#573: Al-ʿAsalī, *Wathāʾiq maqdisīya* II, 164.
#574: Al-ʿAsalī, *Wathāʾiq maqdisīya* II, 152–4; Little, *Six Fourteenth Century Purchase Deeds*, 298–313.
#577: Lutfi, *Al-Quds al-Mamlûkiyya*, 41–3.
#586: Al-ʿAsalī, *Wathāʾiq maqdisīya* II, 158–63.
#591: Little, *Documents Related to the Estates of a Merchant*, 111–26.
#593: Richards, *Glimpses of Provincial Mamluk Society*, 54–5.
#595: Al-ʿAsalī, *Wathāʾiq maqdisīya* II, 137–8.
#596: Richards, *Qasāma in Mamlūk Society*, 279–82.
#603: Al-ʿAsalī, *Wathāʾiq maqdisīya* II, 167.
#607: Lutfi, *Al-Quds al-Mamlûkiyya*, 54–60; Lutfi, *Documentary Source*, 216–26.
#609: Al-ʿAsalī, *Wathāʾiq maqdisīya* II, 51–2.
#613: Al-ʿAsalī, *Wathāʾiq maqdisīya* II, 142.
#616: Little, *Two Petitions and Consequential Court Records*, 185–7 (recto only).
#620: Maḥāmīd, *Dirāsāt fī tārīkh al-Quds al-thaqāfī*, 207–9.[147]
#628: Müller, *Crimes without Criminals*, 159–61.
#635: Al-ʿAsalī, *Wathāʾiq maqdisīya* II, 33–5.
#636: Al-ʿAsalī, *Wathāʾiq maqdisīya* II, 66; Ṣāliḥīya, *Min wathāʾiq*, 77–82; Richards, *Qasāma in Mamlūk Society*, 270–3; Little, *Ḥaram Documents related to the Jews*, 257–62.
#640: Al-ʿAsalī, *Wathāʾiq maqdisīya* II, 62–3.
#642: Müller, *Crimes without Criminals*, 161–6; Al-ʿAsalī, *Wathāʾiq maqdisīya* I, 224–6.
#645: Al-ʿAsalī, *Wathāʾiq maqdisīya* II, 129–30.
#646: ʿAbd al-Raḥmān/Anas, *ʿAqdā zawāj*, 303–10; Hagedorn, *Domestic Slavery*, 224–5.
#647: Al-ʿAsalī, *Wathāʾiq maqdisīya* II, 53–7.
#648: Al-ʿAsalī, *Wathāʾiq maqdisīya* II, 28.

---

147 We thank Umar Jamal Muhammad Ali (Sohag University) for drawing our attention to this edition.

#649: Al-ʿAsalī, *Wathāʾiq maqdisīya* II, 25–6; Little, *Two Fourteenth-Century Court Records from Jerusalem*, 18–21.
#650: Little, *Two Fourteenth-Century Court Records from Jerusalem*, 30–5.
#653/1: Al-ʿAsalī, *Wathāʾiq maqdisīya* II, 19–20; Little, *Court Record of a Divorce Hearing*, 76–7.
#653/2: Little, *Court Record of a Divorce Hearing*, 79.
#654: Little, *Two Petitions and Consequential Court Records*, 174–5.
#676: Aljoumani/Hirschler, *Owning Books and Preserving Documents*, Appendix 2.
#688: Little, *Six Fourteenth Century Purchase Deeds*, 321–5.
#691: Richards, *Qasāma in Mamlūk Society*, 256–9.
#694: Lutfi, *Al-Quds al-Mamlûkiyya*, 51–3.
#695: Al-ʿAsalī, *Wathāʾiq maqdisīya* II, 48.
#697: Al-ʿAsalī, *Wathāʾiq maqdisīya* II, 74; Richards, *Qasāma in Mamlūk Society*, 276–9.
#699: Aljoumani/Hirschler, *Owning Books and Preserving Documents*, Appendix 2.
#703: Al-ʿAsalī, *Wathāʾiq maqdisīya* II, 64; Richards, *Qasāma in Mamlūk Society*, 262–4.
#706: Al-ʿAsalī, *Wathāʾiq maqdisīya* II, 127.
#710: Al-ʿAsalī, *Wathāʾiq maqdisīya* I, 260.
#712: Richards, *Qasāma in Mamlūk Society*, 252–6.
#719: Muḥammad, *Ijrāʾāt jard al-mawārīth al-ḥashrīya*, 87–91.
#720: Müller, *Écrire pour établir la preuve*, 94–7.
#763: Muḥammad, *Idārat amwāl awqāf al-Ḥaram*, 265–6.
#767j: Lutfi, *Al-Quds al-Mamlûkiyya*, 64–6.
#768: Muḥammad, *Ijrāʾāt jard al-mawārīth al-ḥashrīya*, 92–8.
#769a/b: Muḥammad, *Idārat amwāl awqāf al-Ḥaram*, 270–9.
#770th: Richards, *Mamlūk Barīd*, 209.
#793: Aljoumani/Hirschler, *Owning Books and Preserving Documents*, Chapter 8.
#800: Aljoumani/Hirschler, *Owning Books and Preserving Documents*, Chapter 8.
#812: Aljoumani/Hirschler, *Owning Books and Preserving Documents*, Chapter 8.
#833: Al-ʿAsalī, *Wathāʾiq maqdisīya* I, 235–6 (recto only).
#840: Lutfi, *Al-Quds al-Mamlûkiyya*, 39–40.
#843: Aljoumani/Hirschler, *Owning Books and Preserving Documents*, Appendix 2.
#847: Richards, *Qasāma in Mamlūk Society*, 267–70; Muḥammad, *Idārat amwāl awqāf al-Ḥaram*, 270–2.
#849: Lutfi, *Al-Quds al-Mamlûkiyya*, 61–3.
#850: Aljoumani/Hirschler, *Owning Books and Preserving Documents*, Appendix 2.
#892: Bhalloo in Aljoumani/Bhalloo/Hirschler, *Catalogue of the New Corpus*, Appendix 1a.

#893: Bhalloo in Aljoumani/Bhalloo/Hirschler, *Catalogue of the New Corpus,* Appendix 1a.
#897: Aljoumani/Hirschler, *Owning Books and Preserving Documents,* Appendix 2.
#898: Bhalloo in Aljoumani/Bhalloo/Hirschler, *Catalogue of the New Corpus,* Appendix 1a.
#906: Bhalloo in Aljoumani/Bhalloo/Hirschler, *Catalogue of the New Corpus,* Appendix 1a.
#911: Bhalloo in Aljoumani/Bhalloo/Hirschler, *Catalogue of the New Corpus,* Appendix 1a.
#913: Bhalloo in Aljoumani/Bhalloo/Hirschler, *Catalogue of the New Corpus,* Appendix 1a.
#922: Aljoumani in Aljoumani/Bhalloo/Hirschler, *Catalogue of the New Corpus,* Appendix 1b.
#923: Aljoumani in Aljoumani/Bhalloo/Hirschler, *Catalogue of the New Corpus,* Appendix 1b.
#942: Bhalloo in Aljoumani/Bhalloo/Hirschler, *Catalogue of the New Corpus,* Appendix 1a.
#945: Aljoumani in Aljoumani/Bhalloo/Hirschler, *Catalogue of the New Corpus,* Appendix 1b.
#946: Aljoumani in Aljoumani/Bhalloo/Hirschler, *Catalogue of the New Corpus,* Appendix 1b.
#966: Aljoumani in Aljoumani/Bhalloo/Hirschler, *Catalogue of the New Corpus,* Appendix 1b.
#968: Aljoumani/Hirschler, *Owning Books and Preserving Documents,* Chapter 8.
#975: Bhalloo in Aljoumani/Bhalloo/Hirschler, *Catalogue of the New Corpus,* Appendix 1a.

Appendix 3a: List of the documents in order of catalogue entry number

Entries in bold are edited in Appendix 1.

(1) Decree, #884
(2) Decree, #973
(3) Report, 795/1393, #966
(4) Petition, before 789/1387, #897
(5) Plea, #908
(6) Petition, #964
(7) *Muṭālaʿa*, #943
(8) *Muṭālaʿa*, #946
(9) Sale contract, 800/1398, #974
(10) Sale contract, 776/1374, #922
(11) Petition, #967
(12) Rent contract, 737/1336, #923
(13) Rent receipt, 778/1376, #948
(14) Accounts, #890
(15) Accounts, #924
(16) Accounts, #940
(17) Accounts, #953
(18) Accounts, #957
(19) Accounts, 792/1389 to 793/1391, #979
(20) Accounts, 788/1386–7 and 789/1387–8, #971
(21) Accounts, #941
(22) Accounts, 1135/1723, #932
(23) Accounts book, 1232/1817 to 1233/1818, #926
(24) Accounts book, 1234/1818 to 1234/1819, #927
(25) Accounts, 1139/1726 to 1139/1727, #936
(26) Authorisation, #949
(27) Debt slip, #962
(28) Receipt of payments, 770/1368, #907
(29) Estate inventory *(wuqūf)*, 795/1393, #901
(30) Estate inventory *(wuqūf)*, 795/1393, #945
(31) Estate inventory *(wuqūf)*, 797/1395, #978
(32) Estate inventory *(wuqūf)*, #939
(33) Estate inventory, #897
(34) Sale of inheritance, #921
(35) List of receivables, 789/1387, #968

https://doi.org/10.1515/9783111330242-009

(36) *Farḍ*, #944
(37) Endowment *madrasa*, #931
(38) Endowment Ḥaramayn, #970
(39) Petition, #937
(40) Petition, #951
(41) Travel permit, #947
(42) Letter of introduction, #889
(43) Merchant's letter, #899
(44) Father's letter, #925
(45) Letter, #935
(46) Persian poetry, 1210/1795–96, #930
(47) *Qaṣīda*, #961
(48) Poetry, #940
(49) *Duʿā* prayer, #952
(50) *Duʿā* prayer, #956
(51) *Duʿā* prayer, #932
(52) Instructions to write prayers, #965
(53) Legal document, #933
(54) Legal document, 753/1352, #976
(55) Koran commentary, #954
(56) Sufi text, #939
(57) *Berat*, 1060/1650, #929
(58) *Berat*, before 1143/1730, #928
(59) *Berat*, before 1143/1730, #934
(60) Letter, 1332/1914, #887
(61) Letters, #972
(62) *Duʿā* prayer, 1237/1822, #903
(63) Archival list, before 731/1331, #891
(64) Purchase contract, 705/1305, #896
(65) Sale contract and judicial decision, 747/1347 and 748/1347, #909
(66) *Iqrār*, 705/1305, #916
(67) Transfer of *iqṭāʿ*, 711/1312, #911
(68) *Iqrār*, 692/1293, #910
(69) *Iqrār*, 705/1306, #914
(70) Marriage contract, 769/1367, #942/#898
(71) Ilkhanid decree, #913/#892
(72) Tax receipt, 681/1283, #918
(73) Loan agreement, 742/1341, #919
(74) *Ishhād*, 715/1315, #888
(75) Decree, 740/1339, #904

(76) Decree, 740/1339, #906
(77) Decree, 748/1347, #969
(78) Decree, 746/1346, #959
(79) Decree, 745/1345, #980
(80) Receipt, #955
(81) Sale contract, 715/1316, #900
(82) Sale contract, 723/1323, #975/#893
(83) Sale contract, #915
(84) Sale contract, 745/1344, #886
(85) Sale contract, #958
(86) Settlement contract, #960
(87) Lease contract, 746/1345, #905
(88) *Iqrār*, 700/1300–1301, #938
(89) Inventory of expenditure, #963
(90) Estate inventory, #977
(91) *Iqrār*, 721/1321–22, #894
(92) Witness clauses, #912
(93) *Iqrār (?)*, 716/1316, #895
(94) Legal document, #917
(95) Armenian legal document, #902
(96) Georgian/Armenian/Persian document, #885/#920
(97) *Du'ā* prayer, #917

Appendix 3b: List of the documents in order of Islamic Museum classmark

#884, Decree: (1)
#885 Georgian/Armenian/Persian document: (96)
#886 Sale contract, 745/1344: (84)
#887 Letter, 1332/1914: (60)
#888 *Ishhād,* 715/1315: (74)
#889 Letter of introduction: (42)
#890 Accounts: (14)
#891 Archival list, before 731/1331: (63)
#892 Ilkhanid decree: (71)
#893 Sale contract, 723/1323: (82)
#894 *Iqrār*, 721/1321–22: (91)
#895 *Iqrār (?),* 716/1316: (93)
#896 Purchase contract, 705/1305: (64)
#897 Estate inventory: (33)
#897 Petition, before 789/1387: (4)
#898 Marriage contract, 769/1367: (70)
#899 Merchant's letter: (43)
#900 Sale contract, 715/1316: (81)
#901 Estate inventory *(wuqūf),* 795/1393: (29)
#902 Armenian legal document: (95)
#903 *Duʿā* prayer, 1237/1822: (62)
#904 Decree, 740/1339: (75)
#905 Lease contract, 746/1345: (87)
#906 Decree, 740/1339: (76)
#907 Receipt of payments, 770/1368: (28)
#908 Plea: (5)
#909 Sale contract and judicial decision, 747/1347 and 748/1347: (65)
#910 *Iqrār,* 692/1293: (68)
#911 Transfer of *iqṭāʿ*, 711/1312: (67)
#912 Witness clauses: (92)
#913 Ilkhanid decree: (71)
#914 *Iqrār,* 705/1306: (69)
#915 Sale contract: (83)
#916 *Iqrār,* 705/1305: (66)
#917 *Duʿā* prayer: (97)
#917 Legal document: (94)

https://doi.org/10.1515/9783111330242-010

#918 Tax receipt, 681/1283: (72)
#919 Loan agreement, 742/1341: (73)
#920 Georgian/Armenian/Persian document: (96)
#921 Sale of inheritance: (34)
#922 Sale contract, 776/1374: (10)
#923 Rent contract, 737/1336: (12)
#924 Accounts: (15)
#925 Father's letter: (44)
#926 Accounts book, 1232/1817 to 1233/1818: (23)
#927 Accounts book, 1234/1818 to 1234/1819: (24)
#928 *Berat,* before 1143/1730: (58)
#929 *Berat,* 1060/1650: (57)
#930 Persian poetry, 1210/1795–6: (46)
#931 Endowment *madrasa:* (37)
#932 Accounts, 1135/1723: (22)
#932 *Duʿā* prayer: (51)
#933 Legal document: (53)
#934 *Berat,* before 1143/1730: (59)
#935 Letter: (45)
#936 Accounts, 1139/1726 to 1139/1727: (25)
#937 Petition: (39)
#938 *Iqrār*, 700/1300–1301: (88)
#939 Estate inventory *(wuqūf):* (32)
#939 Sufi text: (56)
#940 Accounts: (16)
#940 Poetry: (48)
#941 Accounts: (21)
#942 Marriage contract, 769/1367: (70)
#943 *Muṭālaʿa*: (7)
#944 *Farḍ*: (36)
#945 Estate inventory *(wuqūf),* 795/1393: (30)
#946 *Muṭālaʿa:* (8)
#947 Travel permit: (41)
#948 Rent receipt: 778/1376, (13)
#949 Authorisation: (26)
#951 Petition: (40)
#952 *Duʿā* prayer: (49)
#953 Accounts: (17)
#954 Koran commentary: (55)
#955 Receipt: (80)

#956 *Du'ā* prayer: (50)
#957 Accounts: (18)
#958 Sale contract: (85)
#959 Decree, 746/1346: (78)
#960 Settlement contract: (86)
#961 *Qaṣīda*: (47)
#962 Debt slip: (27)
#963 Inventory of expenditure: (89)
#964 Petition: (6)
#965 Instructions to write prayers: (52)
#966 Report, 795/1393: (3)
#967 Petition: (11)
#968 List of receivables, 789/1387: (35)
#969 Decree, 748/1347: (77)
#970 Endowment Ḥaramayn: (38)
#971 Accounts, 788/1386–7 and 789/1387–8: (20)
#972 Letters: (61)
#973 Decree: (2)
#974 Sale contract, 800/1398: (9)
#975 Sale contract, 723/1323: (82)
#976 Legal document, 753/1352: (54)
#977 Estate inventory: (90)
#978 Estate inventory *(wuqūf)*, 797/1395: (31)
#979 Accounts, 792/1389 to 793/1391: (19)
#980 Decree, 745/1345: (79)

Bibliography

Abdul-Rahman, Muhammad N.: An Arabic Marriage Contract and Subsequent Divorce from Mamluk Jerusalem: The Ḥaram al-Sharīf No. 302, *Mamlūk Studies Review* 22 (2019), 121–36.

ʿAbd al-Raḥmān, Muḥammad Naṣr: al-Taʿāmulāt al-qaḍāʾīya li-ahl al-dhimma fī al-Quds al-mamlūkīya fī ḍawʾ wathāʾiq al-Ḥaram al-qudsī, *Annales islamologiques* 50 (2016), 343–63.

ʿAbd al-Raḥmān, Muḥammad Naṣr/Ashraf Muḥammad Anas: ʿAqdā zawāj wa-lawāḥiqihā fī wathīqa ghayr manshūra min wathāʾiq al-Ḥaram al-qudsī al-sharīf, *Annales islamologiques* 53 (2020), 299–325.

Aljoumani, Said/Konrad Hirschler: *Owning Books and Preserving Documents in Medieval Jerusalem. The Library of Burhan al-Din al-Nasiri*, Edinburgh 2023.

Amin, Muhammad Muhammad: *Catalogue des documents d'archives du Caire, de 239/853 à 922/1516 (depuis le IIIe/IXe jusqu'à la fin de l'époque mamlouke)*, Cairo 1981.

Al-ʿAsalī, Kāmil: *Wathāʾiq maqdisīya tārīkhīya*, 3 vols., Amman 1983–89.

Al-Asyūṭī: *Jawāhir al-ʿuqūd wa-muʿīn al-quḍāh wa-l-muwaqqiʿīn wa-l-shuhūd*, M. ʿA. al-Saʿdanī (ed.), Beirut 1996.

Atıl, Esin: *Kalila wa Dimna: Fables from a Fourteenth-Century Arabic Manuscript*, Washington, D.C. 1981.

Atiya, Aziz S.: *The Arabic Manuscripts of Mount Sinai: A Hand-List of the Arabic Manuscripts and Scrolls Microfilmed at the Library of the Monastery of St. Catherine, Mount Sinai*, Baltimore 1955.

Barakat, Bashir: *Tārīkh al-qaḍāʾ wa-al-iftāʾ fī bayt al-Maqdis*, Riyadh 2015.

Bauden, Frédéric: Mamluk Era Documentary Studies: The State of the Art, *Mamlūk Studies Review* 9/1 (2005), 15–60.

Bhalloo, Zahir: A Pre-Mongol New Persian Legal Document from Islamic Khurāsān dated 608 A.H./1212 C.E., *Bulletin of SOAS*, (in press 2023).

Bhalloo, Zahir and Ryoko Watabe: A Fourteenth-Century Persian Archival List from al-Ḥaram al-Sharīf in Jerusalem (in preparation for submission to *Der Islam*).

Bhalloo, Zahir and Yoichi Yajima: Two Anatolian Tax Receipts from al-Ḥaram al-Sharīf in Jerusalem dated 658/1259 and 681/1283 (in preparation for submission to *Annales islamologiques*).

Biran, Michal: Jovaynī, Ṣāḥeb Dīvān, *Encyclopaedia Iranica* vol.XV, Fasc.1, 71–74.

Burgoyne, Michael H.: A Chronological Index to the Muslim Monuments of Jerusalem, in: *The Architecture of Islamic Jerusalem: An Exhibition Prepared on Occasion of the World of Islam Festival, London, 1976*, Jerusalem 1976, no pagination.

Burgoyne, Michael H./Amal Abul-Hajj: Twenty-four Mediaeval Arabic Inscriptions from Jerusalem, *Levant* 11/1 (1979), 112–37.

Clark, Kenneth W.: *A Checklist of Manuscripts in St. Catherine's Monastery, Mount Sinai*, Washington, D.C. 1952.

Conrad, Lawrence I.: The Khalidi Library, in: Sylvia Auld/Robert Hillenbrand (eds), *Ottoman Jerusalem: The Living City: 1517–1917*, London 2000, 191–209.

Diem, Werner: Philologisches zu Mamlūkischen Erlassen, Eingaben und Dienstschreiben des Jerusalemer al-Ḥaram aš-Šarīf, *Zeitschrift für arabische Linguistik* 33 (1997), 7–67.

Dozy, Reinhart Pieter Anne: *Supplément aux dictionnaires Arabes*, Leiden 1881.

El Shamsy, Ahmed: *Rediscovering the Islamic Classics. How Editors and Print Culture Transformed an Intellectual Tradition*, Princeton 2020.

Ernst, Hans: *Die mamlukischen Sultansurkunden des Sinai-Klosters*, Wiesbaden 1960.

Frenkel, Yehoshua: *The Relationship Between Mamluk Officials and the Urban Civilian Population. A Study of Some Legal Documents from Jerusalem* in: Johannes Pahlitzsch/Lorenz Korn (eds), *Governing the Holy City*, Wiesbaden 2004, 91–108.

https://doi.org/10.1515/9783111330242-011

Ghawānma, Yusūf Darwīsh: *Tārīkh niyābat Bayt al-Maqdis fī al-ʿaṣr al-mamlūkī*, Amman 1982.
Gotein, Shelomo D.: *A Mediterranean Society: The Jewish Communities of the Arab World as Portrayed in the Documents of the Cairo Geniza*, 6 vols., Berkeley 1967–93.
Gronke, Monika: *Arabische und persische Privaturkunden des 12. und 13. Jahrhunderts aus Ardabil (Aserbeidschan)*, Berlin 1982.
Gronke, Monika: *Derwische im Vorhof der Macht: Sozial und Wirtschaftsgeschichte Nordwestirans im 13. und 14. Jahrhundert 1993*, Stuttgart 1993.
Haarmann, Ulrich: The Library of a Fourteenth Century Jerusalem Scholar, *Der Islam* 61 (1984), 327–33.
Hagedorn, Jan: *Domestic Slavery in Syria and Egypt, 1200–1500*, Göttingen 2020.
Herrmann, Gottfried: *Persische Urkunden der Mongolenzeit*, Wiesbaden 2004.
Hirschler, Konrad: From Archive to Archival Practices: Rethinking the Preservation of Mamluk Administrative Documents, *Journal of the American Oriental Society* 136/1 (2016), 1–28.
Hirschler, Konrad: *A Monument to Medieval Syrian Book Culture: The Library of Ibn ʿAbd al-Hādī*, Edinburgh 2020.
Hirschler, Konrad: A (Mostly) Local Story: The Translocations of al-Jazzār's Manuscripts in the Nineteenth and Twentieth Centuries, in: S. Aljoumani/G. Burak/K. Hirschler/D. Sajdi (eds), *Al-Jazzar's Library. Book Culture in Ottoman Syria* (for publication in 2024).
Hope, Michael: The Political Configuration of Late Ilkhanid Iran: A Case Study of the Chubanid Amirate (738–758/1337–1357), *Iran* (2021), DOI: 10.1080/05786967.2021.1889930.
Ibn Ḥabīb: *Tadhkirat al-nabīh fī ayyām Manṣūr wa-banīh*, 2 vols., Cairo 1976–82.
Al-Jarawānī, Muḥammad: *al-Kawkab al-mushriq fī mā yaḥtāj ilayhi al-muwaththiq*, Jeddah 2015.
Jefferson, Rebecca: *The Cairo Genizah and the Age of Discovery in Egypt. The History and Provenance of a Jewish Archive*, London 2022.
Kessler, Christel: *The carved masonry domes of mediaeval Cairo*, Cairo 1976.
Khālidī, Walīd: *al-Maktaba al-Khālidīya fī al-Quds: 1720–2001*, Beirut 2002.
Liebrenz, Boris: An Archive in a Book: Documents and Letters from the Early-Mamluk Period, *Der Islam* 97/1 (2020), 120–71.
Little, Donald: The Significance of the Ḥaram Documents for the Study of Medieval Islamic History, *Der Islam* 57/2 (1980), 189–219.
Little, Donald: Six Fourteenth-Century Purchase Deeds for Slaves from al-Ḥaram aš-Šarīf, *Zeitschrift der Deutschen Morgenländischen Gesellschaft* 131 (1981), 297–337.
Little, Donald: Two Fourteenth-Century Court Records from Jerusalem Concerning the Disposition of Slaves by Minors, *Arabica* 29 (1982), 16–49.
Little, Donald: *A Catalogue of the Islamic Documents from al-Ḥaram aš-Šarîf in Jerusalem*, Beirut/ Wiesbaden 1984.
Little, Donald: Ḥaram Documents Related to the Jews of Late Fourteenth Century Jerusalem, *Journal of Semitic Studies* 30/2 (1985), 227–64.
Little, Donald: Five Petitions and Consequential Decrees from Late Fourteenth-Century Jerusalem, *Al-Majalla al-ʿArabīya lil-ʿUlūm al-Insānīya* 14/54 (1996), 348–94.
Little, Donald: The Use of Documents for the Study of Mamluk History, *Mamlūk Studies Review* 1 (1997), 1–13.
Little, Donald: Documents Related to the Estates of a Merchant and His Wife in Late Fourteenth Century Jerusalem, *Mamlūk Studies Review* 2 (1998), 93–192.
Little, Donald: Two Petitions and Consequential Court Records from the Ḥaram Collection, *Jerusalem Studies in Arabic and Islam* 25 (2001), 171–94.

Little, Donald: A Fourteenth-Century Jerusalem Court Record of a Divorce Hearing. A Case Study, in: Little, Donald/Üner Turgay: Documents from the Ottoman Period in the Khālidī Library in Jerusalem, *Die Welt des Islams* 20/1 (1980), 44–72.

Lutfi, Huda: A Study of Six Fourteenth Century Iqrārs from al-Quds Relating to Muslim Women, *Journal of the Economic and Social History of the Orient* 26 (1983), 246–94.

Lutfi, Huda: *Al-Quds al-Mamlûkiyya: A History of Mamlûk Jerusalem Based on the Ḥaram Documents*, Berlin 1985.

Lutfi, Huda: A Documentary Source for the Study of Material Life: A Specimen of the Ḥaram Estate Inventories from al-Quds in 1393 A.D., *Zeitschrift der Deutschen Morgenländischen Gesellschaft* 135 (1985), 213–26.

Lutfi, Huda/Donald P. Little: "Iqrārs from Al-Quds": Emendations, *Journal of the Economic and Social History of the Orient*, 28/3 (1985), 326–30.

Maḥāmīd, Ḥātim Muḥammad: *Dirāsāt fī tārīkh al-Quds al-thaqāfī fī al-ʿaṣr al-wasīṭ*, Amman: Dār Ward al-Urdunnīya, 2009.

Massoud, Sami: *Studies in Islamic Historiography. Essays in Honour of Professor Donald P. Little*, Leiden 2020.

Muḥammad, Mīrzā Khwāja and Nabī Sāqī (eds.): *Barg-hā-yī az yak faṣl ya asnād-I tārīkhī-yi ghūr*, Kābul: Intishārāt-i Saʿīd, 1388 sh./2010.

Muḥammad, Umar Jamāl: Marsūm al-Sulṭān al-Ashraf Īnāl al-khāṣṣ bi-ḍabṭ al-bayʿ wa-al-taqbīn fī dār al-wakāla wa-sūq al-bāshūra bi-al-Quds al-sharīf, *al-Rūznāma* (Cairo) 14 (2016 [published 2019]), 154–82.

Muḥammad, Umar Jamāl: Idārat amwāl awqāf al-Ḥaram al-nabawī al-sharīf fī Bilād al-Shām ʿaṣr salāṭīn al-Mamālīk, *Waqāʾiʿ tārīkhīya* 33/1 (2020), 243–322.

Muḥammad, Umar Jamāl: Ijrāʾāt jard al-mawārīth al-ḥashrīya wa-bayʿihā fī al-Quds ʿaṣr salāṭīn al-mamālīk, tarikat Yaḥyā al-ʿAjamī shaykh zāwiyat Muḥammad Bāk namūdhajan, *Majallat al-dirāsāt al-tārīkhīya wa-al-ḥaḍārīya al-mīsrīya* 21/1 (2021), 67–134.

Müller, Christian: Constats d'héritages dans la Jérusalem mamelouke: les témoins du cadi dans un document inédit du Ḥaram al-Šarīf, *Annales Islamologiques* 35 (2001), 291–319.

Müller, Christian: Écrire pour établir la preuve orale en Islam. La pratique d'un tribunal à Jérusalem au xive siècle, in: Akira Saito/Yusuke Nakamura (eds), *Les outils de la pensée: Étude historique et comparative des «textes»*, Paris 2010, 63–97.

Müller, Christian: The Ḥaram al-Šarīf Collection of Arabic Legal Documents in Jerusalem: A Mamlūk Court Archive?, *al-Qanṭara* 32/2 (2011), 435–59.

Müller, Christian: *Der Kadi und seine Zeugen. Studie der mamlukischen Ḥaram-Dokumente aus Jerusalem*, Wiesbaden 2013.

Müller, Christian: Crimes without Criminals? Legal Documents on Fourteenth-Century Injury and Homicide Cases from the Ḥaram Collection in Jerusalem, in: Maaike van Berkel/Léon Buskens/ Petra Sijpesteijn (eds), *Legal Documents as Sources for the History of Muslim Societies: Studies in Honour of Rudolph Peters*, Leiden 2017, 129–79.

Müller, Christian: Document JerH_333 on endowed villages (Mamlūk Ḥaram editions 1), *The Documents of Islamic Law. Studies on Arabic Legal Documents*, published 16/05/2021, https://dilih.hypotheses.org/664.

Northrup, Linda S.: *From Slave to Sultan: The Career of al-Manṣūr Qalāwūn and the Consolidation of Mamluk Rule in Egypt and Syria (678–689 A.H./1279–1290 A.D.)*, Stuttgart 1998.

Northrup, Linda S.: Qalawun's Patronage of the Medical Sciences in Thirteenth Century Egypt, *Mamlūk Studies Review* 5 (2001), 119–40.

Northrup, Linda S.: Documents as Literary Texts: Mamluk Historiography Revisited, in: Stephan Conermann (ed), *Mamluk Historiography Revisited – Narratological Perspectives*, Bonn 2018, 121–36.

Northrup, Linda S./Amal Abul-Hajj: A Collection of Medieval Arabic Documents in the Islamic Museum at the Haram al-Šarīf, *Arabica* 25 (1978), 282–91.

Al-Nuwayrī, Aḥmad: *Nihāyat al-ʿarab fī funūn al-adab*, Cairo 1923–97.

Onimus, Clément: *Les maîtres du jeu: Pouvoir et violence politique à l'aube du sultanat mamlouk circassien (784–815/1382–1412)*, Paris 2019.

Posegay, Nick: Searching for the Last Genizah Fragment in Late Ottoman Cairo: A Material Survey of Egyptian Jewish Literary Culture, *International Journal of Middle East Studies* 54/3 (2022), 1–19.

Paul, Jürgen: Archival Practices in the Muslim World prior to 1500, in: Alessandro Bausi (ed), *Manuscripts, Archives, Comparative Views on Record-Keeping*, Berlin 2018, 339–60.

Pringle, Denys: Michael Hamilton Burgoyne 1944–2021, *Levant* 54/1 (2022), 1–4.

Publications of Donald P. Little, *Mamluk Studies Review* 9/1 (2005), 1–14.

Al-Qalqashandī: *Ṣubḥ al-aʿshā fī ṣināʿat al-inshāʾ*, Beirut: Dār al-kutub al-ʿilmīya ^{2}2012.

Rajabzadeh, Hashem: Jovayni Family, *Encyclopaedia Iranica* vol. XV, Fasc. 1, 61–63.

Reinfandt, Lucian: Mamluk Documentary Studies, in: Stephan Conermann (ed), *Ubi sumus? Quo vademus?: Mamluk Studies – State of the Art*, Bonn 2013, 285–310.

Richards, Donald: The Mamlūk *Barīd*. Some Evidence from the Haram Documents, in: Adnan Hadidi (ed), *Studies in the History and Archeology of Jordan III (3. International Conference on the History and Archeology of Jordan, Universität Tübingen 1987)*, Amman/London 1987, 205–9.

Richards, Donald: A Mamlūk emir's 'square' decree, *Bulletin of the School of Oriental and African Studies* 54/1 (1991), 63–7.

Richards, Donald: The Qasāma in Mamlūk Society: Some Documents from the Ḥaram Collection in Jerusalem, *Annales Islamologiques* 25 (1991), 245–84.

Richards, Donald: Primary Education under the Mamlūks: Two Documents from the Ḥaram in Jerusalem, *The Arabist: Budapest Studies in Arabic* 24–25 (2002), 223–32.

Richards, Donald: Glimpses of Provincial Mamluk Society from the Documents of the Haram al-Sharif in Jerusalem, in: Amalia Levanoni/Michael Winter (eds), *The Mamluks in Egyptian and Syrian Politics and Society*, Leiden 2004, 45–57.

Risciani, Norberto: *Documenti e Firmani*, Jerusalem, 1931.

Salameh, Khader: Primary Sources on Social Life in Jerusalem in the Middle Ages, in: Pahlitzsch, Johannes/Lorenz Korn (eds), *Governing the Holy City*, Wiesbaden 2004, 1–11.

Salameh, Khader: The Renovations of Sultan Mahmud II (r. 1808–1839) in Jerusalem, in: Eyal Ginio/Elie Podeh (eds), *The Ottoman Middle East*, Leiden 2014, 25–44.

Ṣāliḥīya, Muḥammad ʿĪsā: Min wathāʾiq al-Ḥaram al-qudsī al-sharīf al-mamlūkīya, *Ḥawliyāt kullīyat al-ādāb* 6 (1985/1406), 3–126.

Stern, Samuel M.: *Fatimid Degrees: Original Documents from the Fatimid Chancery*, London 1964.

Al-ʿUlaymī, Mujīr al-Dīn: *al-Uns al-jalīl bi-l-tārīkh al-Quds wa-l-Khalīl*, ʿAdnān Nubāta (ed.), Amman: Maktabat Dandīs 1999.

Al-ʿUmarī, Ibn Faḍlallāh: *Al-Taʿrīf bi-muṣtalaḥ al-sh*arīf, Beirut 1988.

Yokkaichi, Yasuhiro: On the Qara Tamgha (Black Seal) of the Ilkhanate: Its Meaning, Image, and Semiosis, (unpublished paper in Japanese), https://www.chuo-u.ac.jp/uploads/2018/11/5824_symposium01_14.pdf Accessed 1 May 2023.

Walls, Archibald G./Amal Abul-Hajj: *Arabic Inscriptions in Jerusalem: A Handlist and Maps*, London 1980.

Wasserstein, David/Ami Ayalon (eds): *Mamluks and Ottomans. Studies in honour of Michael Winter*, London 2006, 67–85.

Index of persons (Arabic script)

اباداد 116
إبراهيم آغا 63–4
إبراهيم بلبيسي 63
إبراهيم بن حسن 61
إبراهيم بن ميكائيل 75
ابراهيم بن يوسف [. . .] 145
إبراهيم الحمال 67
إبراهيم الداوودي 64
إبراهيم دورار 63
إبراهيم [الزوجني؟] 138
إبراهيم قسطندي 63
إبراهيم المغربي 63
إبراهيم الناصري 74
ابراهيم ولى بن يوسف 135, 167
ابن الجماعين 54
ابن الجوسكا 54
ابن حجرين 54
ابن الزركشية 87
ابن سليم 57
ابن شرف الدين 57
ابن الشماعة 54
ابن العربي 98
ابن الفارس 87
ابن قاسم 91
ابن الموكاني 87
ابن النوري 56
ابن يونس 76
أبو إسحاق 57
أبو بكر بن محمد [. . .] 122
أبو بكر بن معد 138
أبو بكر الخليلي 148
أبو بكر العرادي 57
أبو حنيفة 98
أبو رشاه بن أحمد 148
أبو سعود 63
أبو سعيد بهادر خان 119, 161
أبو سعيد المرواني 109–10
أبو الفرج مدبر الممالك الإسلامية 38, 171
أبو المرجا بن علي بن أبو المرجا 148
اتا بک بن [مسامر؟] 109
أحمد إسماعيل 63
أحمد الثالث 101
أحمد حمو 63
أحمد المصري 63
أحمد المصري زوج مريم 58
أحمد بن [الربعي؟] 72
أحمد بن رسول القيصري 123
أحمد [بن عبد الله؟] بن سعد 36
أحمد بن عبد الله بن محمد 35
أحمد بن كرد أمير 141
أحمد بن ميكائيل النخجواني 118, 158
أحمد سمقة 63
أحمد عسلي 64
أخى صلاح الدين صالح ابن مرحوم عز الدين يوسف 135, 167
آدوجى آقا 111, 113
[ارمنج بن كوانى؟] 116
[اروچ؟] بن چريكتمور 141
إسحاق ابن عثمان 61
إسحاق بن يوسف 138
إسحاق الجلودي 54
إسحق ابن صالح اللطيفي 101
[اسعملش؟] 116
اسلان بن [گران؟] أمير 135, 167
اسماعيل ابن ملك شاه 135, 167
اسماعيل أحمد [. . .] 115
إسماعيل أفندي 64
إسماعيل بن حجي بن إبراهيم 51, 179
إسماعيل بن خليل 77
اسماعيل بن محمد 111
إسماعيل شراباتي 64
[اغلجه؟] بن [قرعاجى؟] 147
الاكواز 111
آل عثمان 66
إلياس بن عمر 138
إلياس التلحمي 63–4
إلياس السلقيني 64
إلياس صحناوي 63
إلياس الفتال 64
إلياس قلفا 64
أمجد بن يوسف القيصري 124
أمير آدوجى بن يازلي 108, 116
أمير أحمد 132
أمير أحمد بن علي 124
أمير أحمد ميرباشى قيصرىه 125
أمير [برات؟] بن الأمير المغفور تمور بغا 110, 136
أمير [بكوداد؟] 108
أمير التنا بک 140
أمير خواجة علي بن الأمير أبي بكر 117–8, 157

https://doi.org/10.1515/9783111330242-012

أمير شاه بن حسن 110
أمير شاه [تماس؟] 115
أمير شيخي بن الأمير المغفور [. . .] 117, 157
أمير كرد 110
أندوني أبو شقرة 64
انطانيوس توما 63
أنطون تلحمي 64
[أورد؟] شاه بن [فخامي؟] 141
[اوروچ؟] 111
الاوسطة يوسف 63
[بادكر؟] بن أمير ألله خواجه 116
البانياسي 54
بدر الدين بن عمر خواجه 118, 158
بدر الدين بن نور [الدين . . .] 83
بدر العجلوني 54
[بدو أحسنجى؟] 116
برهان الدين إبراهيم العراقي 44
بشارة بن عبد الله 70
بشير العكاري 63
بطرس لطفي 63
البعلبكي 50, 57
بكتاش بن شادي الالباوت 158
بكتاش بن غازي الألباوت 118
بكتاش بن محمد بن أحمد 138
[بكليک؟] بن محم الثابت 133
بلال بن عمر بن أبي القاسم 45
[بلياق؟] 115
البليغي الأمجدي الحاكمي 37
بني فارس 90
[بوعاچى؟] 111
[بولاد؟] بن محمد حسين 145
پير محمد جماقلو 116
تاتر بک بن اسماعيل 141
تاج الدين شيخون السايس 45
تاج النساء بنت الخطيب 138
تغلق بن چريكتيمور 141
التقوي الصالحي 82
تقي الدين أبو بكر بن المرحوم الجناب العالي الشمسي شمس الدين محمد بن إبراهيم الظاهري 72
تمور بن [. . .] طغا جار 108
توبكشاه بن علي 141
[توبي] بن حسن 114
تيمور بوغا 138
الجارية سعيد[ة . . .] 72
جرجس بن سمعان 64
جرجس منسا الكاتب 63–4
جرجس نصر 63
جرجس نظيلي 64
جرجس يناكي أسطفاني 64
[جعفر؟] بن اروج بک 142
[جعفر؟] حسن بن [. . .] 142
چريك 111
الجلودي 54
الجمال 54
جمال الدين محمد بن أحمد بن عبد القادر 138
جمال [؟] الملک 113
الجناب العالي العلائي متولي القدس الشريف 36
چنكيز مؤيد 142
چوبان محمد الأمير [. . .] 124
الحاج إبراهيم أدرو 85
الحاج إبراهيم المصري 63
الحاج أحمد بن إبراهيم بن محمد الحمصي القطان 47, 175
الحاج أحمد الشخمي 85
الحاج أحمد المتوكلي 85
الحاج حسن 85
الحاج خليل 40
الحاج سعيد 63–4
الحاج عمر 63
الحاج عمر بن محمد بن عمر [الخضري/الحصري؟] العلاف 46–8, 175
الحاج محمد الزغبي 63
الحاج محمد قيشانجي 64
الحاج محمود الشخمي 85
الحاج يوسف الورّاق 54
حاجي أحمد بن شاه [. . .] 109
حاجي الخازن بن بواروق 118
حاجي الخازن بولدوق 158
حاجي بک بن موسى [. . .] 142
حاجي بن خواجه محمود [كدوا؟] 146
حاجي عبد الله 138
حاجي عزيز 109
حاجي علي معروف چوپان 125
حاجي مطرب 108
حاجي يعقوب بن يوسف 117–8, 157
[حاروق؟] 116
حبش بن [توكاى؟] 109
حسان عبد الكريم آغا 64
حسن ابن الزغلي 54
حسن ابن علي المصري 54
حسن البقاعي 45
حسن بن علي المغربي 54
حسن بن محمد بن حاجي فقيه 148
حسن بن يوسف ابن حسام الدين [الحافظ جده؟] 138
حسن الرومي 68

حسن سعسع معلم الطواحين 63
حسن نجار 64
الحسين بن الحسن الخطيب 124
حسين بن حسن المؤذن بجامع بيلقان 146
حسين بن نوشيران 146
حسين رزاري 63
حسين سقلاوي 4–63
حسين طحان 63
حسين طنطش 64
حسين الفضلي 63
حسينك أمير [. . .] 116
حمد بن [شباب؟] 142
حمدان الحمد 63
حمدان حميدان 64
حنا ناصر 64
حيدر بن [. . .] شاه 141
حيدر بن حاجي [التا؟] 142
خاصكى سلطان 101
خديجة بنت برهان الدين إبراهيم الناصري 74
خرّم خاتون بنت الحاج [. . .] 138
خرَّمشاه خاتون بنت الأمير كرد 118
خضر بن [البوسجى؟] 141
خضر التركماني 38
الخطَّابي 54
خليل بن بو بكر 144
خليل بن حسن الصواف 72
خليل بن مكي 54
خليل بن يوسف بن حسن 97
خليل درعطاني 63
خليل شاهين أفندي 64
خليل غندور 63
خليل قلفا 63
خليل الياسوري [الياصوري] 54
خواجه باروجى 147
خواجه بن اسماعيل 141
خواجه بن اغل 141
خواجه حسن بن حاجب 144
خواجا شمس الدين لمشا 69
خواجه صالح ابن عز الدين [اردساى؟] 108
خواجه عزيز [مخلده؟] 110
خواجة عمر البزاز 138
خواجه محمد بن عز الدين بن [. . .] 108
خواجه موسى 116
خواجه موسى بن ابراهيم 167
خواجه مير جمله تمربغا 135
دانشمند بن الياس 144
داود بن ميكائيل 109
درويش بن شير بيك 115
درويش بن طغاى 147
الدرويش حسين 63
دولات بنت عبد الله 69
[ديلنجى؟] بن محمد 141
رجب بن حسن 115
ريحان 54
زكريا بن محمد جوينى 113, 153
زين الدين بن الحاجب 36
زين الدين عبد الرحمن 72
زين الدين عبد الرحمن بن محمد بن أحمد بن محمد التوريزي 69
سابق الدين بن أبي بكر بن أمير الحسن الحنبلي 124
سالم بن محمد بن محرز 51, 179
ستاي بن [واحوق؟] 115
سعد الدين بن محمد [. . .] 154
سعيد آغا 65
السكاوي 54
سلمان جحا 54
سليمان أبو زرفة 64
[سمهر؟] بن على 109
سهل بن عبد الله التستري 99
[سوجنک؟] بن كرد أمير 141
السيد رحيم 64
سيف الدين أمير ابن المرحوم شيخ ارسلان بن جمال بن قتلغبک 136
سيف الدين جقمق الدوادار 38
سيف الدين خضر بن محمد بن أحمد 138
شادى بن [جادل؟] 141
شادى بن [زكه نبى؟] 135
شاهين 63
شبل بن خلف بن سبع 51, 179
شجاع الدين رمضان 4–123
شرف خاتون 69
شرف الدين ابن غانم 42
شرف علي 54
شمس الدين زكريا 154
شمس الدين العجمي 69
شمس [الدين؟] محمد أبي الفضل [السينجاني؟] 108
شمس الدين محمد بن أحمد بن غانم المقدسي 51, 179
شمس الدين محمد بن حسن [. . .] 138
شمس الدين محمد بن شهاب الدين أحمد بن شمس الدين محمد التوريزي 69
شمس الدين محمد بن نجود بن قاسم الأصبهاني 70
شمس الدين محمد شاه 111
شهاب الدين أحمد 71, 182
شهاب الدين بن حامـ[ـد] 83

شهاب الدين الحنفي 40
شهاب الدين صبحي 72
شهاب الدين كهمان 75
الشهابي 42
الشيخ إسماعيل 75
شيخ زنكى 7–134–5, 166
شيخ عادي 110
الشيخ فضل الله 70
شيخ قاران 7–134–5, 166
شيخ بابا بن [مه كان؟] 167
صالح أفندي معمار 63
صالح خليفة 63
صالح النامي 63
صدر الدين بن محمود بن [. . .] 148
صدر الدين علي 40
صدقة 54
صلاح الدين خليل بن الشيخ جمال الدين يوسف 70
الصّيداوي 54
الصيرفي 54
[طابا؟] 111
الطرابي 54
عبد الحميد أسطة 64
عبد الرحمن بن محمد [. . .] 8–46, 175
عبد الرحمن بن محمد [الحبراني؟] 77
عبد الرحمن [الظاهري؟] 42
عبد السلام تركية 64
عبد الصمد 64
عبد الكريم آغا 63
عبد الله باشا 63
عبد الله بن خضر الحنفي 97
عبد الله بن سليمان 145
عبد الله بن عيسى 125
عبد أللە بن محمد شاه 109
عبد الله بن محمد المصري 70
عبد الله بن يحيى 36
عبد الله الجرداني 66
عبد الله السمان 63
عبد الله القانوع 63
عثمان آغا متسلم الرملة 4–63
عثمان بن حسن 111
عثمان بن علي بن إبراهيم العجمي 54
عثمان الشافعي 122
عز الدولة أمير يوسف بن ناصر الدولة نصر الله 4–123
عكاشة بن [بيرم؟] 122
علاء الدين ألطنبغا البريدي 38, 171
علاء الدين بن كمال الدين 42
علاء الدين تاج [. . .] القصارى 109
علاء الدين دوادار 38
علاء الدين [الطبري؟] 139
علاء الدين علي التوريزي 70–69
علي باشاه ابن نساب 142
علي بن إبراهيم البقاعي 45
علي بن إسماعيل بن شاكر 8–46, 175
علي بن [بدير؟] 54
علي بن حسن 70
علي بن عثمان 111
علي بن عليم 63
علي بن كاتب 125
علي بن محمد البخاري 135, 166
علي بن محمد الحجازي 45
علي بن مصطفى 147
علي شاه بن أبو بكر 146
علي الفضلي 4–63
علي محسن السقلاوي 64
علي المليجة 63
علي مير [. . .] 116
عماد الدولة و الدين أبي الفرج بن داود بن يعقوب 4–123
عماد الدين عارف ابن المرحوم قتلغا [. . .] 136
عمر الآدمي 68
عمر بن أبو فارس 61
عمر العجمي 45
عوض حمد [. . .] بن [أمير؟] أحمد 124
عيسى تلحمي 64
عيسى شيخ الخانقاه الصلاحية 6–35
عيسى عبده 64
عيسى الياسوري [الياصوري] 54
عين الدين [. . .] بن حسين بن أحمد 148
غازان بن شادي الألباوت 118, 158
غازى بن سليمان قتلغبغا ابن عمر 135, 167
غرس الدين خليل [الحكمي؟] 39
غريب سعده 108
[فاجورا؟] 111
فاطمة زوجة برهان الدين إبراهيم الناصري 74
الفتياني 64
فراج ابن إسماعيل 61
القاضي أحمد 122
قتلغ [. . .] بن أمين الدين 141
قتلغ بوغا 116
قتلغبغا ابن عمر 167
قتلغبك 111
قتلغبک بن [اكو؟] 141
قتلغبك بن عيسى 125
[قره؟] بن [كوكداس؟] 109
القساطلي 63

قطلو بنت عبد الله 71, 182
القلفا بوغوز 63
القلفة بوجوس 63
قمر بنت محمد 72
[قمري؟] 115
[قويدان؟] 126
كاتب أحمد بن يوسف 124
گرجى بک بن كرد أمير 141
كرداباجي 116
كريم الدين حاجي بك بن كمال [. . .] 138
كمال ابن برهان الدين إبراهيم الناصري 74
كمال الدلّال 54
كمال الدين بن توبک 136
كمال الدين يوسف بن قتلوبک 121
كمبا يونس بن أمير شير بن گرجى 125
]كوجنكى؟] 116
لاجن [شيوسوجى؟] 115
ماجد بن خضر 97
[متكلي؟] بن عبد الله الثابت 133
مجد الدين [مخلس؟] 116
محمد آغا 4–63
محمد آغا باش جاويش 63
محمد آغا جاويش 63
محمد الاسكندري النساج 72
محمد أفندي 64
محمد بكر بن النجک 142
محمد بن إبراهيم [البرنيسي؟] 138
محمد بن إبراهيم بن محمد 138
محمد بن إبراهيم (الرابع) 100
محمد بن أبي بكر الشافعي 97
محمد بن أحمد [. . .] 52
محمد بن أحمد بن حسن الرملي الصبان 72
محمد بن أحمد الشافعي 97
محمد بن بوبكر 111
محمد بن حاجي محمود بن إبراهيم 148
محمد بن الحريري 52, 179
محمد بن حسن بن ياسين العجمي 47, 175
محمد بن حسين العلوى 135, 167
محمد بن حمزه صفّار بيلقاني 146
محمد بن خطّاب 146
محمد بن [زروف؟] 94
محمد بن سعيد 73
محمد بن عبد الرحيم الحسيني ابن أبي اللطف 81
محمد بن عبد العزيز الحجاجي 97
محمد بن عبد الفتاح 103
محمد بن علي [بري؟] 146
محمد بن محمد [البخاري؟] [. . .] 108
محمد بن محمد بن يحيى 54
محمد بن ناصر 58
محمد جاويش 64
محمد جمال بن محمود أبوالقاسم 146
محمد الحلاق 64
محمد الحلبي الصبان 72
محمد الدماميني 44, 173
محمد الرطوني 73
محمد الطويل 61
محمد العجمي 49
محمد المهدي 69
محمد شاه [. . .] 111
محمد شاه بن خليل [. . .] 108
محمد غلام خليل 58
محمد قاسم 64
محمد قدسي الرهاوي النقشبندي 89
محمد كامل الحسيني 103
محمد كردي 63
محمد يوسف 63
محمود أحمد 108
محمود بن حسن بن بوبكر بيلقاني 146
محمود بن خلف بن محمود [السعيدي؟] 52, 179
محمود بن خليل بن محمود 97
محمود بن محمد شاه السمرقندى 133
محمود بن محمود بن أحمد بن محمود [الخالداري؟] 146
محمود مؤذن 135, 167
المرداوي 54
مرزوق باورقة 63
[مرهم؟] حاجي إلياس 146
مسيحي بن جواد علي 118, 158
المصري الأعمش 57
مصطفى بن إسحق [البرنيسي؟] 138
مصطفى بن محمد بن أحمد 138
مصطفى السمان 4–63
مصطفى شعبان 63
مصطفى علي أفندي 63
مصطفى قسطلاوي 63
المعلم جرجس 63
المعلم سمعان 63
مقيم بن شاه 127
ملكشاه بن [سوبدک؟] 141
المملوك زين الدين 40
منصور بن نصار 61
موسى بن [. . .] 148
موسى بن إبراهيم 135
موسى السقا 138
موسى النحاس 72

موسى قندلفت 63
المولا باعلي فقيه ابن حاجي فقيه بن حسين فقيه 148
مولا تمور بن [بويكساى؟] حاجي بن [سووبدک؟] 141
مولانا شافعي بن محمد شاه النخجواني 146
مولانا الشيخ يوسف بن الشيخ رضي الدين 100
مؤيد ابن أمير ارسلان جمال بن قتلغبک 136
ميخائيل 64
ميخائل حجار 63
ميخائيل داراني 63
مير حسن بن أحمد 111
مير شاه بن علي 124
ناصر بن سالم الحنفي 70, 72, 97
ناصر الدين الحموي 53
نجم الدين أبو بكر نواده كمال بيلقاني 146
نصرت زوجة عثمان 138
نصرة [الدين؟] أمير چوپان 108
نظام بن چوپان قيصرى المعررف بشجاع 125
نعمة بن بشارة النصراني 48, 49, 175, 176
نقولا روماني 63
نكودنى 134–5, 166
نمير من العيساوية 58
نور الدولة سوريك بن صفي الدولة بن أبي الغنائم 123–4
نور شاه بن [قارباعدي؟] 133
هبة الله بن حميد بن سراج الحسيني 97
هبة الله بن محمود بن محمد الخوارزمي 138
هندو 116
هومان بن كمباى 124
واكيم 63
ولد سعد الدين جلبي 139
ولي الدين بن أمير بک 141
يحيى بن أشرف 138
يعقوب بن غازي التركماني 54
يعقوب نسيبة 64
يوسف ابن أبو طعمة 63
يوسف بن حسن بن إبراهيم 97
يوسف بن محمد 147
يوسف بن نصر الله 124
يوسف دحلان 63
يوسف شطها 63
يوسف مرداور 64
يوسف الوعري 63
يونس بن أبي الفتح المنصوري 124
بيرمز يدى 111

Index of persons (Latin script)

ʿAbd Allāh al-Jurdānī 66
Abū al-Faraj 38
ʿAbd al-Karīm al-Qushayrī 73
ʿAbd al-Raḥmān 42–3, 188–9
ʿAbd al-Razzāq 80
Abū Saʿīd al-Marwānī 109
Abū Saʿīd Bahādur Khān 29, 119–20
Abul-Hajj (Hull), Amal A. IX, 1–2, 4, 6–8, 12–3, 16–17, 20, 24
Abul-Hajj, Wasilah 6
Abul-Hajj, Ali 6
ʿĀdī b. Amīr Kurd (b. Amīr Ādūjī?) 110
Ādūjī family 22, 25–6, 28–9
Aḥmad b. Ibrāhīm al-Ḥimṣī al-Qaṭṭān 46
Aḥmad b. Mīkāʾīl al-Nakhjawānī 118
ʿAlāʾ al-Dīn Alṭunbughā 38
ʿAlāʾ al-Dīn Ibn Kamāl al-Dīn 42
ʿAlī b. Muḥammad al-Bukhārī 134
ʿAlī b. Muḥammad al-Ḥijāzī 25
ʿAlī b. ʿUthmān 115
Amin, Muhammad Muhammad 4
Amīr Ādūjī b. Amīr Yāzilī b. al-Nāʾib 28, 106, 108, 111, 115–6, 113
Amīr Altunā (?) Bek 140
Amīr Barāt (?) b. al-Amīr al-Maghfūr Tīmūr Būghā b. Jingāj (?) 110, 136–7
Amīr Shaykhī b. Amīr Khwāja ʿAlī b. Amīr Abū Bakr 117
Arghūn 28
Aristakes 149
Aslān b. Girān (?) Amīr 135
al-Asyūṭī 15
Atıl, Esin 2
Awwad, Issam 15
Ayalon, David 11
Aziz Atiya 16

Banū Fāris 90
Barakat Khān 18
Bennett, Chrystal M. 1, 13–4
Bilāl b. ʿUmar Ibn Abī al-Qāsim 45
Būlād b. Muḥammad Ḥusayn 145
Burgoyne, Lynda 1
Burgoyne, Michael H. 1, 2, 9
Burhān al-Dīn al-Nāṣirī 7, 22, 25–6, 31, 68, 74, 76
Burhān al-Dīn Ibrāhīm al-ʿIrāqī 44

Chubanids 28
Chūpān Beg/Amīr Chūpān 28–9
Clark, Kenneth 16
Creswell, Keppel Archibald Cameron 2, 9, 11

Dakkak, Ibrahim 15

Emmel, Stephen 1
Ernst, Hans 16

Fāṭima, wife of Burhān al-Dīn al-Nāṣirī 25, 74

Georg son of Bakht 149
al-Ghazālī 73
George, James 13
Gippert, Jost V, 21
Goitein, Shelomo D. 16

al-Ḥajj Maḥmūd al-Shakhmī (?) 85
Ḥājji Yaʿqūb b. Yūsuf 117
Ḥasan al-Rūmī 68
Ḥasan b. ʿAlī 108
Hawass, Zahi 5
Hull, Edmund J. 1
Hūmān b. Kambay (?) 124

Ibn al-ʿArabī 98
Ibn al-Jawzī 73
Ibn al-Marzubān 73
Ibn al-Nūrī 56
Ibrāhīm al-Ḥammāl 67
Ibrāhīm b. Mīkāʾīl 75
ʿImād al-Dawla wa-al-Dīn b. Abī al-Faraj b. Dāwūd b. Yaʿqūb 123
ʿImād al-Dīn ʿĀrif b. al-Marḥūm Qutlughā (?) 136
Isḥāq b. Ṣāliḥ al-Laṭīfī's (?) 101
Ismāʿīl b. Ḥajjī 51
Ismāʿīl b. Khalīl 77
Ismāʿīl b. Malik Shāh 135
ʿIzz al-Dawla Amīr Yūsuf b. Nāṣir al-Dawla b. Naṣrullāh 123

https://doi.org/10.1515/9783111330242-013

Jalal 149
al-Jarawānī 15
al-Jazāʾirī, Ṭāhir 23

Kamāl al-Dīn Yūsuf bin Qutlūbak 121
Kamāl b. Tūbak 136
Kamāl, son of Burhān al-Dīn al-Nāṣirī 74
Karmraykel (Gamrekeli?) 149
Kawamoto, Masatomo 21
Kessler, Christel 1–2
Khadīja, daughter of Burhān al-Dīn al-Nāṣirī 74
Khalidi, Haydar 18
Khiḍr al-Turkmānī 38
Khurram Shāh Khānum bt. Amīr Kurd b. Amīr Ādūjī 117
Khwāja Mīr Jumla Tīmūr Būghā 134, 137

Little, Donald P. 1, 12, 16, 20–1, 24
Lutfi, Huda 15–6
Lyons, Martin 1

Maḥmūd b. Muḥammad Shāh al-Samarqandī 133
Mālik b. Anas 73
Muʾayyad b. Amīr Arslān Jamāl b. Qutlughbak 136
Muḥammad b. ʿAbd al-Raḥīm al-Ḥusaynī Ibn Abī al-Luṭf 80
Muḥammad b. Aḥmad b. Ḥasan al-Ramlī 72
Muḥammad b. Amīr Kurd (b. Amīr Ādūjī?) 110
Muḥammad b. Ḥasan al-ʿAjamī 47
Muḥammad b. Ḥusayn al-ʿAlawī 134
Muḥammad Kāmil al-Ḥusaynī 103
Muḥammad Qudsī al-Rahhāwī al-Naqshabandī, *naqīb* of Aleppo 89
Muḥammad al-Raṭūnī 73, 99
Muḥammad b. Saʿīd 73
Muḥammad b. Shaykh ʿAbd al-Fattāḥ Efendi 103
Muḥammad b. Z-r-w-f (?) 94
Mujīr al-Dīn 15
Müller, Christian 30, 42, 53, 185
Muqīm b. Shāh 127
Mūsā (Prophet) 89

Nāṣir al-Dīn al-Ḥamawī 22, 53
Natel 150
Niʿma b. Bishāra al-Naṣrānī 48
Northrup, Linda V, IX, 2, 4, 6–9, 12, 17, 19–20, 24
Nūr al-Dawla Sūrayk (?) b. Ṣāfī al-Dawla b. Abī al-Ghanāʾim 123
al-Nuwayrī 15

Polotsky, Hans Jakob 1
Posegay, Nick 23

al-Qalqashandī 15, 37
Qūydān (?) 125
Qurra (?) b. Kukādās (?) 109
Quṭlūwa bt. ʿAbd Allāh 71

Rogers, Michael 2

Sābiq al-Dīn Abū Bakr b. Amīr al-Ḥasan al-Ḥaydarī (?) 123
Salameh, Khader 21
Sālim b. Muḥammad 51
Sayf al-Dīn Amīr b. al-Marḥūm Shaykh Arslān b. Jamāl Qutlughbak 136
Sayf al-Dīn Jaqmaq al-Ẓāhirī 38
Sayf al-Dīn Khiḍr, Muḥammad b. Ibrāhīm 138
Shāfī b. Muḥammad Shāh al-Nakhjawānī 146
Shams al-Dawla wa-al-Dīn Maḥmūd Shāh b. al-Marḥūm Muḥammad b. al-Saʿīd 111
Shams al-Dīn (?) Muḥammad Abī l-Faḍl al-Sīnjānī (?) 108
Shams al-Dīn Muḥammad al-Maqdisī 51
Shams al-Dīn Muḥammad al-Tabrīzī al-ʿAjamī 69
Shams al-Dīn Muḥammad b. Muḥammad Juwaynī 28, 113, 150
Sharaf al-Dīn ʿĪsā b. Ghānim 7, 17, 22, 30–1, 35, 42–3
Sharaf al-Dīn Muḥammad al-Damāmīnī 44
Shams al-Dīn (?) Zakariyā 114
Shaykh ʿAlī 128
Shaykh Ḥasan 131
Shaykh Qārān 134–5
Shaykh Zankī 134–5
Shibl b. Khalaf 51
Shihāb al-Dīn Aḥmad b. Muḥammad al-Yaghmūrī 42–3
Shihāb al-Dīn Kahmān 75
Shujāʿ al-Dīn Ramaḍān 123
Snoy(?) 149
St. Stephen 19

Stanley-Price, Nicholas 1
Stern, Samuel M. 15
Sultan Ahmed III, 101–2
Sultan al-Manṣūr Qalāwūn 4–5, 12
Sultan Mehmed IV, 100
Sultan al-Ẓāhir Baybars 5, 18

Timur Bughā 134–5, 137–8
Tīmūr Būghā b. Jingāj 137

ʿUmar al-Ādamī 68
ʿUmar b. Muḥammad b. ʿUmar al-Ḥuṣrī (?) al-ʿAllāf 46–8
al-ʿUmarī 15

Yūsuf b. Muḥammad 147
Yūsuf b. Shaykh Raḍī al-Dīn 100

al-Ẓāhir Barqūq 38
Zakariyā b. Ṣāḥib Dīwān Shams al-Dīn Juwayni XI, 28, 114, 150, 184
Zakī Sharaf al-Dīn 151
Zayn al-Dīn ʿAbd al-Raḥmān b. Ṣārim al-Dīn Ibrāhīm al-Khalīlī al-Fakhrī 43

Index of places (Arabic script)

أبواب الأقصى 65
اريغي 113, 153
ازاد 134–5, 166
إسلامبول 66
الأعمال الساحلية 35–6
اغورس 111
اق كوى 142
باب الأسباط 65
باب الحديد 65
باب حطة 65
باب الدويدارية 65
باب الرباط 65
باب الرحمة 65
باب السلسلة 65
باب الغوانمة 65
باب القطانين 65
باب المتوضى 65
باب الناظر 65
البقعة 59
بيت دجن 83
بيت لحم 64
بئر الصرارة 36
تبريز 133
توريز 70
جامع سيدنا عمر 64
جامع المغاربة 65
جفنا الجوز؟ 48, 175
جورة زين الدين الحاجب 36
جورة القباب السفلى 36
جورة القباب العليا 36
حارة المغاربة 71, 182
الحرم الشريف 63
حلب 70, 89
حمام البترك (حمام البطرك) 51, 179
حمام ستي مريم 64
حمام السلطان 64
حمام العين 64
الحنبلية 65
خاغريش كوچل؟] 136
الخانقاه الصلاحية 35–6, 51, 179
الخليل 63–4
درب الخليل 36
دمشق 42, 70
دير أبو ثور 36
دير المجاذمة 36
ديه [نسودان؟] 124
الرملة 63–4, 72
رواق الشيخ منصور 65
الرواق الغربي 65
روكسر؟ 134–5, 166
زاوية البراك 85
زاوية الجنيد 70
زبارت ارتوغ؟ 135
ساحل آغروس 79
سطوح الصخرة 64
سلواد 103
سلوان 63
سيواس 121–2
الشام 41
صحن الحرم 64
صخرة الله أو الصخرة المشرفة 63, 65, 105
الطريق الآخذ إلى الطاحون 78
عبوين 103
عثمان كوى 142
العفيفية 65
عكا 63–4
عمر كوى 142
العوجا 58
غزة 35–6, 63
القاهرة 39, 82
قبة السلسلة 65
قبة المعراج 65
قبة موسى 65
قبر سليمان 65
القدس الشريف أو القدس 35–6, 38–9, 42, 44–5, 51, 63–4, 69–72, 77, 81, 86, 96, 100, 103, 171, 173, 179, 182
قرية [سيبكوش؟] 124
القناة السلطانية 36
قوشون؟ 135, 166
قيصرية 123–4
كرسي سليمان 65
كسرطاش؟ 136
كللسيا؟ 108
كوزه بک؟ 135, 166
المدرسة الحجازية بالقاهرة 82

https://doi.org/10.1515/9783111330242-014

المدرسة الخاتونية 69–70
المدرسة الصلاحية 73
مربعة البنات 36
مربعة النساء 36
مرج عرب 45
المسجد الأقصى أو الأقصى الشريف 65, 100, 105
مكرود 111
نابلس 64
نسودان؟ 124, 125, 126
يافا 63–4

Index of places (Latin script)

ʿAbawīn (close to Ramallah) 103
ʿAfīfīya Madrasa 65
Aghūrs 111–12
Aleppo 33, 69, 89
Alexandria 44
Allenby Bridge 1
American University in Beirut 2
American University in Cairo 2
Amman V, 1, 3, 5, 13–4
Anatolia VII, 14, 24, 27, 29–30, 33, 106, 119, 121–3
Aq Kūy 131, 142
Aqsa Mosque 2–3, 14, 65, 100, 105
Ardabīl 113
Arīghī 113–4
Azād IX, 29, 134–5, 166, 168–9
Azerbaijan 113

Bāb al-Silsila (Chain Gate) 18
Bāb al-Ẓahra 6
al-Baqʿa 59
Bayt Dajan 32, 83
Berdaa 113
Beylagan 146
Bilād al-shām VII, 25, 32–3, 35, 41, 85

Cairo VII, 1–5, 7, 10, 12, 16, 25, 33, 35, 44, 82
Church of the Holy Sepulchre 19, 51

Damascus 6, 42–3, 69
Dayr Abū Thūr 35
Dome of the Rock 19, 65

Gates of the Ḥaram al-sharīf 22
Gaza 33, 35

Ḥanbalīya Madrasa 65
Ḥijāzīya Madrasa (Cairo) 82

Iran VII, 14, 24, 27–30, 33, 106, 112–3, 128, 135
Islamic Library (Jaffa) 23
Islamic Museum (Jerusalem) V, VIII, IX, 2, 4, 6, 8–9, 17, 20–3, 30, 33–4, 153, 157, 161, 164, 166, 171, 173, 175, 179, 182, 197

al-Jazzār Library (Acre) 23

Kahrīz-i Khwāja ʿAzīz 109
Kasrtāsh (?) 136
Khāghuraysh-i Kūchal (?) 136
Khalidi family library 18, 23
Kilākūn 113
King Hussein Bridge 1

L.A. Mayer Museum for Islamic Art (Jerusalem) 11
Libya 33, 85
London 2, 23

Maghāriba Mosque 65
Maghāriba quarter 71
Maghribi gate 9, 12
Makrūd 111–2
Marj ʿArab 45
Māzandarān 112
McCord-Stewart Museum (Montreal) 11
McGill University (Montreal) 3, 13, 15–6, 18, 20
Montreal 2–3, 5, 11, 12
Middle East 2, 16–7

Nakhchivan 146
Nasūdān (?) 123–5
National Palace Hotel 6
Northwestern Iran VII, 14, 27, 33, 106
Pool of the Patriarch's bath 51

Qarafa (Cairo) 2
Qayṣarīya (Kayseri) 29, 119, 123
Qubbat al-Miʿrāj 65
Qubbat Mūsā 65

Rochester (N.Y) 1
Robarts Library (University of Toronto) 15

Ṣalāḥīya Khānqāh 25, 31, 35, 51, 75
Ṣalāḥīya Madrasa 73
Shaykh Jarrah neighbourhood (Jerusalem) 2
Sībkūsh (?) 123–4
Silwād 103

https://doi.org/10.1515/9783111330242-015

Sīwās (Sivas) VII, 29, 119, 121–2
St. Cross College (Oxford) 2, 13
Syunik Province 112

Tabrīz 69, 133
Ṭarīq Bāb al-Silsila 18
Textile Museum (Washington, D.C.) 2
Tihama 11
Transcaucasia VII, 14, 24, 27–8, 30, 33, 106
Toronto V, 1–2, 15

ʿUmar Kūy 142
University of Jordan 15
ʿUthmān Kūy 142

Wailing Wall 9, 14, 18
West Azerbaijan province (Iran) 29, 135
West Bank 1, 13

Yemen 5, 9, 11

Zangezur (Armenian: Զանգեզուր) 111–2
Zangezur of Arrān 111
Zāwiyat al-Burāk (Libya?) 85
Zāwiya al-Fakhriyya 9

www.ingramcontent.com/pod-product-compliance
Lightning Source LLC
Chambersburg PA
CBHW070828300426
44111CB00014B/2492